THE GREAT
NORTH OF SCOTLAND
RAILWAY

The History of the Railways of the
Scottish Highlands—Vol 3

by

H. A. VALLANCE

Revised by the Great North of Scotland Railway Association

DAVID ST JOHN THOMAS PUBLISHER

AN APPRECIATION

This revised and enlarged edition of 'Vallance' owes much to the unstinting efforts of Norris Forrest, honorary secretary of the GNSR Association for the first twenty-five years of its existence, and for most of that time also the editor of its journal, *Great North Review*.

British Library Cataloguing in Publication Data

Vallance, H. A. (Hugh Aymer) 1902–1967
The Great North of Scotland Railway – Rev. and enl.
ed. – (The History of the railways of the Scottish
Highlands v 3)
1. Scotland. Railway services, history
I. Title II. Series III. The Great North of Scotland
Railway Association
385′.09411

ISBN 0–946537–42–9 (hbk)
0–946537–60–7 (pbk)

First published 1965
New edition published 1989
Paperback edition first published 1991

Printed in Great Britain by Redwood Press Limited,
Melksham, for David St John Thomas Publisher
PO Box 4, Nairn, Scotland IV12 4HU

THE GREAT NORTH OF SCOTLAND
RAILWAY

THE HISTORY OF THE RAILWAYS
OF THE SCOTTISH HIGHLANDS:

Vol 1 – *The West Highland Railway*
by John Thomas

Vol 2 – *The Highland Railway*
by H. A. Vallance

Vol 3 – *The Great North of Scotland Railway*
by H. A. Vallance (updated by the Great North of Scotland
Railway Association)

Vol 4 – *The Callander & Oban Railway*
by John Thomas (updated by John Farringdon)

Vol 5 – *The Skye Railway*
by John Thomas (updated by John Farringdon)

Contents

FOREWORD 9
FOREWORD TO 1989 EDITION 10
PHOTOGRAPH ACKNOWLEDGEMENTS 11

1 AN AMBITIOUS START   13
   Rival schemes · parliamentary victory · the Aberdeenshire Canal

2 PROGRESS UNDER DIFFICULTIES   19
   Lack of capital · construction begun · opening to
   Huntly · the Waterloo branch

3 THE INEVITABLE SEQUEL   29
   The Inverness companies · the junction at Keith ·
   board room quarrels · the Highland Railway

4 THE MORAYSHIRE RAILWAY   37
   From Elgin to Lossiemouth · the Craigellachie extension · through the Glen of Rothes · amalgamation
   with the Great North

5 THE BANFFSHIRE RAILWAY   48
   Early schemes · construction and opening · the Great
   North takes over

6 EXPANSION AND CONSOLIDATION   53
   The Keith & Dufftown Railway · through Strathspey
   · the Macduff line · the old Meldrum branch · into the
   Alford Valley · the Formartine & Buchan Railway ·
   consolidation

7 ABERDEEN JUNCTION CONTROVERSY   67

Waterloo and Guild Street · two abortive schemes ·
the Denburn Valley line

8 THE DEESIDE RAILWAY   74

Formation of the company · opening to Banchory ·
extensions into Upper Deeside · leasing and amalgamation · Royal trains

9 CRISIS AND RECOVERY   87

Grave financial difficulties · towards better times · the
Moray Firth Coast line · the Cruden Bay branch ·
continued progress · after fifty years

10 THE ROAD TO INVERNESS   103

Enterprise leads to warfare · a seven-year traffic agreement · the long struggle continues · after the race to
Aberdeen · the feud is ended

11 LIGHT RAILWAYS AND BUS ROUTES   117

An unpromising start · the St Combs branch · more
fruitless schemes · pioneer bus services · route mileage
trebled · tourist services · services during the war · after
the war · the 1918 committee

12 YEARS OF MATURITY   129

Modernisation continued · enterprise ill-rewarded ·
the Highland amalgamation scheme · long-distance
excursions · breaks with the past · train service
developments · the Great North at war · the last years
of independence

13 LOCOMOTIVES AND ROLLING STOCK   144

Daniel Kinnear Clark: 1853-1855 · John Folds
Ruthven: 1855-1857 · William Cowan: 1857-1883 ·
the Morayshire Railway · the Banffshire Railway · the
Deeside Railway · James Manson: 1883-1890 · James
Johnson: 1890-1894 · William Pickersgill: 1894-1914
· Thomas Heywood: 1914-1922 · rolling stock

14 UNDER LNER AEGIS 168

After the grouping · Sunday services · road services and
competition · the Royal Commission on Transport ·
economic depression and recovery · staff changes ·
locomotive changes · rolling stock changes · through
war to nationalisation

15 BRITISH RAILWAYS AND RETRENCHMENT 184

The first years · diesel replaces steam · the Beeching
Report · goods traffic · track and signalling

16 NORTH SEA OIL AND THE FUTURE 192

Oil to the rescue · charter trains · service improvements · Great North remains

APPENDICES 199

1 Authorisation and opening dates for rail and road
motor services
2 Doubling and singling of line
3 Closures
4 Route information
5 Officers
6 Summary of train services
7 Rolling stock
8 Non-GNSR locomotives
9 Selected altitudes
10 GNSR Association

INDEX 213

Foreword

Of the five completely independent Scottish railways embraced by the grouping of 1923, the Great North of Scotland alone included the word 'Great' in its title; yet, strangely enough, it was the smallest. Nevertheless, this apparently misnamed company, after an obscure and troubled youth, had emerged into a vigorous middle age, and had given the lead to other and larger railways by a progressive policy that had earned for it the name of 'Little and Good'.

It is in an attempt to do justice to the struggles and achievements of this remarkable railway that I have prepared this history. It is a story of initial success, speedily marred by prolonged financial embarrassment, of slow recovery, of fierce disputes with the Highland Railway, and of an all too brief period of prosperity that ended so tragically in 1914. The record has been brought up to date by a review of the four decades since the company lost its independence.

As on so many previous occasions, the library of the Railway Club has been a valuable source of reference. I must also express my appreciation of the assistance I have received from the Archivist's Department of the British Railways Board, and especially from Mr R. M. Hogg, Custodian of Records at the Edinburgh office, who read the proofs. I am grateful to Mr M. D. Greville for delving deeply into railway and other records to discover obscure details.

My thanks are due to Mr J. G. Carr for allowing me to reproduce items from his extensive collection of tickets; to Mr J. H. Court, Deputy Editor of *The Railway Magazine*, for making available photographs from his personal collection; and to the Public Relations Officer of the Scottish Region of British Railways for permission to use photographs from his files. Finally, I must record my appreciation of the work of Mr C. Hamilton Ellis in preparing the oil painting for the frontispiece.

H.A.V.

The Railway Club
320 High Holborn
London, W.C.1
September 1965

Foreword to the 1989 Edition

It is perhaps extraordinary that getting on for two thirds of a century after it ceased to exist, The Great North of Scotland Railway is the subject of rising rather than decreasing interest. It is also almost a quarter of a century since the late H. A. Vallance wrote his classic history of the line.

This new edition was conceived not only to fill the bookshelves of those unable to obtain the original edition but also to bring the story up to date. The first edition was published when the effects of the 'Reshaping of British Railways' (the 'Beeching' Report) were beginning to be felt in the north east of Scotland. Today, only the main line between Aberdeen and Keith remains in full operation but it now has the prospect of a far healthier future than for many years as it shares in the general buoyancy found throughout ScotRail.

In preparing this new edition, much of the original edition has been left intact. New material has been incorporated where it was felt useful and some revisions have been made to add information which has come to light since the original publication. Two new chapters have been added, one to describe the contraction of the system in the sixties and the other to bring the story fully up to the present time.

This edition has been prepared with the enthusiastic support of several members of the Great North of Scotland Railway Association, which itself celebrated its 25th anniversary in March 1989 and worked on this book as part of its activities to mark that occasion. The principal sources of original material used include the Scottish Record Office in Edinburgh, the O'Dell Collection at Aberdeen University and the National Newspaper Collection of the British Museum at Colindale, London.

Photograph Acknowledgements

H A Vallance – plates 1, 2, 3, 5, 6, 7, 8, 9, 21
LGRP – plates 10, 11, 14, 15, 16, 18, 19, 24, 26, 32, 36, 39, 47, 48, 54
N Forrest – plates 17, 20, 25, 28, 59, 60, 61, 64
GNSRA – plates 22, 27, 34, 35, 42, 43, 49, 50, 51, 53, 56, 57
K Fenwick – plates 37, 38, 58, 62, 66
B E Timmings – plate 40
W A Camwell – plate 41
British Rail – plates 45, 46
B E Morrison – plate 52
K Jones – plate 63
R Kinghorn – plate 65

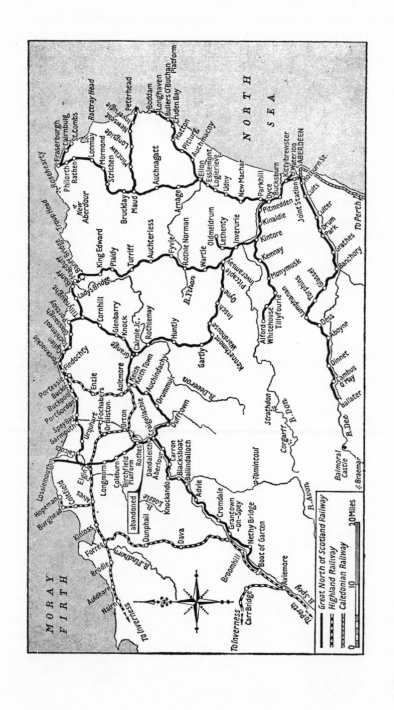

CHAPTER 1

An Ambitious Start

RIVAL SCHEMES

The early railway history of Scotland reflects clearly the unequal distribution of that country's natural resources. Until the middle 1840s, development had been almost wholly confined to the industrial and relatively well-populated Lowlands, and save for some short isolated lines serving Dundee and the County of Angus, the whole country north of the Forth still awaited the coming of the iron road. However, the year 1845 saw a great step forward; for not only was the Caledonian Railway authorised to link Edinburgh and Glasgow with Carlisle, but three other railways—the Scottish Central, the Scottish Midland Junction and the Aberdeen—forming the remaining links required to complete an unbroken chain of communication between Aberdeen and the south, received their Acts of Incorporation.

Some time before all the bills for the lines south of Aberdeen had been deposited with Parliament, meetings were held in that city with a view to securing support for a railway through the country lying to the west and north. The idea took definite shape early in 1845, when the Great North of Scotland Railway Company was formed, with Thomas Blaikie, Lord Provost of Aberdeen, as chairman, and William Leslie as interim secretary. William Cubitt was appointed engineer-in-chief, but he acted only as a consultant, and the resident engineer, Alexander Gibb, was responsible for the preparation of the surveys and plans.

The name Great North of Scotland Railway was not new. It had been chosen some 12 months earlier for a scheme to place the whole route between Perth and Aberdeen to Inverness in one ownership; and an extension of this line from Aberdeen to Inverness had also been considered. These proposals for a single company to undertake the construction of such a long line through districts with only limited natural resources did not inspire sufficient confidence to ensure success. The result was that the Aberdeen and the

Scottish Midland Junction Companies secured the country south of Aberdeen, and the scheme for continuing the line to Inverness was deferred.

In March 1845 the company issued its first prospectus for a railway from Aberdeen to Inverness on a route that differed but little from that suggested a year earlier. Starting from a junction in Aberdeen with the already authorised railway to the south, the main line ran inland in a north-westerly direction, beside the River Don, to the Royal Burgh of Inverurie, and across the hills to Huntly, whence it followed the River Deveron and its tributary, the Isla, to Keith. Crossing the Spey some eight miles west of the latter town, the line turned northwards to Elgin, and reached Inverness by way of Forres and Nairn. The line was 108¼ miles long, and was a route of fairly easy gradients and few outstanding engineering works.

The coast towns of Banff and Portsoy were to be served by a branch from Grange, four miles east of Keith, and shorter branches were to run from Orton to Garmouth, and from Alves to Burghead. The total length of these subsidiary lines was 30½ miles. These proposals were not received with general satisfaction, but the opposition was sharply divided.

On the one hand, it was considered that the fishing havens of Banffshire and Morayshire should be placed on the main line; and the Aberdeen, Banff & Elgin Railway was promoted for this purpose. It was proposed that the railway should run north from Aberdeen to Ardo, and thence north-west to Banff, via Udny, Fyvie and Turriff. Turning to the west at Banff, the line would follow the coast through Portsoy, Cullen and Buckie to Portgordon, whence it would turn inland to Elgin. A separate company, the Inverness & Elgin Junction, was to link Elgin with Inverness, following almost the same line as that already chosen for the Great North of Scotland Railway. The distance from Aberdeen to Elgin by this route was about 78 miles, and to Inverness 114 miles. The districts of Formartine and Buchan were to be served by a branch from Ardo to Peterhead, which, in its turn, put off branches from Longside to Fraserburgh, and Logierieve to Newburgh. There was also to be a shorter branch from the main line near Banff to Macduff. The total length of the branches was about 46 miles.

On the other hand, in Inverness and the northern Highlands the demand was for a more direct route to the south. Despite the engineering difficulties, and high cost of construction inseparable from such an undertaking, a railway across the Grampians to Perth was proposed, and actively supported. Starting from a junction with the Inverness & Elgin Junction Railway at Nairn, the company's engineer, Joseph Mitchell, surveyed a route across the hills to Grantown, and thence for several miles up Strathspey. The Grampians were to be surmounted by the Druimuachdar Pass, nearly 1,500 ft above sea-level, whence the line would descend to Blair Atholl and the Pass of Killiecrankie, and passing through Dunkeld, join the Scottish Midland Junction Railway some seven miles from Perth. No sooner was this scheme fairly launched, than the Inverness & Elgin Junction severed its alliance with the Aberdeen, Banff & Elgin, and threw in its lot with the new company.

PARLIAMENTARY VICTORY

All three companies prepared to introduce bills into Parliament. However, the struggle resolved itself into a straight fight between the Great North of Scotland and the Perth & Inverness, because internal dissensions and failure to raise funds brought about the collapse of the Aberdeen, Banff & Elgin.

The opposition to the bill for the direct line from Inverness to Perth was chiefly directed against the high altitudes to be reached by the railway—upwards of 1,300 ft above sea-level between Nairn and Grantown, and approaching 1,500 at the Druimuachdar Pass. Against this it was argued that a railway had already been authorised to cross Shap Fell at an altitude of 915 ft, and that Beattock Summit on the Caledonian Railway exceeded 1,000 ft and was approached by gradients scarcely less severe than those proposed between Nairn and Perth. There remained, however, the long stretches of single line across the mountains which, taken in conjunction with the gradients, were considered especially objectionable. The bill was rejected, and the promoters of the Great North of Scotland Railway were left to seek their powers almost unopposed.

The Act received the Royal Assent on 26 June 1846. At that time, the authorised mileage exceeded that of any other Scottish railway, and the title Great North of Scotland Railway was not ill-chosen. But the victory had been dearly bought at a price of at least £80,000. Moreover, costly stipulations were inserted in the Act. There was to be a gate-keeper and a lodge at each of the numerous level-crossings, and the trustees of the toll bridges carrying the main road from Aberdeen to Inverness over the Spey, near Orton, and the Findhorn, at Forres, were to be compensated for loss of revenue. On the other hand, the maximum charges allowed for the conveyance of passengers were distinctly generous. Provided the speed of a train exceeded 25 m.p.h., the company was entitled to demand 2¾d, 2d and 1½d a mile from first, second and third class passengers respectively. By slower trains, the fares were not to exceed 2d, 1½d and 1d per mile. Accommodation for second and third class passengers was to be provided on at least two-thirds of the trains.

THE ABERDEENSHIRE CANAL

The advent of the railway sealed the fate of the Aberdeenshire Canal, authorised on 26 April 1796, to link Inverurie with the sea at Aberdeen. Although the earthworks were reduced to a minimum by following the winding course of the River Don closely—with the result that the journey of 16 miles by road became 19 by canal—not only was considerable difficulty experienced in raising the necessary money, but the cost of the undertaking had been underestimated. In 1801 the company was forced to seek powers to raise additional capital.

Another four years elapsed before through communication was established, while even then the works were by no means completed, and much of the masonry in the locks was found to be defective, and had to be replaced. In 1809 further powers to raise additional capital had to be obtained. The average width of the canal was 23 ft and the depth 3 ft 9 in. The difference in level of 168 ft between Inverurie and sea-level at Aberdeen was overcome by means of 17 locks, grouped in three flights, at Kintore, Stoneywood and Kittybrewster. At Aberdeen the canal ended at the harbour, but the western terminus was one mile from Inverurie, at a point named Port Elphinstone in honour of Sir Robert Elphinstone, who had from the outset been a generous supporter of the undertaking.

The opening ceremony took place on 31 May 1805, when the directors and a party of local celebrities embarked at Port Elphinstone for Aberdeen in a gaily decorated barge named *Countess of Kintore*. According to a contemporary account, the party was greeted with loud cheers by the people assembled on the banks, while those on board responded to these expressions of goodwill by firing salutes on a small cannon mounted in the bow.

Goods traffic was carried partly by the canal company, and partly by private contractors. In addition, a passenger service was maintained by two iron fly-boats which made two trips in each direction daily. The right to operate this service was periodically put up for

BRIDGES—1

(1) Bridge carrying the main line over the River Don, south of Inverurie. Looking upstream, 1964.

(2) The longest of the viaducts at Cullen. The town is on the left.

(3) The main span of the Spey Bridge at Garmouth, looking upstream. Also known as Barnett's Monument after the designer, this bridge is now a public footpath.

BRIDGES—2

(4) Bridge over the Spey at Carron, carrying both rail and road side by side. Looking upstream, 1958. Still in use for road traffic.

(5) Another bridge over the Spey, at Ballindalloch, with the station to the right. Looking downstream. The bridge now carries the Speyside Way.

(6) The Ythan Bridge at Ellon, looking upstream in 1955. The small span on the left was added after the south abutment collapsed in 1861.

AS THE DRIVER SAW THE SPEY BRIDGES

(7)   Looking through the Spey Bridge at Craigellachie. Loop points in the
foreground, Dandaleith in the distance.

(8)   The bridge at Ballindalloch, looking north. This viaduct is also shown
in plate 5.

(9)   The Spey Viaduct, looking towards Garmouth. See also plate 3.

ABERDEEN JOINT

(10) Exterior of the station, 1937. The buildings remain much the same today from the outside although inside they have been completely modernised.

(11) North end of the station, 1937, looking towards Schoolhill from Union Street.

(12) The south end of the old station, with a Deeside train on the right and a Caledonian train on the left. The Deeside train is headed by class T, no 93.

auction. Because of the time required to negotiate the locks at Kittybrewster, the boats did not work through to Aberdeen harbour but terminated at the Boat House, between Kittybrewster and Woodside, some two miles from the city. Although the maximum speed was about 8 m.p.h., such was the time lost in passing through the locks at Kintore and Stoneywood that the journey of 17 miles occupied three hours. As it was feared that floating ice might impede the boats, the service was suspended during the winter.

Traffic, of which the chief items were granite from the neighbouring quarries, fertilisers and farm produce, continued satisfactorily until the end of the Napoleonic Wars; but with the return of peace came a serious depression from which the company never recovered. In 1834, the basin at Aberdeen was connected with the harbour by a tide lock; but this improvement did not revive the diminishing traffic. Eleven years later, the position was such that an offer by the Great North to purchase the canal for £36,000, and use most of its course for the railway, was readily accepted. That this figure was subsequently considered unduly generous is evident from the caustic remarks passed at the meeting of the railway shareholders in November 1849, when the propriety of allowing two of the directors who were also prominently identified with the canal to express an opinion on the matter was questioned in no uncertain fashion. However, the objectors were mollified, and the two directors—Alexander Jopp, the secretary of the canal company, and Sir James Elphinstone, an influential shareholder—retained their seats on the board. Shortly afterwards, the latter succeeded Thomas Blaikie as chairman, and held that office for 17 years.

Although the Act of 1846 had established the Great North of Scotland Railway strongly in the country north and west of Aberdeen, it was realised that the company would be dependent for its through traffic on the Aberdeen Railway, which had secured the outlet to the south, and immediate steps were taken to amalgamate the two undertakings. The Act authorising the fusion received the Royal Assent on 9 July 1847, and the combined system was to be known as the Great North of Scotland Railway. However, in accordance with the resolution governing railway amalgamations and sales, recently adopted by Parliament in view of the increasing shortage of money, it was stipulated that the fusion should not become effective until one half of that company's authorised capital of £1,500,000 had been subscribed. This clause gave great satisfaction to the shareholders of the Aberdeen company, who were apprehensive not only because much of the capital for the railway north of Aberdeen remained to be subscribed, but also because it had been decided not to attempt any construction until the works on their own line were nearing completion. The wisdom of such a proviso was to become only too apparent during the next few years.

CHAPTER 2

Progress Under Difficulties

LACK OF CAPITAL

When the Great North of Scotland Railway was authorised, the extraordinary wave of railway speculation known in after years as the Railway Mania was sweeping over the country. The depression which had characterised the early 1840s had yielded to a period of recovery, and money had once more become plentiful. The time was ripe for the provision of additional railway facilities, and during the preceding 18 months an unprecedented number of schemes had passed successfully through Parliament. However, by the end of 1846, there were unmistakable signs that the promotion of new lines had proceeded at too great a pace, but it was not until the autumn of 1847 that a series of domestic events, entirely unconnected with the railway world, precipitated a nation-wide financial panic. Money was not to be had at any price. Faced with this crisis, Parliament conceded some relief by an Act granting an extension of time, up to a maximum of two years, for the purchase of land and the completion of works to those companies which made application.

The Great North of Scotland Railway was particularly hard hit. Although negotiations with the landowners had been proceeding since the passing of the Act, lack of funds had so far precluded any attempts to construct even a portion of the line, and there appeared to be little prospect of completing the undertaking before the company's powers expired in 1852. Application was made for the maximum concession allowed by Parliament, but meantime lack of confidence on the part of investors produced a state of complete stagnation.

The Aberdeen company fared better than its northern neighbour. Construction was slowed down, but by April 1850 the railway had been completed to a temporary station at Ferryhill, on the outskirts of Aberdeen. Meantime, the policy of the company had undergone an important change. Previously it had been intended to work the

Aberdeen Railway in close association with the lines on the east coast of Scotland and England; but early in 1850 some influential shareholders, interested in the Caledonian Railway and its associated companies, pressed for a new arrangement whereby traffic should be sent over that route. Their efforts were successful, and the arrangement with the east coast companies was annulled by mutual consent. The capital which those companies had agreed to contribute was raised by an issue of preference shares among shareholders of the Aberdeen Railway.

Far more serious for the Great North of Scotland Railway was a persistent demand for the repeal of the Amalgamation Act of 1847. The measure had never been favourably received by many of the Aberdeen Railway shareholders, who considered that their company should look south, rather than north, for an alliance. The financial difficulties of the Great North strengthened this opinion, and it was decided to seek powers to annul the fusion. The Act was passed on 29 July 1850, and all prospects of carrying the Great North of Scotland Railway south of Aberdeen vanished for the time being. The Aberdeen company already had leased the Arbroath & Forfar Railway, and had established friendly relations with the Scottish Midland Junction Company, whose main line extended from Perth to Forfar. This policy bore fruit six years later, when the two systems were amalgamated on 29 July 1856 as the Scottish North Eastern Railway.

Meantime, there were signs that the Great North was emerging from its state of stagnation, although complete recovery seemed as far off as ever. At the general meeting held in November 1849, it was stated that £650,789 would be required to construct the main line from Aberdeen to Inverness, if a maximum gradient of 1 in 100 was adopted. On the other hand, if gradients as steep as 1 in 70 were allowed, rather more than £66,000 could be saved on the earthworks. In each case, a single line, with passing loops at most stations, was proposed in place of the originally-intended double track.

There was also placed before the meeting a separate estimate of £375,334 for making the railway only between Kittybrewster (1½ miles from Aberdeen) and Keith, 52 miles distant and mid-way to Inverness. This figure was for single track, but with bridges and earthworks made wide enough to accommodate a second track as soon as required. Although it was emphasised that nearly £94,500 could be saved by restricting the works to the width of one track, after considerable discussion, the estimate for works made wide enough for a second track to be added was strongly recommended.

By fixing the eastern terminus in the outskirts of Aberdeen, the heavy expense of carrying the line through the city to join the Aberdeen Railway would be obviated until the financial position had still further improved. Keith was the obvious western terminus for the time being, as not only was it a town of considerable importance, situated approximately halfway to Inverness, but the most expensive section of the whole route, through the hilly country of lower Strathspey, lay immediately ahead.

In November 1850 it was proposed to place the company's finances on a new basis. The total capital was to be reduced from £1,500,000 to £1,000,000; and the existing £50 shares, 27,686 in number, were to be reduced to ordinary, or postponed shares of £10 each, the holders being credited with the £2 10s already paid thereon. The balance of the capital was to be made up by the creation of 72,314 new 4 per cent preference shares of £10 each. These proposals were amended to increase the preference share capital to £830,580, and the total share capital authorised in the following year became £1,107,440.

It was also announced at the meeting in November 1850 that complete agreement had been reached with the landowners, and that it was intended to proceed with construction from Kittybrewster to Keith at the earliest opportunity. Tenders for the work were invited, and that submitted by Mitchell & Dean was accepted. However, the necessary capital was still not forthcoming, and a further delay appeared inevitable. The contractors then offered to take up one quarter of the shares, and subsequently proposed that they should lease the railway for 21 years for a payment of 5 per cent on the sum expended on its construction. This offer was not accepted, as there were, at long last, signs of a distinct improvement in the prospects.

CONSTRUCTION BEGUN

The position did, in fact, improve steadily, although not to the extent that had been hoped. At length, in the summer of 1852, the directors were able to authorise the contractors to begin, although it was deemed advisable still further to curtail the undertaking by stopping short at Huntly, 39¼ miles from Kittybrewster, and 12½ miles from Keith. To allow the Aberdeenshire Canal to remain open as long as possible, it was decided that the 24 miles from Inverurie to Huntly should be completed before a start was made on the remainder of the line. It was even suggested that this section should be opened separately.

Meantime, the engineer, Sir William Cubitt, who had been knighted in 1851 for his services in connection with the erection of the buildings for the Great Exhibition, had resigned, and had been succeeded by Benjamin Hall Blyth.

The first sod was cut amid scenes of great rejoicing on 25 November 1852 in a field near Oyne, on the estate of Westhall, the seat of Sir James Elphinstone, the chairman. A large crowd had assembled from places as far afield as Elgin and Banff, while Aberdeen, as fitted the headquarters of the company, was represented by its Lord Provost and Bailies and a number of prominent townsfolk. After the first sod had been turned by Lady Elphinstone, Sir James and several of the distinguished guests continued the ceremony by removing barrow-loads of earth.

Construction was carried on with all possible speed; but the fine dry weather of the late autumn was followed by an exceptionally severe winter, during which work was brought virtually to a standstill for weeks on end; and it was not until 25 April that the contractor was able to report that construction had been fully resumed. These delays destroyed all hope of completion by the summer of 1854, and appear to have led to the decision not to open the railway in two sections, as had been proposed.

With the improvement in the position of the railway company, the chequered history of the Aberdeenshire Canal drew to its close. Throughout the years of depression it had been worked on behalf of its new owners, but the final transfer to the Great North had not yet been completed. By an extraordinary oversight, the Act authorising the railway contained no reference to the canal, and its purchase had not been confirmed by Parliament. In consequence, when the waterway was abandoned, not only were the claims for compensation inordinately high, but it was deemed necessary to settle with each shareholder and mortgagee individually, a task that proved difficult and complicated in the extreme. The result was that the conveyance was still uncompleted when the contractors were ready to commence operations east of Inverurie.

Faced with the prospect of a further delay, Mitchell & Dean took the drastic step of breaching the canal bank at Dalwearie, near Kintore, and a number of barges were stranded in the reach between Kintore and Stoneywood. Temporary repairs were carried out at once; but the incident had the beneficial effect of hastening the lawyers in their task, and the transfer was soon completed. Whether the directors connived at this extreme action, or even inspired it, never emerged; but local opinion evidently considered them blame-worthy, as the company was in bad odour in the district for some time.

For the most part, the railway followed the course of the canal closely, but at several points, particularly between Pitmedden and Kinaldie, the sharp curves of its many windings necessitated devia-tions. The abandoned portions were left to decay, and have become considerably overgrown although still traceable.

The tardiness of the lawyers in securing possession of the canal was the last serious delay experienced, and thereafter the works progressed steadily. Save for the bridge of five girder spans on timber piles over the Don at Port Elphinstone, there were no out-standing engineering works, although some of the cuttings between Inverurie and Huntly were at that time considered to be quite extensive. For the first 19 miles the gradients were easy, but there followed an almost unbroken ascent of 11 miles to the summit of the line at Kennethmont, which included several stretches of 1 in 100, 120 and 150. The descent from the summit was easier, and save for rather more than a mile at 1 in 100, east of Gartly, few of the gradients were steeper than 1 in 200.

At a special meeting, held on 23 June 1854, the directors reported that the railway would be opened within three months. It was also announced that a contract had been signed with the Electric Tele-graph Company for the provision of the telegraph at all stations. In this respect, the Great North was far ahead of many other railways, both in Scotland and in England.

OPENING TO HUNTLY

Early in September 1854, the works were inspected by Col Yolland on behalf of the Board of Trade. He found the railway single throughout, with passing places at Kintore, Inverurie and Insch, in addition to those at either terminus. At Kittybrewster the loop was placed clear of the platforms to enable engines to run round incoming trains, and push the coaches into the station. The telegraph had been installed, but was as yet only available at those stations provided with crossing loops. Although most of the signals had been erected, many were still unusable, while no signals had been provided at the level crossings. Criticism was chiefly directed against the crossing loop at Insch, which the inspector considered should be re-aligned, and the dangerously insufficient clearance at

Kintore, where the trains would have come within 2 ft of a wooden shed.

Goods traffic began on 12 September; and such was the progress made with the completion and improvement of the works that by the 14th the inspector was able to declare his entire satisfaction. The railway was officially opened on 19 September, when a special train of 25 carriages, drawn by two engines, left Kittybrewster at 11 a.m. for Huntly. It was estimated that at least 400 persons travelled from Aberdeen, and that this number was increased to upwards of 650 by those joining the train at intermediate stations.

At Huntly the preparations for the arrival of the visitors had brought business in the town almost to a standstill. Long before the train was due, a large crowd had assembled at the station; and when, at about twelve minutes past one o'clock, the long line of carriages drew slowly up to the platform, the people gave vent to their pent-up excitement in round upon round of deafening cheers. A few minutes later there emerged from the station such a throng of visitors as the sedate old capital of Strathbogie had never before been called upon to welcome.

Regular services began on 20 September, with three passenger trains and one goods train in each direction. The former called at all stations, and were allowed 2h. for the journey of 39 miles. The up goods train, which also conveyed passengers and mails, was allowed 3h., but the down service was some 40m. slower. Sunday services were restricted to the mail trains in each direction, which ran to their weekday schedules. For some time great difficulty was experienced in maintaining even these meagre services, because of delays in the delivery of locomotives and rolling stock. Not only were the trains very unpunctual, but the company was prevented from developing its traffic in goods and cattle as quickly as had been hoped. However, these troubles had been largely overcome by the spring of 1855. By this time the number of trains on weekdays had been increased to four in each direction.

For these distinctly mediocre services the fares were fixed at approximately 1¾d and 1¼d a mile for first and third class passengers respectively. The mail trains were first class only, although servants accompanying their employers were admitted to them at third class fares. By one service only in each direction was it possible to travel at the statutory fare of 1d per mile. Although the company had refrained from imposing the maximum rates allowed by the Act, the charges for both passengers and goods were considered excessive, and evoked widespread complaints; but it was not until 30 years later that they were finally reduced.

Although second class fares were expressly mentioned in the Act, such bookings were conspicuous by their absence. In deciding to provide only two classes of accommodation, the directors were probably influenced by the shortage of rolling stock, and by the precedent established a year earlier on the neighbouring Deeside Railway, where the step had been taken for similar reasons.

Intermediate stations were provided at Bucksburn (spelled Buxburn until 1897), Dyce, Kinaldie, Kintore, Inverurie, Pitcaple, Oyne, Buchanstone, Insch, Wardhouse, Kennethmont, and Gartly. Although several of them were in an unfinished state when Col Yolland carried out his inspection, by 20 September all save three were sufficiently far advanced to be brought into use; but it was not until 1 December that trains were advertised to call at Kinaldie, Buchanstone or Wardhouse. The last-named was remarkable in that it was built specially for Mr Gordon, whose mansion of Wardhouse adjoined the railway. Buchanstone, situated one mile west of Oyne, had a life of only 12 years as a passenger station, although the neighbouring meal mills continued to provide goods traffic. The platforms and buildings were subsequently demolished. Additional stations were opened at Inveramsay in 1857; Woodside in 1858; Pitmedden in 1874; Don Street, Bankhead and Stoneywood in 1887; and Persley in 1903.

The railway had been open for only three days when a serious accident occurred at Kittybrewster. On 23 September the 4.25 a.m. up mixed train was delayed at Huntly, after the tender of the engine had become derailed, and did not reach Kittybrewster until 9.10 a.m. Although steam was shut off, and the brakes applied, about three-quarters of a mile from the station, the greasy state of the rails made it impossible to reduce speed quickly, and the driver reversed his engine at about 300 yd from the platform. Unfortunately, the reversing lever slipped back into forward gear, and speed was increased when steam was applied. This added impetus carried the train past the home signal and into the station, where it came into collision with the coaches of the 8.35 a.m. down train, which had been placed at the platform, with no engine attached, to await the arrival of the up train. The leading third class carriage of the stationary train was completely wrecked, and a lady seated in it was thrown on to the track and killed. Several other passengers were severely injured.

An examination of the causes of the accident reveals the slipshod methods of operation then in vogue. That the driver had shown himself over-zealous in attempting to regain the time lost by the late start there can be no doubt. In the course of the journey he had over-run three stations by almost a quarter of a mile, and the speed of the train when approaching the terminus was certainly excessive. There is even a suggestion that the driver was not completely familiar with his engine, and that his failure to realise that the gear lever had returned to the forward position was not due to a pure mischance. On the other hand, the station staff at Kitty-brewster were guilty of a breach of the rules in allowing the coaches of the down train to be brought into the station without warning the driver that the platform was already occupied. At the half-yearly meeting held in the following November, the chairman expressed regret that such a lamentable accident had almost coincided with the opening of the railway, and added that the special safety measures since introduced should effectually prevent its recurrence.

THE WATERLOO BRANCH

Although financial stringency was the primary reason for the decision not to carry the railway right into Aberdeen for the time being, even had funds been more plentiful there would have remained the difficulty of coming to terms with the Aberdeen company for the provision of a joint station. Originally, it had been intended to provide a high-level station for the use of both companies in Market Street, a short distance north of the junction of the Aberdeen Railway with the Great North. The trains of the latter company would have had to reverse at the junction in both directions, but at that time this was not considered objectionable. Largely because of the extortionate price demanded for the site, this plan was abandoned; and in 1850 powers were obtained to extend the Aberdeen Railway from Ferryhill to a terminus in Guild Street, adjacent to the harbour. Not only did this alteration fail to improve the approach from the north, but the site chosen for the station was cramped, and by no means central.

The disadvantages of having to reverse in and out of a terminal station had now been realised, and the Aberdeen company was pressed to contribute towards a larger and more convenient joint station, designed for through working. To this end a site north of the junction, but on the main line of the Great North, was acquired in 1852; but it soon became evident that negotiations between the two companies were progressing far from smoothly. In the next year powers were obtained to refer to arbitration points still outstanding when both railways had been completed up to the boundary of the proposed station; and until this work had been carried out neither company was to undertake any construction on the site of the station.

Meantime, the approaching completion of the railway from Kittybrewster to Huntly called for access to the harbour and physical connection with the Aberdeen Railway. At the half-yearly meeting in November 1853 it was announced that powers would be sought for a branch, 1¾ miles long, following the course of the canal round the outskirts of the city from Kittybrewster to the Waterloo Quay, where a passenger and goods station was to be

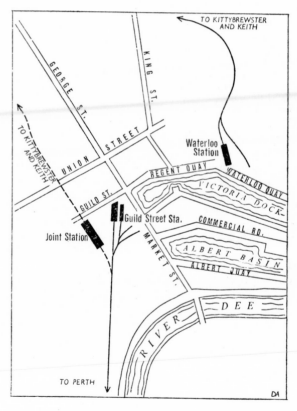

Relative position of Guild Street and Waterloo Stations
in Aberdeen

built on the site of the canal basin. The chairman added that negotiations were proceeding with the harbour trustees for the provision
of lines along the quays to link the new branch with the Aberdeen
Railway at Guild Street. As the use of locomotives on the quays was
prohibited, traffic on these connecting lines was to be worked by
horses.

The Act authorising the branch received the Royal Assent on
24 July 1854, but the work of construction had already been started,
as the canal had by that time passed into the hands of the railway.
The gradients were severe, and included nearly half a mile at 1 in
62 and 64, in addition to shorter stretches at 1 in 56 and 80. For the
most part the line was in a cutting, supported by retaining walls
and spanned by several bridges. The branch was opened for goods
traffic on 24 September 1855, but accommodation for passengers,
comprising waiting rooms, a booking office, and a single extremely
narrow island platform partly covered by a wooden over-all roof,
was not provided until 1 April of the next year. At the same time
the company's offices were moved to the new station from the
original premises at 75 Union Street. At Kittybrewster, the passenger terminus was replaced by a new station with platforms on the
branch.

Whatever may have been the merits of the new line in providing
improved access to the town and the harbour, the facilities for
exchanging traffic with the Aberdeen Railway left much to be
desired. The two stations of Waterloo and Guild Street were about
half a mile apart, and the difficulties and delays inseparable from
working goods wagons over the connecting lines with horses became increasingly serious as traffic developed. Passengers were conveyed between the stations in a special omnibus, and mails in a
Post Office van. Both the omnibus and the mail van soon acquired
unenviable notoriety.

CHAPTER 3

The Inevitable Sequel

THE INVERNESS COMPANIES

In Inverness, the varying fortunes of the Great North of Scotland Railway had long been regarded with a critical eye. It had become obvious that a considerable time must elapse before the company could complete its main line, and that a continued absence of railway facilities would inevitably react adversely on trade. On the other hand, it was impossible to take immediate steps to remove this danger. Quite apart from the great cost of the undertaking, the time was not yet ripe for a resuscitation of the scheme for a direct line across the mountains to Perth. Equally, any attempt to place part of the route to Aberdeen in the hands of an independent concern would be doomed to failure until the powers of the Great North expired in the summer of 1854. However, when it became clear that a complete revival of the Act of 1846 would not be sought, a company was floated in Inverness for the construction of a railway to Nairn, a distance of 15 miles.

Opposition to the scheme came from the Great North, on the grounds that it was an invasion of the territory assigned to that company by Parliament; but in view of all that had transpired during the past eight years, it may be doubted whether such an objection would have been upheld. At any rate, it was withdrawn on the understanding that as soon as a physical connection between the two railways had been established, the Great North should be granted running powers into Inverness. An agreement to this effect was, in fact, prepared, but never completed. However, it was quite clear that the directors of the Great North regarded the new undertaking as one over which their company would exercise a large measure of control, even though it retained its nominal independence. The Act received the Royal Assent on 24 July 1854; and the railway was opened on 6 November of the next year.[1]

[1] For the complete story of railways to Inverness, see *The Highland Railway*, by H. A. Vallance, published David & Charles

Shortly before the Inverness & Nairn Railway was authorised, another company was floated to continue the line for 22 miles from Nairn to Elgin, where it was proposed to wait for the Great North to undertake an extension of 31 miles from Huntly. The name chosen for the new undertaking, the Inverness & Elgin Junction Railway, was that adopted for one of the ill-fated projects of 1845. Strong protests against the proposals, coupled with threats of opposition in Parliament, were received from Aberdeen, on the grounds that the resources of the Great North would be unduly strained if that company was called upon to carry the railway across lower Strathspey unaided. As a compromise, it was agreed that each company should construct its line up to the River Spey, and that the cost of the connecting bridge should be jointly defrayed. The title of the newcomer was then changed to the Inverness & Aberdeen Junction Railway.

Although the two companies had negotiated a general basis of agreement, they had yet to reach a final understanding with regard to the Spey bridge. That this would prove difficult had been foreseen by the directors of the Great North, as they had insisted that unless complete agreement had been reached by the spring of 1855 they should be left free to limit the scope of their bill to a line from Huntly to Keith. In the event, agreement was not reached, and it appeared that the Inverness & Aberdeen Junction would stop short at Elgin, 18 miles from Keith.

The 12½-mile extension of the Great North from Huntly to Keith was authorised on 25 May 1855, and was opened, with intermediate stations at Rothiemay and Grange, on 10 October of the next year. For the most part, the gradients were easy, and the only major engineering work was the masonry bridge of five skew arches over the River Deveron at Rothiemay. Five services (subsequently reduced to four) were provided in each direction between Aberdeen and Keith, the journey time varying from 2h. 40m. to 3h. 5m.

Soon after the opening of the extension to Keith, the engineer, Benjamin Hall Blyth, resigned, and was succeeded by Alexander Gibb, who had had almost complete charge of the work of construction. Some months earlier, the board had decided to appoint a general manager, and Robert Milne, who had succeeded William Leslie as secretary in 1851, was chosen. For the next 12 years he acted in the dual capacity of general manager and secretary, but after the amalgamation of the Great North with its subsidiary companies, he relinquished the secretaryship in favour of William B. Ferguson, former general manager of the Deeside Railway.

THE JUNCTION AT KEITH

Throughout the summer of 1855, efforts were made to raise extra capital for carrying the Inverness & Aberdeen Junction Railway through to Keith, and negotiations were reopened with the Great North. An agreement was reached whereby the latter company was to subscribe £40,000 towards the construction of the line, and in return was to nominate two of its directors to the board of the Junction Railway. However, it was stipulated that no calls on the shares held by the Great North were to be made until £80,000 (that is, twice the amount of the agreed total subscription) had been expended on the works between Elgin and Keith, and on the Spey bridge.

The railway from Nairn to Keith was authorised on 21 July 1856, three months before the opening of the extension of the Great North from Huntly. At that time it was hoped to complete the section from Nairn to Elgin by the end of 1857, and the remainder of the line in the following spring; but the construction of the bridges over the Findhorn, at Forres, and the Spey, at Orton, was delayed by unexpected difficulties. To save expense, the design of the latter differed considerably from that proposed in 1846. Not only had the height of the bridge been much reduced, but the deep cuttings by which it was approached had been abandoned in favour of lighter earthworks. These modifications inevitably led to the adoption of steeper gradients than originally intended.

The railway was opened from Nairn to a temporary station at Dalvey (near Forres) in December 1857. It was extended to Elgin three months later, and the opening to the junction with the Great North at Keith took place on 18 August 1858. The Junction company at once took over the working of the Inverness & Nairn Railway, and the two undertakings were fully amalgamated in 1861.

The completion of the railway from Inverness to Keith did not occasion substantial changes in the timetables of the Great North. Three services in each direction were provided between Aberdeen and Inverness. The time for the journey of 108½ miles varied from 5h. 55m. (by the up mail) to 6½h. However, by March 1859, as the result of improvements south of Aberdeen, the down mail had been altered to start 1¾h. earlier. It now passed a few stations, but still required 2h. 40m. to reach Keith. At the same time, the number of trains between Aberdeen and Keith was restored to five in each direction, but the number of services to and from Inverness remained unaltered, although there were some slight improvements in journey times.

On the Great North, the mail trains remained first class only, and for a short period during 1860 and 1861 the fares by them were increased to 2d a mile. On the other hand, all trains west of Keith carried first and third class passengers at fares similar to those charged for the ordinary and parliamentary trains on the Great North. Through coaches were probably provided between Aberdeen and Inverness from the first[1], but the Great North did not attempt to insist on running powers west of Keith.

Thus was through railway communication established between Aberdeen and Inverness, but not in the manner so confidently expected 12 years earlier. Indeed, it must be admitted that the promoters of the Great North of Scotland Railway had failed lamentably in their undertaking. In place of the promised double line throughout the 108 miles, a single track had, with great difficulty, been provided for barely half the distance, while the remainder of the route had passed into the hands of a virtually independent concern. Nor by any stretch of the imagination could the connection with the Scottish North Eastern Railway at Aberdeen be considered satisfactory. A sorry enough picture, and one that could scarcely bring gratification, even to the most optimistic shareholder.

BOARD ROOM QUARRELS

The long-continued difficulties which had clouded the company's early years had served to alienate those who had given but grudging support to the scheme. Indeed, it had long been obvious that as soon as the time was opportune, the western end of the line would be placed in the hands of a company controlled from Inverness. The acquiescence of the Great North directorate in this development was made clear by the chairman at the opening ceremony of the extension from Huntly to Keith when he remarked that 'the company had been relieved of the duty of carrying the line through to Inverness by the parties to whom the influence in that part of the country legitimately belonged'. Yet, notwithstanding this pronouncement, steps had already been taken to secure representation on the board of the Inverness & Aberdeen Junction Railway. Moreover, active preparations were being made to extend the company's sphere of influence westwards to Elgin, the county town of

1 Contemporary timetables are obscure on this point

Morayshire, and south-westwards into the wooded and pastoral uplands of Strathspey.

In such circumstances, the chances of harmony at the board meetings in Inverness were slender. Nor were they enhanced by the high-handed attitude adopted by the directors from Aberdeen, who appear to have regarded the Junction Railway as their subsidiary. To make matters worse, there was an ever-growing demand for a more direct line from Inverness to Perth across the Grampians. Not only was the closest possible co-operation with the Inverness & Aberdeen Junction Railway envisaged, but many of that company's most influential shareholders had pledged their whole-hearted support.

It had been realised for a considerable time that a railway through the central Highlands was a necessity, for which a company would sooner or later be promoted in Inverness; but there can be no doubt that hopes were entertained in Aberdeen that by the time the scheme came to fruition the Great North would be in a position to secure some control of the undertaking. With this end in view, support was given to the Keith & Dufftown Railway, whose promoters readily accepted the suggestion that their purely local line of less than ten miles should be extended into Strathspey, at least as far as Grantown, where it would be certain to meet any direct railway from Inverness to Perth. Powers for the railway from Keith to Dufftown were obtained in 1857, and a working agreement was arranged with the Great North; but at this stage inability to raise funds caused the company to fall into a state of suspended animation. It was at this juncture that the agitation of the Inverness party was brought to a head by the intolerable position which had arisen at Aberdeen.

The interval between the arrival of a train at Guild Street and the departure of the connecting service from Waterloo was ample for crossing the half-mile of quays separating the two stations, provided the train from the south was not late. However, the Scottish North Eastern Railway enjoyed a rather doubtful record for punctuality, and the most important train of the day, the morning mail from Perth, with connections with the south of Scotland and England, was that most liable to be late. The train for Keith frequently had to be detained at Waterloo until the mails (for which it was bound to wait) could arrive.

To reduce these delays to a minimum, the convenience of passengers appears to have been deliberately disregarded; instructions were issued that the entrance gates of the station were to be closed at the advertised starting time, and only reopened to admit the mail van. Moreover, for some time after the opening of the Inverness & Aberdeen Junction Railway, this was the last train of the day for Inverness. It was even alleged that on more than one occasion, when the arrival of passengers at the last moment threatened to delay the train, the station gates were closed shortly *before* starting time.

By January 1860 the position had been improved by the provision of an additional service on the Inverness & Aberdeen Junction Railway, running in connection with the later train from Aberdeen. Although passengers who had missed the mail train were thus enabled to proceed beyond Keith that same evening, those arriving at Guild Street by the midday service from Perth were by no means certain of reaching Waterloo before the gates were closed.

Such high-handed treatment occasioned endless storms of complaint, and a persistent demand for a joint station in Aberdeen. In the absence of any definite moves in this direction, the directors of the Great North were accused of neglecting a vital obligation which, in view of the company's improved financial position, they were now well able to fulfil; for the dividends on the ordinary shares had risen from 1¼ per cent in 1855 and '56 to 4½ per cent in the next two years, and had reached 5 per cent in 1859. The Inverness party therefore redoubled efforts to secure support for a direct line across the mountains to Perth.

The agitation for improved facilities was speedily carried into the board room at Inverness, where the position of the two Great North directors became more and more invidious. The dissensions at the meetings were intensified, and the breach between the opposing factions threatened to become complete when, early in 1860, the Great North announced its intention of disposing of its holding in the Inverness & Aberdeen Junction Railway, and withdrawing its directors from the board.

Although this step was ostensibly precipitated by the refusal of the directors from Aberdeen to agree to an increase in the capital of the Junction Railway, other reasons were not far to seek. It had become obvious that the construction of a direct line from Inverness to Perth could no longer be delayed, and that the Inverness & Aberdeen Junction Railway would become completely independent of Aberdeen by entering into a working agreement with the new concern. Moreover, the Great North was committed to financial support of a number of nominally-independent companies that had recently obtained Acts for the construction of the branches in

Aberdeenshire and Banffshire originally authorised in 1846. In these circumstances the decision to release the capital invested in the Inverness & Aberdeen Junction Railway was scarcely surprising.

THE HIGHLAND RAILWAY

The scheme for the line through the central Highlands was launched under the title of the Inverness & Perth Junction Railway, and Joseph Mitchell, who had been appointed engineer, surveyed a route which differed from his ill-fated line of 1845 only in that the junction with the Inverness & Aberdeen Junction Railway was at Forres instead of Nairn. The short section of some eight miles from the Scottish North Eastern Railway at Stanley to Dunkeld had already been constructed by a local company, the Perth & Dunkeld, which it was proposed to merge with the new undertaking. Despite strong opposition, the line was authorised on 22 July 1861, and the railway was opened in sections during the summer of 1863, and completed on 9 September. The agreement with the Inverness & Aberdeen Junction Railway was so close that the two systems were worked as one from the outset. An Act authorising complete fusion was passed in 1865, and in August of that year the combined undertaking became known as the Highland Railway, with headquarters at Inverness.

On the completion of the direct line to Perth, the Inverness companies attempted to secure a monopoly of the traffic to and from the south by refusing to quote through rates and fares via Aberdeen. Second class accommodation was provided on the principal trains at fares approximately equal to those previously designated third class, and third class passengers were admitted to all trains at 1d a mile. On the other hand, in January 1864 the passenger fares by all trains on the Great North, save the solitary parliamentary service, were raised to 2d a mile first class, and 1½d a mile third class, at which level they remained for the next three years. The only concession was that the mail trains were made available to third class passengers.

Although the opposition to the consolidation of the Highland Railway was unavailing, clauses regulating and protecting through traffic passing via Aberdeen and Keith were inserted in the Act. To prevent undue preference being given to the direct route to the south, the Great North was to have its own booking office at Inverness, and its through traffic was to be treated equally with that of the Highland company. The latter was to co-operate in fixing the rates for this traffic but, in any case, was to receive the same mileage rate for traffic passing *via* Aberdeen as for that on its own main line. The maximum mileage was also granted to the Highland Railway by making Keith the point of exchange with the Great North, although the latter already controlled an alternative route to Elgin (see Chapters 4 and 6).

These arrangements were of little benefit to the Great North, because almost all traffic between Perth and the south and places west of Keith had already passed to the new and shorter route. The loss of the valuable contract for the mails resulted in the Sunday trains between Aberdeen and Keith being withdrawn at the end of 1864.

The effect of this diversion of traffic on the finances of the company was immediate and severe, and the dividend on the ordinary shares, which had risen to 7¼ per cent in 1862, and declined only fractionally to 7 per cent in the next year, dropped to 5 per cent in 1864, and was passed altogether a year later. By that time, the company had become heavily involved with its subsidiary undertakings, several of which were in need of substantial assistance. Whatever the potentialities of these branches, their traffic was not yet sufficiently developed to make good the loss of traffic on the main line.

This set-back in the company's prosperity was the final repercussion of the disasters which had attended its earliest years. Inability to raise capital had brought about the repeal of the Act for amalgamation with the Aberdeen Railway; and now failure to reach Inverness had resulted in the railway through the central Highlands being constructed under independent ownership. With dividends dwindling, and the prospect of hard times ahead, many a shareholder must have looked back with regret to the summer of 1846, when the company's future seemed assured, and the title *Great* North of Scotland Railway was in no danger of becoming a misnomer.

CHAPTER 4

The Morayshire Railway

FROM ELGIN TO LOSSIEMOUTH

The possibility of connecting the city of Elgin with the port of Lossiemouth by rail was first considered in 1841, but although a preliminary survey revealed that the line could be constructed easily and cheaply, the necessary support was not forthcoming. Some four years later, thanks to the efforts of James Grant, a local banker and distiller, and subsequently Lord Provost of Elgin, the scheme was revived as the Morayshire Railway; and it was then proposed to extend the line for 16 miles beyond Elgin to Craigellachie, in Strathspey. It was even optimistically suggested that the railway should be double track.

Preparations were made to seek parliamentary powers in 1846, but before the bill was lodged the Great North of Scotland Railway had been promoted. It was therefore decided to connect the two railways at Elgin, and to construct the Craigellachie extension from Orton, ten miles to the east, leaving the main line of the Great North to form the connecting link. Powers for this scheme were obtained on 16 July 1846, three weeks after the passing of the Act for the Great North. However, before construction could be started the company was involved in the financial panic of 1847; and for the next four years the undertaking lay dormant.

In 1851, changes in the directorate were followed by a crisis. The board announced that powers would be sought to abandon the extension to Craigellachie; but a number of shareholders in Edinburgh, who disagreed with such a step, immediately attempted to secure the abandonment of the whole line, under the Abandonment of Railways Act of 1850. Although the continued existence of the company was assured by the defeat of the motion for complete abandonment at a meeting held in Edinburgh on 24 February, the disgruntled faction withdrew its support, and for the time being the financial position became extremely critical. The Railway Commissioners granted a warrant for the abandonment of the extension to

Craigellachie on 10 July; but it was not until the Elgin town council had agreed to increase its already considerable holding by £1,000, and Col Brander of Pitgaveny, a local landowner, who had throughout been one of the company's staunchest supporters, had made a substantial addition to his subscription, that the contract for the 5½ miles from Elgin to Lossiemouth could be let to Hutchings & Company of London.

The first sod was cut by Mrs Grant, the wife of James Grant, at Bareflat Hills, near Elgin, on 28 November 1851, and construction was pushed forward with all possible speed. The line passed through flat country on easy gradients, and a bridge over the River Lossie was the principal engineering work. Originally, the shallow Loch Spynie was crossed on an embankment, but the part of the loch lying to the west of the railway was drained in 1861.

The chief difficulty encountered by the contractor appears to have been caused by an influx of Irish navvies, who were willing to accept very low wages. The local men previously employed not unnaturally resented this invasion. Matters reached a climax one evening in April 1852, when a large force of Morayshire men assembled on the outskirts of Elgin with the intention of ejecting the Irish from the district. Although no serious injuries appear to have been received in the ensuing fracas, the sheriff appointed ten extra constables, at the expense of the railway company, to keep order along the line.

The railway was opened on 10 August 1852. In Elgin, the day was observed as a general holiday, and a procession, headed by the directors of the company, marched through the streets to the station, where a delay of more than an hour occurred while defects in the engine of the special train provided for the distinguished guests were rectified. At length, all was in readiness, and amidst the cheers of the crowd, the train started on its journey. On arriving at Lossiemouth, the directors were entertained by the members of the harbour board at the new Steamboat & Railway Hotel, where several enthusiastic speeches were made, and the prosperity of both undertakings toasted. The party then returned to Elgin, where the rejoicings concluded with a banquet.

Regular services began next morning. For some time five trains were provided in each direction, on weekdays only, but this was subsequently reduced to four before being increased to six in 1857. The journey of 5½ miles occupied 15m., with conditional stops at Linksfield Level Crossing and Greens of Drainie. No permanent station buildings appear to have been erected at these points, and both names disappeared from the timetables at the end of 1859.

Two classes of accommodation—'first' and 'second' until 1855, and subsequently 'first' and 'third'—were provided, the fares for which were 1½d and 1d a mile respectively. However, it would appear that the difference between the two standards of comfort was not great, because one of the earliest coaches to be delivered was described by the local newspaper as running on four wheels, and seating 40 passengers, in one first and three second class compartments—an average of ten per compartment. Obviously the first class passenger was afforded no more space than his more plebian neighbour, although doubtless his compartment boasted somewhat superior upholstery.

Although a dividend of 5 per cent was declared after the first year's working, this was the highwatermark of the company's prosperity, and thereafter its history was a continual struggle to turn the proverbial corner. For some years the line was entirely isolated from all other railways, and dependent for its revenue on local traffic. Thus, in 1855, when Lossiemouth harbour was almost closed for four months while improvements were carried out, traffic fell off to an extent that called for special mention at the annual meeting in the following October. At this meeting James Grant, to whose efforts the company owed so much, was elected chairman.

THE CRAIGELLACHIE EXTENSION

When the original powers for the Great North of Scotland Railway lapsed in 1854, proposals were afoot for the completion of the line from Elgin to Orton and Craigellachie under the sole ownership of the Morayshire Railway. However, with the advent of the Inverness & Aberdeen Junction Railway it was decided to revert to the plan of 1846, and use that company's track between Elgin and Orton. Negotiations with the Junction company were successfully concluded; and on 14 July 1856 the Morayshire was again authorised to construct the extension from Orton to Craigellachie, and to connect its line with that of the Inverness & Aberdeen Junction Railway at Elgin. This Act antedated that of the IAJR by seven days.

The junction at Orton was a short distance west of the bridge over the Spey. Originally it was intended to provide a passenger station with platforms on both lines at this point, but to save the expense of constructing the extra platforms for the Morayshire trains, the site was moved about a quarter of a mile to the west. This alteration occasioned some delay, and the works at the junction were by no means complete when Capt Tyler carried out a preliminary inspection on behalf of the Board of Trade in July 1858. By the time the Inverness & Aberdeen Junction Railway was extended from Elgin to Keith on 18 August the inspector had expressed his satisfaction with the works, provided the junction at Orton was used only by passenger trains until a goods siding had been completed. With this stipulation, the 3½ miles of the Moray-shire extension from Orton to Rothes were opened on 23 August. For the most part, the line skirted the Spey, and there were no outstanding engineering works. There was one intermediate station, at Sourden, at which the trains called conditionally.

The completion of the railway from Rothes to Craigellachie was delayed until 23 December 1858. To avoid a costly bridge over the Spey the terminus was placed on the west bank of the river, a short distance from Telford's famous iron bridge, built in 1815. The opening of the extension was marked by an increase in the fares —to 2d a mile first class and 1½d a mile third class—by all trains except a parliamentary service in each direction.

The station on the Morayshire Railway at Elgin was situated some 300 yd from that of the Inverness & Aberdeen Junction Railway. To facilitate the transport of materials and plant required for the construction of the line from Elgin to Keith, and Orton to Craigellachie, which arrived by sea at Lossiemouth, a temporary connection between the two railways was hurriedly completed and brought into use a few weeks after the opening of the railway from Forres to Elgin in March 1858. When reporting on his inspection of the works some three months later, Capt Tyler commented sharply on the fact that no formal notification of this step had been sent to the Board of Trade, and added, with almost pained surprise, that his enquiries as to the reason for this omission had only elicited the reply that neither company had thought of it. The inspector recom-mended that a passenger platform for the Morayshire trains should be provided adjacent to the station of the Inverness & Aberdeen Junction Railway; and the opening of the connecting line was deferred, pending the completion of the permanent track and the bridge carrying the main road over the railway.

Another surprise awaited Capt Tyler when he returned in Sep-tember, some days after a certificate to the effect that the works were now complete had been received from the engineer. He found that the company had anticipated his permission to open the line, and that it was already in regular use by passenger trains. Although there remained no further grounds for criticism of the works, he felt bound to draw attention to this apparent disregard of authority. The result was that the company received a pointed enquiry from the Board of Trade as to why such action had been taken, together with a request that any reasons for the non-enforcement of the penalties incurred thereby should be advanced.

In his reply, the secretary emphasised that the position had arisen through a misunderstanding. The temporary connection had never been used by locomotives or passenger trains, and such goods wagons and empty passenger coaches as had passed over it had been hauled by horses. Capt Tyler had recommended certain alterations and improvements in the layout and the signals, and the engineer understood that it only remained to fulfil these requirements before the line was brought into full use, and that no further inspection would be necessary. As soon as the work was completed, notification had been sent to the Board of Trade, and thereafter locomotives had been used and passengers had been allowed to keep their seats while passing to and from the Inverness & Aberdeen Junction Railway. This explanation apparently satisfied the Board of Trade, for we hear no more of the incident.

Under the agreement with the Inverness & Aberdeen Junction Railway, the Morayshire company was to work its own trains between Elgin and Orton, and pay 40 per cent of the rates for the traffic calculated on a mileage basis for the use of the track. Its trains were not to call at the intermediate stations. This arrangement only remained in force for about six weeks, by which time it had become clear that the Morayshire engines were quite unsuited to the far from easy gradients on the Junction Railway. The company's engineer and locomotive superintendent, James Samuel, had made extravagant claims for his design of light engines, but few, if any, had been realised. Even while the line extended only from Elgin to Lossiemouth, cases of engine failure had not been uncommon; and it was now alleged that dislocation of traffic between Elgin and Keith, resulting from the unpunctuality of the Morayshire trains, was almost an everyday occurrence. After strong representations from Inverness, a new agreement was made, whereby the Morayshire coaches were to be attached to the trains of the Junction company between Elgin and Orton, and the latter was to receive an additional 10 per cent of the receipts.

The revised agreement had not been in force for long when a serious dispute arose between the two companies. The Inverness & Aberdeen Junction claimed that the proportional rates should apply only to traffic from Craigellachie and Rothes to Lossiemouth and *vice versa*, and that traffic for all other places should pass completely out of the hands of the Morayshire company at Elgin or Orton. The latter strongly resisted these demands, and when steps were taken to enforce them diverted traffic away from the Junction Railway. Goods consigned to places west of Elgin were carried on to Lossiemouth, and dispatched thence by carriers' carts, at rates considerably below those charged by the Inverness & Aberdeen Junction Railway, while traffic for Inverness was forwarded by sea from Lossiemouth, frequently without the knowledge or consent of the consignor. Matters dragged on for some time without a settlement, until on 15 September 1859 the Junction company intimated that all traffic, both passenger and goods, except that actually passing between stations on the two sections of the Morayshire Railway, must be rebooked at Elgin or Orton.

The dispute aroused considerable local feeling, and when the terms of the agreement for the common use of the line between Elgin and Orton were called into question, the Junction company issued a statement in justification of its action. Decidedly restrained in tone, this explanation contrasted sharply with the reply of the Morayshire directors, who sought to impute the blame for their unfortunate position to the parliamentary solicitor who had acted for both companies. They alleged that insufficient care had been exercised in the preparation of the agreement, with the result that it was ambiguous to an extent which allowed the owning company to insist on the rebooking of traffic. In conclusion, they announced their intention to connect the two portions of the system by means of a line through the Glen of Rothes.

THROUGH THE GLEN OF ROTHES

Whether the Inverness & Aberdeen Junction company hoped by insisting on the strict letter of the agreement to acquire the Morayshire Railway, having first made its position untenable, must remain an open question. If such was the expected outcome of the dispute, the result must have caused disappointment, if not consternation. The smaller company lost no time in promoting its line from Elgin to Rothes and, to make the break with Inverness complete, opened negotiations for an agreement with the Great North. The latter not only expressed its willingness to take over the working of the railway for 45 per cent of the receipts, as soon as the two systems were physically connected, but offered to subscribe £20,000 towards the cost of the new line.

For the moment, a gap of 15 miles separated the western terminus of the Great North at Keith, from the Morayshire Railway at Craigellachie, but the greater part of it was soon to be bridged by the nominally-independent Keith & Dufftown, and Strathspey Railways. Provided that the Morayshire company's bill was successful, it would only remain to construct the connecting link at Craigellachie, less than one mile in length, for the Great North to gain access to Elgin.

The Act for the line through the Glen of Rothes received the Royal Assent on 3 July 1860; and the railway was opened for goods on 30 December 1861, and for passengers on 1 January 1862. The junction with the Lossiemouth line faced towards Elgin, necessitating a reverse for through trains. There was one intermediate station, at Longmorn; but on 5 June 1863 a platform, at which trains called conditionally, was opened at Coleburns. By 1871 this stop had been replaced by another, also conditional, at Birchfield Platform, 1½ miles nearer to Rothes.

None of the engineering works could be considered outstanding, but the gradients were severe. From Elgin there was an unbroken climb for over five miles, for the most part at 1 in 66, 50 and 74, to the summit of the line at Coleburns. The corresponding rise from Rothes, although shorter, included more than a mile at 1 in 50. By reducing the distance from Elgin to Rothes to ten miles, the new line saved more than three miles over the route *via* Orton.

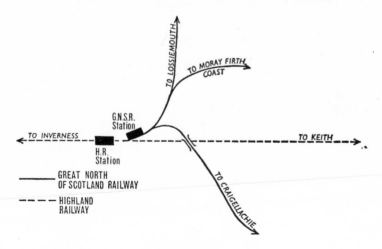

Lines at Elgin

At Elgin, alterations and additions were made to the passenger station. The primitive accommodation that had sufficed for the local traffic to and from Lossiemouth had already been supplemented by the platform on the connecting line adjoining the station of the Inverness & Aberdeen Junction Railway; and now the altered traffic arrangements, and the necessity of providing accommodation for the Great North of Scotland Railway in the not far distant future, called for further additions. Impecunious as ever, the company reduced the cost to a minimum, with the result that many of the buildings were constructed almost wholly of timber, and the platforms were left unprotected from the weather. This lack of amenities was excused on the grounds that the premises were of a temporary nature, and would be replaced as soon as circumstances permitted. Nevertheless, with a few minor alterations and additions, they were destined to last for 40 years.

Before the opening of the direct line to Rothes, three trains in each direction had been provided between Elgin and Craigellachie on weekdays only, with an additional service on Fridays and Elgin fair days. As the coaches were attached to the trains of the Inverness & Aberdeen Junction Railway between Elgin and Orton, good connections were assured to passengers travelling between Craigellachie and stations west of Orton; but it was otherwise for those proceeding to or from Keith, who had to change at the junction. Nor were the connections at Elgin well arranged, for most of the trains to and from Lossiemouth waited a considerable time at that station. The reason for these delays is not clear, because the junction with the Inverness & Aberdeen Junction Railway faced towards the west, and it was a simple matter to detach the Morayshire coaches from westbound trains, while even in the opposite direction the shunting operations could scarcely be described as complicated. In addition to the through trains, there were a few local trips between Elgin and Lossiemouth.

The opening of the new line did not occasion any sweeping changes. The through trains between Lossiemouth and Craigellachie were diverted via Longmorn, but there were still only three daily. The average journey time was reduced from about 55m. to 45m. Three trains continued to run between Craigellachie and Orton, but the connections at Orton were intended solely for passengers to and from Keith and the Great North of Scotland Railway. A journey between Craigellachie and Elgin by this route became almost impossible.

On 17 May 1861 the Morayshire company was authorised to

extend its line across the Spey at Craigellachie to join the Strathspey Railway, authorised on the same day from Dufftown to Abernethy, near Grantown-on-Spey. At Dufftown the latter line joined the Keith & Dufftown Railway, at that time under construction. The bridge over the river had three plate girder spans of 57 ft, and one lattice girder span of 200 ft across the main channel, supported on masonry piers, the foundations of which were carried down to a depth of 14 ft.

The construction of the line proceeded slowly, and occupied over two years. Meantime, the Keith & Dufftown Railway was completed and opened for traffic. At length, the extension of the Morayshire Railway and the Strathspey Railway were opened simultaneously on 1 July 1863, and an alternative route from Keith to Elgin, entirely independent of the Inverness & Aberdeen Junction Railway, became available. However, as the distance between the two towns by the latter railway was only 18 miles, as against 27½ via Craigellachie, the older route retained practically all the through traffic. The working agreement with the Great North came into force forthwith, and to all outward appearances the Morayshire Railway lost its separate identity.

Four trains in each direction were run between Elgin and Keith by the new route, three of which had through coaches, or connections, to or from Aberdeen. The trains called at all stations, and the journey time varied from 84m. (by one eastbound train) to 110m. The average time was about 98m. However, this poor performance was quite in keeping with that on the Great North of Scotland and the Inverness & Aberdeen Junction Railway with their far easier gradients. The disparity in the length of the two routes inevitably led to timetable difficulties. Two trains leaving Keith at approximately the same time, in connection with a service from Aberdeen, could not connect with each other at Elgin, and passengers changing there faced long waits. Similarly, in the opposite direction, a train running via Craigellachie had to leave Elgin more than half an hour before the arrival of the corresponding service from Inverness to make its connection at Keith.

AMALGAMATION WITH THE GREAT NORTH

The importance of the branch from Rothes to Orton had now completely declined. Local traffic was of the scantiest, and the Great North was naturally unwilling to improve the connections, especially because the distance from Rothes to Keith via Orton was six miles less than that *via* Craigellachie. On more than one occasion it was strongly represented from Aberdeen that the line was redundant, and being worked at a loss. However, for the time being the services were continued in deference to the wishes of the Morayshire company.

By the end of 1865 the Great North was seeking to consolidate its position by amalgamating with its subsidiary companies, whose traffic it had always worked, and whose independence had never been more than nominal. Such were the financial ties binding these undertakings to the parent company, that in most cases fusion presented little difficulty. On the other hand, despite a desire on both sides to embrace the Morayshire Railway in the scheme, an examination of that company's finances revealed serious obstacles. However, when the Act for the consolidation of the Great North received the Royal Assent on 30 July 1866, the Morayshire company simultaneously obtained powers to amalgamate with the Great North as soon as terms had been agreed.

On the day following the passing of this Act (31 July) the Great North suspended all services between Rothes and Orton, on the grounds that they were no longer required. This action was taken without notice, and aroused considerable local resentment. When the matter was referred to the Railways Department of the Board of Trade, it was disclosed that the Morayshire company had agreed to accept a small annual payment from the Great North as compensation for the withdrawal of this unprofitable service, and that this arrangement was to come into force as soon as the Act paving the way for amalgamation was passed. The protest subsided after this explanation, but whether the owning company or the working company was at fault for failing to give notice that the line was to be closed does not appear to have been established. Regular services were never restored, and the junction with the Highland Railway at Orton was soon removed; but for some years goods wagons were worked as required between Rothes and Sourden siding. Thereafter the line lay derelict, and became completely overgrown. The permanent way was not removed until 1907.

The chequered history of the Morayshire Railway had now reached its final stage, the tranquillity of which contrasted sharply with the stormy times that had characterised its early years. On the death of James Grant in 1872, the deputy chairman, Alexander Urquhart, was elected chairman, and remained in office throughout the remainder of the company's separate existence.

Although the hope had been expressed in 1866 that the difficulties standing in the way of an amalgamation with the Great North would soon be removed, more than 14 years elapsed before the scheme came to fruition. In 1876 the Great North secured powers to meet the outstanding debts of the smaller company in case of necessity. Four years later negotiations for an amalgamation were resumed, and the Act authorising the fusion, as from 1 October 1880, received the Royal Assent on 11 August 1881.

Among the officers of the Morayshire Railway who came to the Great North was Alexander Watt, the secretary, who had entered the service of the company in 1853. In 1861 he was appointed to the dual position of general manager and secretary, but relinquished the former office when the Great North took over the working of the line in 1863. Thereafter he was closely associated with the negotiations for amalgamation with the Great North, and it was largely through his efforts that they were brought to a successful conclusion. When the winding up of the Morayshire company was completed Watt succeeded George Morison, the former manager of the Banffshire Railway, as superintendent of the Northern Section of the Great North of Scotland Railway, and continued in that office until his retirement in 1906.

CHAPTER 5

The Banffshire Railway

EARLY SCHEMES

The need for railway communication along the Banffshire coast was realised at an early date. In this district, the heights of Aultmore and the Knock, between Keith and the sea, render the construction of branches to the coast from an inland main line far less easy than is the case farther west. The promoters of the Aberdeen, Banff & Elgin Railway of 1846 solved the difficulty by proposing a line along the coast, although by so doing they had necessarily to avoid Keith. Failure to serve a market centre of such importance constituted a cogent argument against that ill-fated scheme.

On the other hand, the original Act for the Great North of Scotland Railway not only provided for the main line to pass through Keith, but also included powers for a branch from Grange to Portsoy and Banff. The course of the latter line was determined by the position of the gap of Glenbarry, lying to the east of the Aultmore highlands. For the moment, at any rate, the company did not contemplate extending its line along the coast to serve the fishing havens to the west of Portsoy.

However, a separate undertaking, the Banffshire Railway, was to run from Portgordon to Dufftown, on a sinuous course of approximately 21 miles by way of Gordon Castle, Fochabers, Forgie, Keith, and the upper glen of the Isla. Although the difficulties inseparable from carrying the line direct across the uplands were avoided by skirting the hills, the section between Fochabers and Keith included long and steep gradients. It is probable that this part of the route was determined by the requirements of the Fochabers estate of the Duke of Richmond, who supported the scheme. As the capital was to be restricted to £120,000, no ambitious standards of construction could be entertained.

Plans were deposited for this line and for the Banffshire Extension Railway, extending from Dufftown through Glenrinnes and into the valley of the Avon. The parent company lodged its bill with

MAIN LINE STATION SCENES

(13) Sketch of the northbound platform at the old station at Inverurie, closed in 1902. From the Aberdeen Daily Journal, 11 February 1902.

(14) Huntly station from the south, showing the overall roof since removed. Note the signal for controlling exit from the sidings.

(15) Keith Junction. Line to Elgin via Rothes on the left, GNSR bays in middle and Highland platform in the distance. The station buildings were completely replaced in 1988.

STATIONS ON THE GLEN ROUTE TO ELGIN

(16)   Keith Town, looking towards the Junction. The wooden building design was used throughout the system with only minor changes in detail from the 1880s onwards.

(17)   The neat ensemble of station buildings at Dufftown. Two signal boxes were provided here, one for each end of the loop.

(18)   Craigellachie from the south. The main platforms are to the right and the Speyside platform is in the centre. The main signal box was behind the photographer.

STATIONS ON THE COAST LINE

(19) The sharply curved station at Cullen, looking west. A more substantial
wooden building than was commonly provided. Houses now occupy the site.

(20) Spey Bay from the south, with the typical style of wooden building
found on this section. The minor signal box on the left dated from the opening
of the line.

(21) Banff Harbour, the terminus of the branch from Tillynaught. There was
no proper run-round for passenger trains here; coaches were gravity-shunted
into the platform.

BUCHAN LINE STATIONS

(22) *Maud from the south in 1955, Fraserburgh platforms on the left, Peterhead ones on the right. The signal box dates from 1935, when the earlier boxes were replaced, and was the only LNER box on the Great North.*

(23) *Philorth in 1955, looking towards Fraserburgh. Originally a private station for Lord Saltoun.*

(24) *Fraserburgh in 1937. The St Combs trains generally used the platform on the right. Engine shed on the left, goods yard on the right.*

Parliament, but at that stage financial collapse occurred, and the undertaking was wound up. The scheme for the extension died a natural death.

However ill-considered these proposals may appear in the light of after years, it must be borne in mind that in the 1840s the glens which the railways would have served had not been seriously denuded of their population by emigration. Moreover, Portgordon was then a flourishing seaport, exporting large quantities of lime from the extensive works at Blackhillock, near Keith, and importing the coal required for the preparation of the lime.

CONSTRUCTION AND OPENING

After the financial crash which followed the Railway Mania, it was obvious that the Great North would not be in a position to embark on the construction of the branches for some considerable time. There was, however, local support for a proposal to place the line from Grange to Banff and Portsoy in the hands of an independent concern, and the Banff, Portsoy & Strathisla Railway was authorised on 27 July 1857. The main line was to run from Grange to Banff Harbour, a distance of 16¼ miles, and there was to be a branch of 3¼ miles from Tillynaught to Portsoy.

The headquarters of the company were in Banff, and most of the directors were local landowners and business men, but the chairman was the Hon Thomas Bruce, the deputy chairman of the Inverness & Aberdeen Junction Railway. Two local men, John Forbes and James Grierson, were appointed secretary and general manager respectively. In 1859 the latter was succeeded by George Morison. The contractors were B. & E. Blyth, of Edinburgh, and construction was supervised by their resident engineer, William Keir, who continued as the company's engineer until the Great North took over the working of the line in 1863.

To avoid heavy earthworks, a ruling gradient of 1 in 70 was adopted for a considerable distance on either side of the summit at Glenbarry, and on the Portsoy branch. Between Tillynaught and Banff the gradients were easier, although there were one or two stretches as steep as 1 in 80. The harbour at Portsoy was approached from the passenger station, at the back of the town, by a steep fall at 1 in 30 for half a mile. Special precautions had to be taken to ensure the safe working of this extreme gradient. The Great North of Scotland Railway rule book for 1867 states that the gate of the level crossing at the foot of the incline was worked by the same lever as the safety points nearby, and that the maximum load for one engine was restricted to four wagons.

The railway was opened throughout on 30 July 1859, but a derailment prevented more than one train from running on that day, and full services did not begin until 2 August. Although the junction with the Great North at Grange faced towards Keith, there was no through running, and the Banff trains were accommodated at a bay on the up platform. On the main line, intermediate stations were provided at Knock, Cornhill, Tillynaught and Ladysbridge. Trains also called conditionally at Millegan, Barry and Ordens, but these names had disappeared from the timetables by 1864. Millegan was closed permanently, but Barry was reopened, and renamed Glenbarry, in 1872. Ordens was retained as a conditional unadvertised stop, although, for some obscure reason, after an interval of more than 50 years, the name reappeared in *Bradshaw* from January 1917 to September 1920. In 1913, halts were opened at Bridgefoot, and Golf Club House, between Ladysbridge and Banff.

The history of the company as an independent concern is mainly one of financial embarrassment. The authorised capital was £90,000 with £30,000 in loans, but great difficulty was experienced in getting the whole paid up. The receipts on the capital account amounted to less than £48,000; and the directors were forced to admit that they could only rely on the continued exertions of the shareholders to assist them in this predicament. As the greater part of the shares were held locally in small blocks, the prospects of the arrears being overtaken in the immediate future were by no means bright. At the end of the first year's working it was stated that the traffic, especially in passengers, had exceeded expectations, and that the receipts were ample to meet the working expenses, but not to cover the whole of the interest charges. A dividend of 2 per cent was declared, but the deficit on the capital account remained.

THE GREAT NORTH TAKES OVER

Matters dragged on for more than three years without a satisfactory solution being found. At length, the Great North agreed to work the line, as from 1 February 1863, for 60 per cent of the receipts. However, it was stipulated that if the receipts reached £7 per mile per week, the proportion paid to the working company should be reduced to 50 per cent. On 21 July the agreement was confirmed by Parliament; and to mark the passing of the old order the undertaking was then renamed the Banffshire Railway.

The Act of 21 July 1863 also authorised the extension of the railway along the coast from Portsoy to Portgordon, a distance of 14¼ miles. Fresh capital was to be raised to the extent of £100,000, with borrowing powers of £33,000. The Great North was authorised to contribute £80,000. The extension was planned to run inland for some two miles from Portsoy, as far as Sandend, whence it was to reach Cullen by skirting the shore at the foot of the cliffs. By this means, several heavy earthworks and high viaducts in the neighbourhood of the latter town were avoided. Between Cullen and Portgordon the line was to follow the coast, at some distance from the shore.

The company's financial troubles continued, for after the Great North had taken its 60 per cent of the gross receipts the balance was insufficient to meet the interest charges. In consequence, it was not found possible to begin work on the extension to Portgordon. Nevertheless, in 1865 the directors reported that 'the line continues to be satisfactorily worked by the Great North of Scotland Railway'.

An Act dated 30 July 1866 extended the time for the completion of the railway to Portgordon by one year, and granted optional powers for amalgamation with the Great North of Scotland Railway. On the same day the latter company was authorised to amalgamate with its subsidiaries; but the fact that the Banffshire Railway had originated as a separate concern, and was still financially embarrassed, precluded immediate fusion.

Some twelve months later, after much negotiation, the local company gave up the unequal struggle, and the amalgamation already foreshadowed was confirmed by the Act of 12 August 1867. At the same time, powers were obtained to abandon the extension to Portgordon. With few exceptions, the officers and staff of the Banffshire Railway entered the service of the Great North, and George Morison, the general superintendent (designated general manager until 1863), became superintendent of the newly-formed northern section, embracing the lines north and west of Keith.

At first, there were three trains between Grange and Banff, and two others between Banff and Portsoy, which reversed at Tillynaught. Connecting trains on the Portsoy branch made up the daily total to six in each direction, so that this was the best-served portion of the line. The schedules were generous, even for those days, and the average time for the journey between Grange and Banff was slightly over one hour, although for some time one up train was scheduled in 45m. Until 1863 all trains carried first and third class passengers at 2d and 1d a mile respectively, but thereafter the third class fares became 1½d a mile, except by one Parliamentary train.

The relatively lavish provision of trains on the Portsoy branch may be explained by the fact that the town was then a flourishing seaport. The importance of its trade justified the expensive extension through the town to the harbour. This line ran in a deep cutting, flanked by retaining walls and spanned by three bridges. Unfortunately, the coming of the railway proved the undoing of Portsoy as a seaport, and the harbour line went out of use about 25 years later, although the track was not removed until the spring of 1910. A connection to the harbour at Banff (easier to construct because the main terminus adjoined the quay) shared a similar fate.

CHAPTER 6

Expansion and Consolidation

THE KEITH & DUFFTOWN RAILWAY

When the Great North of Scotland Railway reached Keith in the autumn of 1856, its total mileage became 54, or slightly more than one-third of that authorised ten years earlier. However, in the course of the next decade this figure was almost quadrupled by branches and extensions, most of which had been projected, if not authorised, in 1846. These lines were built as nominally-independent undertakings, but were financially assisted by the Great North, and worked by that company from the outset.

To serve upper Strathisla, part of the Banffshire Railway scheme of 1845 was revived as a line from Keith to Dufftown, a distance of ten miles. The support of the Great North was secured, and a complete working agreement speedily followed. By securing control of the line, not only did the Great North ensure that it should not be absorbed by the Inverness & Aberdeen Junction Railway, but paved the way for an extension westwards from Dufftown to Grantown-on-Spey. As the western portion of the railway from Aberdeen to Inverness had passed into the hands of an independent company, the strategic value of such an extension was beyond question.

Powers for the Keith & Dufftown Railway were obtained on 27 July 1857. The line joined the Great North immediately to the east of Keith station, and according to the company's prospectus, the works were 'as easy as the country would allow', with a maximum gradient of 1 in 70. The authorised capital was £50,000, with £16,000 in loans. The Great North was to subscribe £1,000, and was to nominate two directors to the board.

The task of raising the capital proved extremely difficult, and for more than two years very little construction could be undertaken. At a special meeting held on 29 October 1859, letters were read from three prominent shareholders, who were together prepared to guarantee £13,500; but despite this public-spirited action there still remained a serious deficiency in subscriptions. At the same meeting it was announced that, as the company's powers would expire in the following July, the opportunity was being taken to secure a more favourable, although somewhat longer line, the surveys for which were then being made. This amended route was authorised on 25 May 1860. The share and loan capital remained unaltered, but the Great North increased its subscription to £25,000, and doubled its representation on the board. Sufficient funds were then forthcoming to allow construction to proceed without interruption; and the railway was opened on 21 February 1862.

Although the amended line was described as more favourable than that originally authorised, the gradients were somewhat harder and the greater part of the ascent from Dufftown to the summit at the western end of Loch Park was at 1 in 60. The engineering works included a masonry viaduct of two spans of 60 ft over the Fiddich, near Dufftown, and several smaller bridges over the Isla. But the most remarkable feature of the line, particularly from the scenic point of view, was at Loch Park, where the railway ran for more than a mile beside the water at the foot of a steep wooded hill.

Intermediate stations were provided at Earlsmill, Botriphnie and Drummuir. Botriphnie was renamed Auchindachy in 1862; and Earlsmill was more appropriately designated Keith Town in 1897.

The early train services call for little comment. At first, four trains were run in each direction on weekdays only, but this number was subsequently reduced to three. The trains called at all stations, the journey time varying from 40 to 50m. After the railway had been extended beyond Dufftown, and had become part of a through route from Keith to Elgin, the services previously withdrawn were restored, and there was a slight improvement in speed.

Financial difficulties continued after the line was opened. Within four months the Great North had to step in as guarantor of the company's mortgage debts; and two years later increased its subscription to the capital account by £10,000. Nevertheless, the subsidiary undertaking maintained its nominal independence until 1866.

THROUGH STRATHSPEY

The reauthorisation of the Keith & Dufftown Railway in 1860 was followed by an announcement that powers would be sought at an early date to extend the line into Strathspey. The Act was obtained on 17 May 1861, but the undertaking was placed in the hands of an independent company, the Strathspey. The Great North of Scotland and the Keith & Dufftown subscribed £100,000 and £25,000 respectively, and nominated directors to the board. The former also undertook to work the railway.

From Dufftown, the line ran north-westwards to Craigellachie (where it met the extension of the Morayshire Railway, authorised on the same day) and thence beside the Spey to terminate at Abernethy, near Grantown, a distance of 32½ miles. To provide an outlet to the south, the Act included powers for a branch from Grantown to a point near Dulnan Bridge, where a junction was to be made with the Inverness & Perth Junction Railway, the bill for which was still before Parliament in May 1861.

The main line was opened throughout to Abernethy on 1 July 1863, but the construction of the branch was not undertaken. In consequence, when the final section of the Inverness & Perth Junction Railway was opened in September 1863, traffic could not be exchanged with the Strathspey Railway, and the revenue of the latter suffered severely. Two years later steps were taken to provide the much-needed connection, and on 5 July 1865 the company was authorised to extend its line from Abernethy across the Spey to the Highland Railway[1], some three miles north of Boat of Garten.

Soon after this extension was brought into use on 1 August 1866, a dispute arose with the Highland Railway over the cost of providing a signalbox at the point between Boat of Garten and Grantown at which the two lines converged. Traffic on the main line from Inverness to Perth had not developed to an extent that called for this intermediate box, and the Highland Railway declined to contribute anything towards its maintenance. Negotiations reached a deadlock, and on 3 March 1868 Abernethy (which had been renamed Nethy Bridge in 1867) again became the terminus of the Strathspey trains. A few weeks later a compromise was reached, and it was agreed on 1 June to use the 'connection' towards Boat of Garten. This was a separate single track owned by the Highland Railway for the sole use of the Strathspey trains beside the Highland main line to the station, where the railways were physically connected.

Although the railway passed through more or less mountainous country, apart from a fall at 1 in 78 and 80 from Dufftown to the Spey, at Craigellachie, the gradients were not severe, and the ascent of Strathspey entailed no gradient steeper than 1 in 75. The summit

[1] The Inverness & Perth Junction and its associated railways assumed the title of the Highland Railway a few weeks later

of the line near Abernethy, 702 ft above sea-level, became the highest on the Great North of Scotland Railway.

On the other hand, the engineering works were varied and heavy. Between Dufftown and Craigellachie, the line followed the narrow and tortuous gorge of the Fiddich. In addition to two bridges over the river, the works on this section included a deep cutting at Corbie's Crag, and a diversion of the river to enable the embankment to be formed on what had previously been the bed of the stream.

At Carron, the railway and the public road were carried across the Spey on an iron bridge of 150 ft span, flanked on either side by a single masonry arch; and at Ballindalloch the railway regained the right-hand bank of the river on a lattice-girder bridge with a span of 198 ft. Between Nethy Bridge and Boat of Garten, the Spey was crossed for the third time on a plate-girder bridge of five spans, supported on masonry piers.

Of the bridges crossing the numerous tributaries of the Spey, the most remarkable was that of three masonry spans—two of 40 ft and one of 50 ft—over the Allt Arder near Knockando. Great difficulty was experienced in securing a solid foundation for the piers, and after the loose shingle of the river bed had been excavated to a depth of 16 ft, timber piles had to be driven for another 15 ft.

Although several of the cuttings exceeded 50 ft in depth, at one point only—about half a mile south of Craigellachie—was it necessary to carry the line through a hillside rising almost sheer from the river in a short tunnel 68 yd long. Open cuttings were substituted for the short tunnels originally proposed at several other points higher up the strath.

When the railway was opened there were intermediate stations at Strathspey Junction, Aberlour, Carron, Blacksboat, Ballindalloch, Advie, Dalvey, Cromdale, Grantown and Abernethy. Strathspey Junction became Craigellachie in 1864, when the original terminus of the Morayshire Railway, on the opposite side of the river, was renamed Dandaleith; and Abernethy was renamed Nethy Bridge three years later. Dalvey (spelled Dalvie in the early timetables) was closed in 1868, and the platform and station buildings were demolished. At the same time Advie station was moved to a new site, about three-quarters of a mile nearer to Cromdale.

To serve the Knockando Estate, an unadvertised private platform was opened in 1869, about 1¼ miles south of Carron. Thirty years later a public station was brought into use at a distillery siding,

1¼ miles nearer to Blacksboat. Known at first as Dalbeallie, this station was renamed Knockando in 1905; and the private platform then became Knockando House Halt.

As part of the route from Keith to Elgin, the northern part of the Strathspey Railway, from Dufftown to Craigellachie, enjoyed the same services as the Keith & Dufftown and Morayshire Railways. The remainder of the line was treated as a branch, and for many years had three services in each direction. The trains called at all stations, and averaged no more than 16 or 17 m.p.h. Although the connections at Craigellachie were commendably smart, a long wait usually was the lot of passengers who had to change from one railway to the other at Boat of Garten. Despite the scenic beauties of Strathspey, tourist traffic was slow to develop, and the railway was largely dependent on the whisky distilleries in the district.

THE MACDUFF LINE

Shortly after the first prospectus for the Great North of Scotland Railway was issued, an attempt was made to secure support for a branch from Inverurie to Macduff and Banff, passing through Old Meldrum, Fyvie and Turriff, a distance of some 30 miles. Although designated the Great North of Scotland (Western Extension) Railway, it was virtually an independent concern, promoted by local interests to serve an extensive agricultural area and the fishing ports of Banff and Macduff. The scheme failed for lack of support; and little or nothing was heard of it in the difficult years which followed.

However, in 1854, the approaching completion of the railway from Kittybrewster to Huntly brought about its revival in a slightly different form, as the Banff, Macduff & Turriff Junction Railway. By moving the junction with the main line to Inveramsay, four miles west of Inverurie, a shorter route with easier gradients, particularly in the neighbourhood of Macduff, was secured, but at the expense of avoiding the town of Old Meldrum. Despite an offer of financial assistance from the Great North, funds for the complete scheme were not forthcoming, and powers were sought only for the 18 miles from Inveramsay to Turriff.

The railway was authorised on 15 June 1855. The Great North subscribed £40,000, and undertook to work the line, and in return for this assistance directors of that company were nominated to the board. The engineering works were by no means heavy; and save for the unbroken descent of four miles from the summit of the line at Rothie Norman to beyond Fyvie, much of which was at 1 in 80, the gradients were not severe. The railway was opened throughout on 5 September 1857. The junction station at Inveramsay was constructed specially for the new line, and there were intermediate stations at Wartle, Rothie Norman, Fyvie and Auchterless.

Meantime, on 27 July 1857, a separate company, the Banff, Macduff & Turriff Extension, had obtained powers to complete the railway from Turriff to Macduff. The Great North subscribed £5,000, and nominated a director to the board. The railway was opened on 4 June 1860, and was worked by the Great North from the outset. Heavy engineering works were avoided at the expense of a ruling gradient of 1 in 66.

There were only two intermediate stations, picturesquely named Plaidy and King Edward.[1] The terminus, designated Banff & Macduff, was high up on the south side of the Hill of Doun, about three-quarters of a mile from Macduff, and a quarter of a mile from the bridge connecting that town with Banff, on the opposite side of the River Deveron. It was by no means conveniently placed for either town, but so steeply did the hillside fall towards the river that a nearer approach to Banff was out of the question. On the other hand, although the engineering difficulties were considerable, improved access to Macduff was only delayed by lack of funds. By the new line, Aberdeen was brought within 50 miles of Banff and Macduff, as against 65 by the Banff, Portsoy & Strathisla Railway; but notwithstanding this material advantage, traffic did not develop as hoped. Four services, with connections to or from Aberdeen, were provided in each direction between Inveramsay and Banff. The trains called at all stations, and the journey time varied from 1½h. to 1h. 50m.

In April 1859 powers had been obtained to adjust the finances of the Banff, Macduff & Turriff Junction Railway, and to change the name of the undertaking to the Aberdeen & Turriff Railway. Despite rigid economies, including reductions in the far from liberal train services, these measures were by no means successful, and within the next three years the company found itself in difficulties with its mortgage debts. The directors sought assistance from Aberdeen, with the result that the Great North became guarantor as from 30 June 1862.

---

[1] King Edward: stated by Dr Milne, in *Celtic Place Names in Aberdeenshire*, to be derived from the Gaelic *cinn* (heads) and *iochdar* (lower)—i.e. 'the lower heads' (or promontories)

Although the Banff, Macduff & Turriff Extension Company fared somewhat better than its neighbour, and was not forced to seek a guarantor for its existing liabilities, further commitments were out of the question, and for the time being all schemes for improvements at Macduff had to be shelved. At length, on 21 July 1863, powers were obtained to carry the railway round the Hill of Doun to Macduff, and for a steeply-graded tramway to the harbour. These extensions were not undertaken, and three years later, when the Great North absorbed its subsidiary undertakings, the parent company announced its intention of abandoning the plan. Clauses to this effect were included in the Act of Amalgamation, but at the same time (30 July 1866) powers were obtained to extend the railway for half a mile to a more convenient terminus on the outskirts of Macduff, but on a considerably higher level than had previously been intended. This alteration would have steepened the gradients on the harbour tramway to an extent that would have prevented the use of locomotives. The scheme was dropped, and all hope of obtaining railway facilities at the harbour was finally abandoned.

The completion of the extension to the new station at Macduff was considerably delayed, and it was not until 1 July 1872 that the line was opened. There was one intermediate station, at Banff Bridge, a quarter of a mile north of the original terminus. The latter was closed to all traffic and demolished.

THE OLD MELDRUM BRANCH

At the end of the 18th century the town of Old Meldrum was a place of some importance on the Banff turnpike road; but after the opening of the Aberdeenshire Canal its prosperity declined in favour of its neighbour, Inverurie. However, with the advent of the railway in north-east Scotland, hopes of a revival were awakened, and the proposals for the main line of the Great North, and for the Western Extension, from Inverurie to Banff, which was to serve the town, were well supported in the district. But when the latter scheme failed, and the Great North found itself unable to undertake any construction, the prospects of improvement in trade vanished for the time being.

By 1854, when the main line from Kittybrewster to Huntly was nearing completion, a branch to Old Meldrum was again proposed. It was at first intended to resuscitate the scheme for a line from Inverurie to Banff, but when it was decided that the branch to Banff and Macduff should leave the main line at Inveramsay and take a more westerly course, a separate branch was projected from Inverurie to Old Meldrum. The Great North agreed to subscribe £2,000 and to work the line.

The branch was authorised on 15 June 1855 as the Inverury & Old Meldrum Junction Railway. In choosing its title, the company adopted the old spelling of Inverurie. With few exceptions, the directors were local residents, and none was appointed by the Great North. The contractors were Locke & Errington, and their resident engineer, John Willet, subsequently became the company's engineer. Construction progressed rapidly, for earthworks were light, and a girder bridge over the Urie was the only outstanding engineering feature. For about three-quarters of a mile near Inverurie the branch ran parallel with the main line.

The official opening took place on 26 June 1856; but regular services do not appear to have begun until 1 July. Although the line was easily graded, the trains were allowed 18 to 20m. for the journey of 5¾ miles. This distance was reduced to 5¼ miles in 1902, when Inverurie station was moved to a new site near the point at which the branch diverged from the main line. Originally, the only intermediate station was at Lethenty, but a platform was opened at Fingask in 1866.

The Great North had undertaken to work the line at cost price, but so slowly did traffic develop that the balance of the receipts was insufficient to meet the debts of the local company. The directors therefore entered into negotiations with the parent company, and on 14 June 1858 the undertaking was leased to the Great North in perpetuity at an annual rental of £650.

INTO THE ALFORD VALLEY

On 3 July 1846, one week after the Act for the Great North of Scotland Railway had been passed, a separate undertaking, the Alford Valley Railway, was authorised from Kintore to Bridge of Alford, 16 miles. Before any construction could be undertaken the financial panic of the next year supervened, and by the time confidence was restored the powers had lapsed. When the construction of the main line from Kittybrewster to Huntly was begun in 1852, an attempt was made to revive the scheme, but for some time no real progress was achieved.

There was also a proposal for a shorter, but more steeply-graded, line running south-westwards to Alford, through Keig, from the Great North at Buchanstone, near Oyne. A variation of this scheme was for a line from Insch (two miles west of Buchanstone), with the junction facing away from Aberdeen. Opinion was still wavering between these alternatives, when it became clear that the Deeside company was preparing to invade the district from the south by means of a line from Drum, eight miles from Aberdeen, to Alford, through Echt (see chapter 8). This threat spurred the supporters of the Alford Valley railway to greater efforts, and a bill for the line from Kintore to Alford was submitted to Parliament in 1856. The route selected differed greatly from that authorised ten years earlier. The Great North subscribed £15,000, and entered into a working agreement with the company. Almost all the members of the board were also directors of the Great North.

The bill for the branch of the Deeside Railway from Drum was rejected in the Commons, but the Alford Valley Railway was authorised on 23 June 1856, and opened throughout on 21 March 1859. The line was steeply graded, with long stretches of 1 in 70 and 1 in 75 on either side of the summit at Tillyfourie, but the engineering works were light. A service of four trains was provided in each direction, all of which called at the intermediate stations of Kemnay, Monymusk and Whitehouse. In 1860 an additional station was opened at Tillyfourie. Traffic receipts were disappointing, and by 1862 the company was no longer able to meet its liabilities. The Great North then entered into a guarantee of the mortgage debts, which remained in force until the passing of the Amalgamation Act of 1866.

THE FORMARTINE & BUCHAN RAILWAY

Although the Great North of Scotland Railway was primarily intended to provide communication between Aberdeen and Inverness, a branch to serve the farming districts of Formartine and Buchan, and the fishing ports of Peterhead and Fraserburgh, was projected by a subsidiary, but nominally-independent, company, the Great North of Scotland (Eastern Extension). The line was to run from Dyce, six miles from Aberdeen, to Peterhead, via Ellon and Mintlaw, and to have a branch from Mintlaw to Fraserburgh. The Act received the Royal Assent on 3 July 1846, but the company collapsed in the subsequent financial disaster.

With the return of more prosperous times, in 1854 an attempt was made to revive the scheme in a slightly altered form. The junction with the Great North was to be at Kittybrewster instead of Dyce, and, for the moment, the branch to Fraserburgh was to be cut short at Strichen. The scheme failed, largely because the directors of the Great North refused to guarantee it financial support. In view of the obvious need for devoting that company's limited resources to the construction of its main line, this decision was scarcely surprising. Nevertheless, it occasioned dissatisfaction, which crystallised into a rival undertaking.

Promoted as the Aberdeen, Peterhead & Fraserburgh Railway, this line was to run from Aberdeen to Peterhead through Logierieve, Ellon and Mintlaw. A branch from Mintlaw was to serve Fraserburgh, and there were to be shorter branches from Logierieve to Newburgh, and from New Leeds to Strichen. Subsequently, the main line was diverted to pass through Newburgh. The terminus in Aberdeen was to be in King Street, adjoining the harbour, but there was an alternative scheme for a junction with the Great North near Waterloo station. In either case, the lines on the quays were to form the connection with the Aberdeen Railway. Foremost among the promoters was John Duncan, chairman of the Deeside Railway, whose policy at this time was one of active opposition to the Great North.

Faced with the prospect of losing the whole district to the newcomer, the Great North revived the scheme for a railway from Dyce to Peterhead as the nominally-independent Formartine & Buchan Railway. Fraserburgh was to be served by a branch from Maud, passing through Strichen, and to the west of the nearby Mormond Hill. The line was three miles longer than that authorised in 1846, and the distance from Dyce to Peterhead became 37 miles, and to Fraserburgh 40 miles.

The rival bills were submitted to Parliament in 1856, but both were rejected—the Formartine & Buchan in the Commons, and the Aberdeen, Peterhead & Fraserburgh in the Lords. They were reintroduced a year later, only to meet with a similar fate at the hands of the Commons. After this second defeat, the promoters of the Formartine & Buchan Railway decided to abandon the branch to Fraserburgh in favour of a line from Mintlaw which practically coincided with that adopted for the Aberdeen, Peterhead & Fraserburgh Railway. It was also decided to seek powers for a 2½-mile branch to serve the town of Ellon.

The parliamentary contest was renewed in 1858, with decisive results. John Duncan and his supporters were again defeated in the Commons; but the bill for the Formartine & Buchan Railway passed successfully through both houses, and the company received its Act of Incorporation on 23 July. No attempt was made to revive the rival scheme.

Although the successive applications to Parliament had afforded ample opportunity for amending the route, no sooner was the Formartine & Buchan Railway authorised, than the company sought powers to abandon the Ellon branch and deviate the main line to serve the town. This alteration, which increased the total length by one mile, was authorised on 19 April 1859; and construction was pressed forward in the hope of opening the first section of the line to Peterhead in the autumn of 1860. But severe weather experienced throughout the ensuing winter gave rise to a series of delays, which culminated on 3 February 1861 in the collapse of the masonry bridge over the Ythan, near Ellon, after a landslip had disturbed the foundations of the abutment on the south bank. The structure was rebuilt with four spans instead of three as originally intended. On its completion, the railway was opened to Old Deer, 29 miles from Dyce, on 18 July 1861; but the final nine miles to Peterhead remained unfinished until 3 July of the next year. The passenger terminus was at the back of the town, but an extension, three-quarters of a mile long, was opened on 9 August 1865, to enable goods trains to reach the harbour.

In addition to the bridge at Ellon, the chief engineering works were the three-span masonry bridge over the Don at Parkhill, near Dyce, and the girder bridge of three skew spans across the South Ugie Water at Longside. Between Dyce and Ellon, a distance of 13½ miles, the gradients were decidedly severe, and included an unbroken climb at 1 in 105, 80 and 75 for five miles from Parkhill to the summit of the line at New Machar, and a fall thence to Ellon, the first three miles of which were at 1 in 80, and the concluding 1¼ miles at 1 in 75. Apart from a two-mile climb at 1 in 75 immediately beyond Ellon, the gradients onwards to Peterhead were relatively easy. At New Machar summit, the railway was carried through the Hill of Strypes in a cutting approaching a mile in length and attaining a maximum depth of 50 ft.

The junction with the Great North at Dyce was about a quarter of a mile on the Aberdeen side of the station, and a new station to serve the village, with platforms for both lines, was provided. The intermediate stations between Dyce and Peterhead originally were designated Parkhill, New Machar, Udny, Newburgh Road, Esslemont, Ellon, Arnage, Auchnagatt, Brucklay, Old Deer, Longside, Newseat and Inverugie. Within three months Newburgh Road had become Logierieve; and Brucklay was renamed Maud in 1865, when it became the junction for the Fraserburgh line, and a station to serve Brucklay was provided on the newly-opened branch. Two years later Old Deer was more appropriately named Mintlaw.

Meantime, lack of funds had prevented the construction of the Fraserburgh branch. Indeed, the question of abandoning the line had been considered. Eventually, it was decided to revert to a line from Brucklay (Maud) passing through Strichen, but keeping to the east side of Mormond Hill. This alteration, which increased the length of the branch from 12 to 16 miles, although the total distance from Dyce to Fraserburgh remained almost unaltered, was authorised on 21 July 1863. The new route was by no means easily graded, and the ruling gradient of 1 in 60 occurred for more than a mile south of Strichen.

The branch was opened on 24 April 1865, with intermediate stations at Brucklay, Strichen, Mormond, Lonmay and Philorth. The last-named was a private station serving Philorth House, the seat of Lord Saltoun, and did not appear in the public timetables until after the grouping, in June 1926.

Under the terms of the Act of Incorporation, the Great North was empowered to work the Formartine & Buchan Railway, and to appoint directors to the board, in return for a shareholding of £50,000. Four years later, powers were obtained to double this amount; and in 1863, when the new line to Fraserburgh was authorised, a further £25,000 was added. On this last occasion the parent company was authorised to guarantee the mortgage debts.

For many years three or four services were provided in each direction between Aberdeen and Peterhead and Fraserburgh. Between Aberdeen and Dyce, the trains ran independently of the main-line services of the Great North. Stops were made at all stations, and the journey time varied from 2½ to 2¾h. These generous schedules allowed time for joining or dividing the Peterhead and Fraserburgh portions of the trains at Maud.

To accommodate this extra traffic, the main line was doubled between Kittybrewster and Dyce. The widening was not extended to Waterloo, because it was hoped that the negotiations with the Scottish North Eastern company for a connecting line through the Denburn Valley would shortly be brought to a successful conclusion. The new track, which was laid on the down (south) side of the existing railway, was ready for use by the autumn of 1860, but normal double-line working was not put into force until the opening of the Formartine & Buchan Railway in the following July. In the meantime, to facilitate the completion of additional engineering works, all traffic in both directions used the old and new tracks alternately for periods varying from a few days to several weeks.

CONSOLIDATION

By 1865 the position of the Great North of Scotland company had become anomalous, in that the lines of its subsidiary undertakings, together with the Banffshire and the Morayshire Railways, made up more than three-quarters of the system. Indeed, the only section owned solely by the company was the main line from Aberdeen to Keith. The subsidiary companies had been promoted with a view to eventual amalgamation, but all had retained their nominal independence. Negotiations for an amalgamation had, in fact, been in progress for some time, and it was decided to seek the necessary powers in the parliamentary session of 1866. The Act received the Royal Assent on 30 July of that year, and the amalgamations became effective two days later.

The Act provided for the amalgamation of all the subsidiary undertakings with the Great North, and for a large measure of financial reorganisation. As far as possible the share capital of the subsidiary companies was cancelled, and like amounts of shares in the amalgamated company were allotted to the shareholders in its stead. The shares created in lieu of those subscribed by the Great North were divided rateably among the original shareholders of that company. The original shares of the Formartine & Buchan Railway were made the subject of a special guarantee; and the annual rent of the Inverury & Old Meldrum Junction Railway was converted into the dividend on a special preference stock which was issued to the shareholders of that company.

The board of the Great North of Scotland Railway remained unaltered by the amalgamations, as those directors of the subsidiary undertakings who were not also directors of the parent company resigned. Nor were any changes necessary among the officers and staff, because none of the local companies had ever worked its own traffic.

The Banffshire and the Morayshire Railways still retained their nominal independence. Although both were worked by the Great North, they had originated as entirely separate undertakings, and thus differed essentially from the railways embraced by the amalgamation. Moreover, their financial difficulties could not be easily overcome. Nevertheless, the opportunity was taken to include in the Consolidation Act clauses granting optional powers of amalgamation, to be exercised at a later date, when circumstances were more favourable. In the event, only twelve months elapsed before the Banffshire Railway was merged with the Great North; but the fusion with the Morayshire company was postponed for more than 14 years.

The Act of 1866 also authorised the Great North to lease the Deeside Railway. Negotiations to this end had been brought to a successful conclusion four years earlier, when there was a prospect that the Deeside would pass into the hands of the Scottish North Eastern company; but an attempt to put into force a temporary working agreement had failed, after action in the Court of Session by dissentient Deeside directors on the grounds that parliamentary sanction had not been obtained. To protect its interests, the Great North then acquired a substantial financial holding in the Deeside Railway, but it was not until 1866 that the lease was ratified by Parliament.

The early history of the Great North of Scotland Railway may be said to end with the amalgamations of 1866. The total mileage of the system then became 207½, and the company leased or worked an additional 68¾ miles. This latter figure was increased to 79¾ miles in October 1866 by the extension of the Deeside line from Aboyne to Ballater (see Chapter 8). East of Keith, all the lines so optimistically authorised in 1846 had been constructed, although the branch to Banff and Portsoy was still in the hands of a nominally-independent company. Moreover, the proposed Western Extension had been undertaken in a modified form, as the branches to Old Meldrum and Macduff. Beyond Keith, however, the position was completely different from that envisaged 20 years earlier; for the western portion of the line from Aberdeen to Inverness, together with the direct route through the central Highlands to the south, had become part of the Highland Railway. On the other hand, the Great North had been extended into Strathspey, and its trains reached Elgin over the lines of the Morayshire Railway.

For the time being, the inconvenient terminus at Waterloo remained the company's only station in Aberdeen for both passenger and goods traffic. But the persistent demand for improved facilities had resulted in powers being obtained in 1864 for a railway from Kittybrewster, through the Denburn Valley, to join the Scottish North Eastern Railway, and for the provision of a joint station. On the completion of these works in November 1867, all passenger and through goods services were transferred to the new line; and the isolation of the Great North, which had provoked such bitter criticisms, and aroused so much ill feeling, was for ever ended.

CHAPTER 7

Aberdeen Junction Controversy

WATERLOO AND GUILD STREET

While the development of the system had progressed steadily in other directions, no progress had been made towards connecting the Great North with the Aberdeen Railway. The already considerable difference in level between Kittybrewster and the junction had been accentuated by the abandonment of the scheme for a high-level terminus in Market Street, and although it was claimed that the new site for the joint station, acquired in 1852, was more convenient, and could be reached with lighter earthworks, prolonged negotiations between the two companies had failed to produce agreement. Meantime, the Aberdeen Railway had reached Guild Street in August 1854, and the Great North had opened its extension to Waterloo—for goods traffic in September 1855, and for passengers six months later.

Such was the position when the Scottish Midland Junction and the Aberdeen Railways were amalgamated as the Scottish North Eastern Railway in July 1856. The new company at once renewed the negotiations with the Great North for the provision of a connecting line through the Denburn Valley—the easiest and most direct route—and a joint station; but despite a hopeful start the scheme did not come to fruition. Quite apart from any differences between the two companies regarding the construction of the station, the proposal to revive the powers for a line through the city evoked determined opposition from the owners of the surrounding property. With the finances of the Great North still in a somewhat parlous state, the directors were unwilling to embark on a prolonged and expensive parliamentary contest, which, even though the company emerged successful, would certainly be followed by inordinately heavy payments for purchase of land and compensation.

During the next few years, several more unsuccessful attempts were made to secure agreement between the two companies for the provision of a joint station, and to overcome the opposition to a line through the Denburn Valley. The inadequate arrangements at Waterloo were fast becoming intolerable, and in view of the high-handed attitude adopted towards passengers when the connecting trains from the south were late, and the improvement in the company's financial position revealed in the yearly-increasing dividends, criticism was mainly levelled at the Great North. Until the company joined the Railway Clearing House in 1859, the position was aggravated by the refusal of the Great North to lower its rates or to agree to an apportionment of the rates for through traffic, and also by deliberate attempts to forward traffic to the south by sea from Aberdeen.

TWO ABORTIVE SCHEMES

The climax was reached in 1861, when the Great North, rather than agree to joint ownership of a connecting line through the Denburn Valley, rejected an offer from the Scottish North Eastern to subscribe £30,000 towards its construction. After this rebuff, the latter company, alarmed at the promotion of the Inverness & Perth Junction Railway, took matters into its own hands, and projected the Scottish Northern Junction Railway to connect its main line at Limpet Mill, some four miles north of Stonehaven, with the Great North at Kintore. At Culter, eight miles west of Aberdeen, the line crossed the Deeside Railway, to which connecting spurs were proposed. Running powers were to be sought from the Deeside company to secure a route between Aberdeen and Kintore entirely independent of the Great North. The distance from Limpet Mill to Kintore was about 22 miles, and from Aberdeen to Kintore, via Culter, about 18 miles.

The prospect of having traffic diverted from the main line at Kintore, and of a further invasion of its territory by a subsequent extension of the Scottish Northern Junction Railway, constituted a serious threat to the Great North that called for immediate action. Negotiations were opened for leasing the Deeside Railway on terms more favourable than those already proposed for the running powers between Aberdeen and Culter. Despite a further offer by the Scottish North Eastern, the Great North's proposals were accepted, and pending the ratification of the lease, an interim working agreement was put into force. Although this arrangement was shortly afterwards suspended as the result of action in the Court of Session by a minority of the Deeside directors and the

Scottish North Eastern company, the Deeside board re-affirmed its intention of completing the lease with the Great North as soon as the necessary parliamentary powers had been obtained. Nevertheless, the Great North considered it expedient to strengthen its position by acquiring a considerable number of Deeside shares.

The Great North opposed the bill for the Scottish Northern Junction Railway, and offered to construct a shorter connecting line from Kittybrewster to Guild Street at its own expense. Although this opposition was not completely successful, and the Act received the Royal Assent on 30 June 1862, provisional powers only were granted to the Scottish Northern Junction. It was stipulated that no construction should be undertaken for six months, and if by that time the Great North had deposited a bill for an alternative line, the powers were to remain in abeyance until it had either been withdrawn or rejected. In the event of such a line being authorised by 1 September 1863, the Scottish Northern Junction Railway was not to be built.

Encouraged by this partial success, the directors of the Great North sought to extend the influence of their company far to the south of Aberdeen. To this end, negotiations were opened with the Montrose & Bervie company, a local undertaking, which had obtained powers in 1860 for a 13-mile line from Inverbervie, on the Kincardineshire coast, to the Montrose branch of the Scottish North Eastern Railway. Although the latter company had undertaken to subscribe £15,000 towards the construction of the line, and had agreed to work it, a considerable portion of the share capital remained unallocated until it was taken up by the Great North on the understanding that powers would be sought to extend the railway northwards from Inverbervie for ten miles, to join the Scottish North Eastern Railway at Stonehaven, and southwards from Montrose to Arbroath, a distance of 12 miles. At Arbroath the southern extension was to join the Dundee & Arbroath Railway, at that time an independent concern, with connection *via* the Broughty Ferry with the Fife lines of the North British Railway.

It was by this means that the directors of the Great North planned to secure a large measure of control over a new route to the south, nearly independent of the Scottish North Eastern Railway. There remained the gap of 16 miles between Stonehaven and Aberdeen to be bridged by the main line of that company, but it was hoped that running powers (or at least favourable rates for the conveyance of through traffic) could be secured. The most important preliminary step was to end the isolation of the Great North

by securing powers for a direct line from Kittybrewster to the
Scottish North Eastern Railway.

No time was lost in promoting this connecting link as the
Aberdeen Junction Railway. In the hope of overcoming local
opposition, the direct route through the Denburn Valley was abandoned in favour of a line following the western outskirts of the
city, and characterised by its steep gradients and sharp curves.
However, far from securing strong support, the line was opposed
because of its inordinate length—2¾ miles, compared with 1¾
via the Denburn Valley; and the local residents, anxious to preserve
the amenities of their district, derisively dubbed it the 'Circum-
bendibus'. Nevertheless, the bill passed successfully through Parliament, and the Act received the Royal Assent on 21 July 1863.

At the same time, so strongly had the advantages of a line
through the Denburn Valley been represented that a final opportunity was given to secure the necessary powers, and the construction of the Aberdeen Junction Railway was postponed for one year
to enable the Scottish North Eastern Railway to promote the bill.
In the event of the Act being obtained, the Great North was to
contribute £125,000 towards the construction of the railway and a
joint station; but should the measure be rejected, the Scottish North
Eastern Railway was to pay £5,000 to the Great North.

On the other hand, the grandiose scheme for extending the
Montrose & Bervie Railway suffered complete eclipse by the rejec-
tion of the bill in the House of Commons. Moreover, the Scottish
North Eastern strengthened its position by obtaining powers to
amalgamate with the Dundee & Arbroath on 28 July 1863. This
Act, which included clauses for the protection of the North British
company's traffic passing *via* the Broughty Ferry, confirmed an
agreement for joint working entered into more than a year earlier.
The Great North then disposed of its financial holding in the
Montrose & Bervie, and devoted its energies to the construction of
the line through the Denburn Valley, and to the establishment of
better relations with the Scottish North Eastern company.[1]

THE DENBURN VALLEY LINE

To overcome an objection that the noise of the trains would
seriously disturb patients in the nearby Aberdeen Royal Infirmary,

[1] Opened in 1865, and worked first by the Scottish North Eastern and then
by the Caledonian Railway, the Montrose & Bervie passed into the hands
of the North British Railway in 1881

the line through the Denburn Valley was diverted slightly to the east, and the Act was passed on 23 June 1864. The Great North subscribed £125,000 and the Scottish North Eastern £70,000.

The railway was double track, for the most part on a gradient of 1 in 72, falling towards the joint station. The engineering works included the sewering of the Denburn, from which the valley took its name, deep cuttings supported by massive retaining walls, and two short tunnels, at Schoolhill and Hutcheon Street, 236 and 270 yd long respectively. The latter was the longest tunnel on the Great North. There were no intermediate stations, but the station at Kittybrewster, which had been moved to a new site in 1856 for the opening of the Waterloo branch to passengers, was again rebuilt to place it on the Denburn line.

The layout of the joint station was remarkable in that, although there were three through roads, only one was provided with a platform face. Four terminal bays, two at each end of the station, completed the accommodation for passenger trains. The platforms, and the three through roads, were partly covered by a glazed iron over-all roof, supported on one side by the station buildings, and on the other by a side wall. On the west side of the station, beyond this wall, were two additional through roads for goods traffic.

Several difficulties and mishaps, not the least of which was the collapse of part of the roof of Hutcheon Street tunnel, delayed construction; and it was not until 4 November 1867 that the railway and the joint station were opened. The passenger services of both companies were diverted to the new station, but goods trains continued to use Waterloo and Guild Street. Although the Scottish North Eastern company had obtained the Act for the railway, and had been largely responsible for its construction, the line from Kittybrewster to the north end of the joint station was handed over to the Great North. The new line was a quarter of a mile shorter than that from Kittybrewster to Waterloo, and the distances from Aberdeen to all Great North stations were shortened accordingly.

There was no substantial alteration in the train services. The interval allowed for connections was reduced now that it was no longer necessary to change stations, but there was little or no improvement in the speed or number of the trains. On the main line, there were five services in each direction between Aberdeen and Keith. The journey time of the down trains varied from 2h. 25m. to 2h. 50m. The best time was by the mail, which left Aberdeen at 1 p.m., but the early morning train leaving at 7 a.m. was only 3m. slower. In the opposite direction, the timings were somewhat easier, and the best train, the 4 p.m. from Keith, required 2h. 38m. for the journey of 53¼ miles. However, this was only 2m. faster than the mail, which left Keith at 9.10 a.m.

Beyond Keith, the Highland Railway, with its shorter route, provided the best connections for Elgin, and the only connections for Inverness. There were three through services daily between Aberdeen and Inverness, and four in the opposite direction, the journey time for the 108¼ miles varying from 5h. 20m. to 6h. 20m. The Great North provided four down and three up services between Keith and Elgin. These trains, which called at all stations, were extremely slow, and the journey time between Aberdeen and Elgin, via Craigellachie, varied from 4h. 5m. to 4¾h. in both directions. The services on the branches, and on the recently leased Deeside Railway, were quite in keeping with those on the main line, many trains averaging barely 20 m.p.h.

One notable innovation came in 1869, when the through coaches already working in the daily mail train between London (Euston) and Aberdeen were extended to Elgin via Craigellachie. At that time, and for many years afterwards, this was by far the longest through coach working in the country; the journey of 620 miles occupied 22h. in the down (northbound) direction, and 43m. less in the up.[1] However, passengers could save time by using the Highland Railway between Keith and Elgin. The through coaches were not well patronised, and ceased to work north of Aberdeen in 1873.

Meantime, the North British and Caledonian companies had been pursuing a policy of expansion and amalgamation with access to Aberdeen as the ultimate objective. By the summer of 1865 each had reached Perth and Dundee, and was seeking to obtain control of the Scottish North Eastern Railway, which held a monopoly northwards to Aberdeen. Although by far the most direct route from Edinburgh to the north had been secured by the North British, it was broken by the ferries across the firths of Forth and Tay, but proposals were already afoot for bridges. Rival schemes for an amalgamation with the Scottish North Eastern Railway speedily followed; but after much negotiation a compromise was reached, and the North British withdrew its bill. The future of the northern company was decided on 10 August 1866, when its absorption by the Caledonian was ratified by Parliament. At the same time the North British was granted running powers over the whole of the

---

[1] It was surpassed in 1984 by the Elgin to Penzance train.

Scottish North Eastern Railway, but several years elapsed before any attempt was made to exercise them.

The proposals for amalgamating the Scottish North Eastern and the Caledonian were followed by others for including the Great North in the fusion. Although some progress was made, the negotiations, which appear to have been instigated by the Great North, were broken off, largely because of the strained and unsatisfactory state of that company's finances. Thus, for the second time within 20 years, an attempt to secure fusion with the company holding the road to Aberdeen from the south failed—and for the same reason.

This critical period saw several changes among the officers. In 1865, William Walker, who had been traffic manager since the opening of the line from Kittybrewster to Huntly, relinquished control of the passenger services to Samuel Bates, although he continued to have charge of goods traffic. Bates resigned after only two years, and was succeeded by Forbes Morrison. In the engineer's department, Alexander Gibb, whose connection with the Great North dated back to its earliest years, resigned in 1867, and was succeeded for a period of barely twelve months by his chief assistant, Alexander Fraser. The directors then appointed as engineer Patrick Barnett, a young man, only 30 years of age, who had entered the service of the company in 1857.

CHAPTER 8

The Deeside Railway

FORMATION OF THE COMPANY

The first proposals for a railway to serve Deeside were made in the summer of 1845. By September it had been decided to seek powers for a line from Aberdeen to Banchory, a distance of 16 miles, and a provisional committee had been formed, with Lord Provost Blaikie (chairman of the Great North) as chairman. William Leslie and William Cubitt, secretary and engineer respectively of the Great North, were appointed to similar positions with the new company. The estimated cost of the works was rather more than £95,000; and it was proposed to limit the capital to £100,000.

After the engineer had reported unfavourably on a line wholly on the south side of the Dee, it was decided to keep as far as possible to the opposite bank, and to extend the railway to Aboyne, 30 miles from Aberdeen. A prospectus was issued for a line branching from the Aberdeen Railway at Ferryhill, on the outskirts of Aberdeen, and passing through Culter, Banchory and Kincardine o' Neil. The engineering works were not heavy, save for two bridges over the Dee, west of Kincardine o' Neil, where the line crossed to the south bank of the river for about a mile. On the other hand, the gradients, particularly west of Banchory, were by no means easy. To meet the cost of the extension to Aboyne, the capital was to be increased to £220,000; and it was proposed to save the expense of providing rolling stock by arranging for the Aberdeen company to work the line.

The railway was authorised on 16 July 1846; but within two months the company had followed the example of the Great North and had decided to defer construction until the Aberdeen Railway was nearing completion. To expedite this work £16,000 of the capital already subscribed was lent to that company in the next year as a debenture bond. Shortly afterwards, however, the general financial instability that followed the Railway Mania culminated in a demand by a large section of the shareholders for the winding up of the Deeside company. This disaster was averted by the prompt action of the Aberdeen company in acquiring the greater part of the Deeside shares so far allocated, having first repaid its loan to enable the disgruntled faction to be bought out. That company thus became master of the situation, to the exclusion of the Great North.

Soon after these changes, interest in the Deeside Railway was stimulated by the purchase by the Prince Consort of the reversion of the lease of the Balmoral estate, and in the autumn of 1848 the Royal Family paid the first of those visits to the castle that were to earn for the district the title of 'Royal Deeside'. The Prince Consort subsequently purchased the estate, and bequeathed it to Queen Victoria. As soon as additional support for the railway was forthcoming, the Aberdeen company disposed of its Deeside shares, and a new board was elected, with John Duncan, a leading Aberdeen advocate, as chairman. The secretary and general manager was William B. Ferguson.

Although the reorganisation of the company was completed in 1849, and Locke & Errington were instructed to prepare new surveys, lack of funds still precluded progress. In the following year an open letter was addressed to the landowners in Deeside by Robert Notman, an Aberdeen accountant, urging their support by reducing the price of the land to a minimum, and waiving all claims for compensation. He proposed the abandonment of the line from Banchory to Aboyne until the traffic between Aberdeen and Banchory had developed; and made suggestions for working the railway as cheaply as possible, particularly by the use of locomotives and rolling stock of special light construction. As an alternative, he recommended a working agreement with the Aberdeen company. In any event, he forecast an annual dividend of at least 9½ per cent.

Despite every effort to raise capital, and a decision to limit the undertaking to a line from Ferryhill to Banchory, it was not until 1852 that the company was able to apply to Parliament to revive its powers. The railway was authorised on 28 May of that year, and the first sod was cut at Park by Mrs Kinloch of Park on 5 July. For the most part, the gradients were easy and the earthworks light. Construction progressed rapidly, and the works were completed in 14 months.

OPENING TO BANCHORY

The formal opening ceremony took place on 7 September 1853, when a special train of 15 coaches, drawn by a locomotive gaily decorated with flags and flowers, left Aberdeen shortly after midday and reached Banchory an hour later. Public traffic began the next day.

Three trains, carrying first and third class passengers at 1½d and 1d a mile respectively, were provided in each direction on weekdays only, and the journey of 16¾ miles took one hour. For the time being, the only station at Aberdeen was the temporary terminus of the Aberdeen Railway at Ferryhill; but on the completion of the extension to Guild Street in the following August, all traffic was transferred to that station. For this facility, an annual payment of £700 for the first three years, and thereafter £1,000, was made to the owning company.

Intermediate stations were provided at Cults, Murtle, Culter, Park and Mills of Drum. There was also a private platform between Mills of Drum and Banchory, serving Crathes Castle. Additional stations were opened at Milltimber and Drum in 1854, and at Ruthrieston two years later. In 1863 Mills of Drum was closed, and replaced by a new station named Crathes on the site of the platform serving the castle. The land required for the new station was granted by the owner of the estate in return for an undertaking that all trains, except privately-chartered specials, should call to pick up and set down passengers.

On the opening of the railway, John Willet, who had supervised the construction for Locke & Errington, became the company's engineer. His position appears to have been peculiar in that he was permitted to accept additional appointments. In 1864 he was succeeded on the Deeside Railway by William B. Ferguson, who for the remainder of the company's independent existence held the triple position of secretary, general manager and engineer.

As was foreshadowed in the prospectus, arrangements were made for the line to be worked by the Aberdeen Railway, but that company was unable to provide enough locomotives and rolling stock to do so properly, despite the fact that additional locomotives were hired from the Scottish Midland Junction and the Scottish Central Railways. These difficulties were reflected in the early time-tables, which were so arranged that the whole of the passenger service could be worked by one train. Moreover, they were responsible for the decision to provide only two classes of accommodation —first and third—an example already set by the Morayshire Railway, and soon to be followed by the Great North (see chapters 2 and 4). So unsatisfactory did the position become that the company decided to provide its own locomotives and rolling stock, and to take over the working of the line. The change-over was effected gradually during the spring and summer of 1854; but a further two years elapsed before the shortage was fully overcome.

The policy pursued by the chairman soon brought the Deeside company into conflict with the Great North. By 1855 attempts were being made to revive interest in the Alford Valley Railway, which had collapsed through lack of funds after it had been authorised in 1846. Although nominally independent, this line was virtually a branch of the Great North, and was supported by that company. Duncan at once advocated an extension of the Deeside Railway from Banchory to Alford, *via* Lumphanan, a distance of 16 miles; but this scheme was dropped in favour of a slightly longer branch from Drum to Alford, passing through Echt and Tillyfourie. In either case, the threat to the Great North was obvious, as an extension northwards from Alford was certain to be projected at an early date. Although the Deeside scheme secured considerable local support, Parliament decided against it, and in favour of the rival line from Kintore to Alford, when the rival bills were presented in 1856.

EXTENSIONS INTO UPPER DEESIDE

Meantime, there were indications that support would be forthcoming for the extension of the Deeside Railway to Aboyne. The undertaking was placed in the hands of a nominally-independent company, the Aboyne Extension, although the Deeside agreed to subscribe £5,000, and to work the line at cost price. It was also agreed to strengthen the Deeside board with two directors elected by the new shareholders, and to amalgamate the two companies as soon as the dividends became equal.

The original line of 1846 through Kincardine o' Neil, with its two bridges over the Dee, was abandoned for one passing northwards, away from the river, through Lumphanan. Although it was claimed that this route, which added some two miles to the length of the line, permitted of substantial savings on the purchase of land and construction costs, some of the earthworks were far from light, and there were long stretches at the ruling gradient of 1 in 70 on each side of the summit, near Torphins.

The railway was authorised on 27 July 1857; and the first sod was cut by the Marchioness of Huntly on 30 October at Rosehall, near Aboyne. The works presented no special difficulties, but at Aboyne the line was continued slightly beyond the authorised limits to secure a more convenient site for the station—a procedure that remained unauthorised by Parliament until 30 June 1862. The railway was opened throughout, with intermediate stations at Glassel, Torphins, Lumphanan and Dess, on 2 December 1859.

Five years elapsed before a separate company, the Aboyne & Braemar, was formed to carry the line through Upper Deeside to Braemar, 28 miles from Aboyne, and 60 from Aberdeen. There was even a suggestion that the line might be extended beyond Braemar, either through Glen Tilt, to join the Highland Railway at Blair Atholl, or through Glen Feshie, to a junction with that railway at Kingussie, whence a railway to Fort William, *via* Loch Laggan and Spean Bridge, had recently been projected. In either case, the mountainous nature of the country would have necessitated heavy engineering works; and the sparseness of the population would probably have precluded all possibility of traffic developing satisfactorily. Indeed, as events proved, the promoters were dubious as to the wisdom of constructing the railway as far as Braemar.

The bill as presented to Parliament was for a line from Aboyne to Braemar, for the most part on the north side of the Dee, but crossing to the south bank at Invercauld Bridge, about two miles from the terminus. However, before the hearing had proceeded very far, not only had any intention of an extension to join the Highland Railway been denied, but it had been decided to limit the undertaking to a line from Aboyne to Bridge of Gairn, a distance of $12\frac{1}{2}$ miles. Even this truncated scheme was modified by a decision to place the passenger terminus at Ballater, and to use the $1\frac{1}{2}$ miles thence to Bridge of Gairn for goods traffic only. It was in this form that the railway was authorised on 5 July 1865, with provisions requiring special legislation before any extension towards Braemar was undertaken. The Deeside company was empowered to subscribe £10,000, and undertook to work the line.

The first sod was cut at Ballater by Mrs Farquharson, of Invercauld, some three months after the passing of the Act. Apart from a short tunnel (127 yd long) at Aboyne, the engineering works were not heavy, nor the gradients severe; and the railway was opened to Ballater on 17 October 1866. For several years the only intermediate station was at Dinnet, but a station was opened at Cambus o' May in 1876.

In the autumn of 1866, the line beyond Ballater was in an unfinished state, and all work on it was then suspended. Some 18 months later the company agreed with James Farquharson, of Invercauld, that the latter should complete the railway to Bridge of Gairn, whence he was proposing to construct a tramway for some

12 miles towards Braemar to exploit the timber in Ballochbuie Forest. After some delay the works, which included a cutting beyond Ballater station and some masonry retaining walls beside the Dee, were completed for about 1¼ miles; but save for the abutments of the bridge over the Water of Gairn, the rest of the line remained unfinished. Construction was then suspended; and no attempt was ever made to complete the line. The rails, which had been laid as far as the Water of Gairn, were subsequently removed, but the course of the derelict line remained clearly traceable. The tramway to Ballochbuie was also abandoned. Apart from some preliminary work at Bridge of Gairn, little or nothing had been done towards its construction.

It has frequently been suggested that Queen Victoria was opposed to a railway in the vicinity of Balmoral Castle, and intervened personally to secure the abandonment of the line beyond Ballater. Possibly the Queen did fear for the amenities of her Highland home, and her wish (conveyed privately to the promoters of the railway) may have been the deciding factor, but there can be little doubt that misgivings already had arisen as to the soundness of the scheme. On the other hand, it may be said that the Queen was responsible for the abandonment of the extension to Bridge of Gairn and Farquharson's tramway to Ballochbuie, because before either was completed Ballochbuie Forest was added to the royal estates, and the need for exploiting its timber was thus removed.

LEASING AND AMALGAMATION

Some time after the opening of the extension to Aboyne, the Deeside directors sought to enhance the company's position by entering the Aberdeen junction controversy, then at its height. Impatient at the repeated failure of attempts to secure agreement with the Great North, the Scottish North Eastern company had projected the line from Limpet Mill (Stonehaven) to Kintore, with two short connecting spurs to the Deeside Railway at Culter—one to provide direct access from the south to the western portion of the Deeside Railway, and the other a route between Aberdeen and Kintore, entirely independent of, and only about five miles longer than, the main line of the Great North. Indeed, this latter loop would have rendered the railway from Limpet Mill to Culter redundant. To complete the scheme, it was necessary to secure running powers over the Deeside Railway between Aberdeen and Culter, and for the moment it appeared as if that company was prepared to accept the terms proposed for granting these facilities. However, while the offer was still under consideration, John Duncan, apparently on his own initiative, and with a view to obtaining a better bargain, opened negotiations for leasing the Deeside Railway to the Great North.

So serious was the threat to the Great North that Duncan's proposals were readily accepted, and a formal offer for leasing the Deeside Railway speedily followed. The terms of the lease were approved by a majority vote at a meeting of the Deeside board held on 13 May 1862, and the Great North was authorised to enter into an interim agreement for working the railway, pending its ratification. This decision was a severe blow to the promoters of the Scottish Northern Junction Railway, and better terms for running powers were promptly offered by the Scottish North Eastern. Although this offer was rejected by a second majority vote of the Deeside board, the Great North felt bound to strengthen its position by the purchase of a large number of Deeside preference shares, the issue of which, in substitution for unallocated Aboyne Extension stock, had recently been authorised.

The dissentient minority of the Deeside board, supported by the Scottish North Eastern, then petitioned the Court of Session against the lease, which was still unconfirmed by Parliament. The application was successful, and an order for the suspension of the temporary working agreement was made in the summer of 1862. However, in announcing this decision, the Deeside directors stated that 'they were confident that it would be in the interests of the shareholders to adhere firmly to the provisions of the agreement entire and unchanged'. On the other hand, it was emphasised that the lease would have to be ratified by Parliament before it could become effective. Meantime, the Act for the railway from Limpet Mill to Kintore had been passed, but in such a restricted form as to be virtually a dead letter.

For the time being the Deeside company regained its independence, and took no part in the final stages of the campaign to end the isolation of the Great North. The ties binding the Deeside Railway to the Great North were strengthened in 1864 by the election of John Duncan to the board of the latter company, and his appointment as deputy chairman. Some twelve months later, when preparations were being made to consolidate the Great North by amalgamation with its subsidiary undertakings, clauses for the ratification of the lease of the Deeside Railway were inserted in the bill.

The Act, which received the Royal Assent on 30 July 1866,

DEESIDE STATIONS

(25)   *Park, looking west. The stone station building design, with the double archway, was used at many Deeside stations.*

(26)   *Cambus O'May in 1937, looking towards Aberdeen. The siding is in the distance beyond the station.*

(27)   *Ballater looking towards the buffers. That this was never intended to be the terminus is shown by the bridge at the end of the station. The earth works extended over a mile to Bridge of Gairn.*

BRANCH LINE STATIONS

(28) *Rothienorman, one of the crossing places on the Macduff branch. Photograph taken after withdrawal of the passenger service.*

(29) *Banff Bridge on the extension to Macduff. The building survives as a private house. The Harbour station was on the right in the far distance.*

(30) *Carron on the Speyside line in 1958, looking north. The site is now part of the distillery, but the station building survives.*

SCENES FROM GNSR DAYS

(31) *Craigellachie in the 1880s, with a freight train in the Speyside platform. Note the two double-armed signals on the up platform. The long shed in the background was later replaced by the two-road goods shed seen in plate 18.*

(32) *0–4–0T, either no 13 or no 14, built Beyer Peacock 1855, and 40 seat third coach no 33, built GNSR in 1871 and withdrawn in 1926. At Aberdeen c1874.*

(33) *Mail train near Gartly in 1910. Only one bogie coach in the train. The leading vehicle is one of two sorting vans built in 1886. TPOs were discontinued in 1916 and never reinstated.*

MOTOR BUSES

(34)   SA338, Maudslay 20/30hp 18 seater. Chain drive to rear wheels. Separate compartment for front row of seats. Entered service June 1907 and withdrawn March 1926.

(35)   SA158, Milnes-Daimler 20/25hp. Example of a convertible vehicle, built as a 2 ton lorry but seen here with a charabanc body. Entered service May 1905 and withdrawn March 1920.

authorised the Great North to lease the Deeside Railway for 999 years, as from 1 September of that year. A dividend of 7½ per cent was guaranteed to the Deeside shareholders, while the Aboyne Extension shareholders were to receive 3 per cent for the first year, and 3½ per cent thereafter. It was also provided that if the gross revenue of the railway exceeded £27,000 in any financial year, half the excess should accrue to the Great North, and the remainder be equally divided between the Deeside and Aboyne Extension shareholders. The difference in the dividends guaranteed illustrated clearly the wisdom of separating the finances of the original company and the extension. The former had always been a prosperous concern, whose dividends had increased from 5 to 8 per cent in the three years immediately preceding the ratification of the lease. The Extension shares had never yielded more than 2 per cent.

The management of the Deeside Railway was vested in a committee composed of three directors from each company. It was agreed that the train service in operation in September 1866 should not be reduced, and that the rates and fares then in force were not to be increased. This latter was a most important proviso, because the charges both for passengers and goods on the Deeside Railway had always been lower than those on the Great North.

The Aboyne & Braemar Railway, which was still under construction as far as Ballater when the lease came into force, was only affected to the extent that it was to be worked by the Great North as lessee of the Deeside Railway. It was an independent and, during its early years at any rate, a by no means prosperous concern.

Some time elapsed before there were many outward signs of the Deeside Railway having lost its independence; but after the opening of the Denburn Valley Railway in November 1867, a number of changes were made which resulted in the line becoming to all appearances part of the Great North. Meantime, traffic increased, until by 1875 a number of improvements—particularly the re-laying of the line with heavier rails, and the provision of extra crossing loops—were overdue. However, it was by no means easy to allocate the necessary capital expenditure between the owning and the leasing companies. Moreover, the position of the Aboyne & Braemar Railway had become somewhat anomalous. To overcome these difficulties, powers were sought to amalgamate both undertakings with the Great North. Although the Act authorising the fusion was not passed until 13 July 1876, its powers were retrospective—to 1 August 1875 for the Deeside, and 31 January 1876 in the case of the Aboyne & Braemar.

John Duncan did not survive to take part in the negotiations for the amalgamation. Early in 1867 he had been elected chairman of the Great North, but ill-health forced him to relinquish his position (but not his seat on the board) five years later. He remained chairman of the Deeside Railway until his death in 1875, and was succeeded in that office by Patrick Davidson, deputy chairman since 1849.

William B. Ferguson, secretary, general manager and latterly engineer of the Deeside Railway, was appointed secretary of the Great North in 1868. When failing health compelled him to resign, after holding that office for 11 years, he accepted a seat on the board, but his illness proved fatal a few months later.

The train services before 1876 call for little comment. By 1855 the number of trains had been increased to five in each direction in the summer, and one less during the winter. On the completion of the railway to Aboyne, and subsequently to Ballater, most of the trains were extended to serve the new line. With few exceptions the trains called at all stations, and although there was some slight improvement from time to time, the schedules remained extremely easy, and the average speed was less than 20 m.p.h.

ROYAL TRAINS

The visits of the Royal Family to Balmoral Castle brought a large amount of traffic to the Deeside Railway. The first recorded instance of a special train being provided was on 10 October 1853, one month after the opening of the line to Banchory, when Queen Victoria's mother, the Duchess of Kent, left Balmoral for the south. The train started from Banchory shortly after 1 p.m., and the journey of 16 miles to Ferryhill took half an hour. Three days later similar arrangements were made for the return to London of the Queen and the Prince Consort. As the Deeside company did not then possess either locomotives or rolling stock, these trains were provided by the Aberdeen company.

Thereafter, Royal specials became a regular feature; and as the railway was extended up Deeside, Aboyne and Ballater became in turn the place of arrival and departure. The first passenger trains to use Ballater station were specials provided for the Prince and Princess of Wales on 20 and 24 September 1866, nearly a month before the opening to the public.

The arrangements for working the trains differed but little from those on other railways, save that no pilot engine was sent in advance of the special. On the other hand, such precautions as clearing the line ahead at least 15 minutes before the train was due, the locking of all facing points and level crossing gates, and closing station platforms to the public were strictly observed. In deference to Queen Victoria's dislike of high speed, no attempt was ever made to reduce the journey time substantially, and the 42½ miles from Ferryhill to Ballater usually took about 75m. The trains were invariably reversed at Ferryhill, and did not enter the passenger station at Aberdeen.

At first, the Royal Family visited Balmoral in the autumn, and travelled to and from Scotland by the East Coast route; but after the death of the Prince Consort in 1861 the West Coast route was used, and the Queen came twice a year to the castle, in the spring and the autumn. The Royal train of the London & North Western Railway was used for these journeys. By the end of the century its weight had increased to 250 tons.

With the accession of Edward VII in 1901, the spring visit was discontinued, and alterations were made in the timing of the special trains. Save on rare occasions, Queen Victoria had travelled to and from Scotland by night, but King Edward preferred to make the return journey by day. The speed of the train was increased, and the journey time from Ferryhill to Ballater became 65m. During the reign of George V, however, the schedule was progressively eased, and the return journey was once more made by night.

The last occasion on which the Great North had to make arrangements for a Royal journey was on 9 October 1922, when the King returned to London from Balmoral. By the autumn of next year the grouping had come into force, and the company had lost its separate identity.

Quite apart from the Royal specials were the so-called 'Messenger Trains', which ran daily in each direction while the Royal Family was in residence at Balmoral for the couriers bearing confidential dispatches to and from London. Until 1865 the couriers travelled between London and Perth by train, and thence by the Cairnwell Road, a long and tedious journey of some 60 miles involving a climb to a height of more than 2,000 ft above sea-level. In that year, however, it was arranged with the Home Office to provide a train between Aberdeen and Aboyne (then the terminus of the Deeside Railway), and a carriage thence to the castle. The daily charge for the combined service was to be £9 2s, and the journey from Aberdeen to Balmoral was to be completed in 3h. 40m.

The service was inaugurated on 8 October 1865. The down train started from Aberdeen at 4 a.m., in connection with the train leaving London on the previous morning, and calling only at Banchory, reached Aboyne at 5.25. It returned at 2.15 p.m., and arrived in Aberdeen at 3.33, to connect with the night train to the south. When the railway was opened to Ballater in the autumn of 1866, the trains were extended to that station, and 1h. 50m. was allowed for the 43¼-mile journey, with stops at Banchory and Aboyne. At first the trains ran on every weekday, except Mondays, but from 1871 they also ran on Sundays. To provide for the delivery and despatch of letters throughout the weekend while the Royal Family was at Balmoral, a Sunday service, subsidised by the Post Office, had been introduced a year earlier. This train started from Ballater in the morning, and returned from Aberdeen soon after midday.

Although they were only run while the Queen was staying at Balmoral, these trains were not special trains in the strictest sense of the term. They were shown in the company's timetables (and also for many years in 'Bradshaw') and were available to first class passengers, and to their servants at third class fares. Nevertheless, they are remarkable, not only for their origin but also as the first in the north of Scotland that did not call at almost every station. The journey time was reduced on more than one occasion, but full advantage was never taken of their light weight to run them at anything like high speed.

Save during the first world war, when the Royal Family did not visit Balmoral, the trains ran regularly for more than 70 years, although latterly they were not advertised in public timetables. In 1938, however, they were discontinued; and thereafter the courier once more travelled between Perth and the castle by road, a journey which the motor car had robbed of its former difficulties.

In 1883, the 'Messenger Trains' figured in a remarkable lawsuit, in which Sir Robert Burnett, who had succeeded to the Crathes estates a few years earlier, sought to enforce his right under the feu charter of 1863 to have all trains stopped at Crathes to pick up and set down passengers. All the subsidised services had been advertised to call, either regularly or conditionally, in 1878, after correspondence had passed between Sir Robert and the railway company; but four years later the Great North declined a request that a Saturday half-day excursion should serve that station. This train called only at Banchory and Aboyne between Aberdeen and Ballater, to set down passengers on the outward journey and to pick up on the return.

ON SATURDAY AFTERNOONS,

UNTIL FURTHER NOTICE,

A FAST EXCURSION TRAIN

WILL BE RUN FROM ABERDEEN TO

BANCHORY, ABOYNE, & BALLATER.

FARES—THERE AND BACK.

BANCHORY, *First Class, 2s. 0d.; Third Class, 1s. 3d.*
ABOYNE, .⎱ *Do.   4s. 0d.   Do.   2s. 0d.*
BALLATER, ⎰

The Train will leave ABERDEEN at 1 o'clock, P.M., and return from BALLATER at 8 o'clock, P.M., ABOYNE at 8·20 P.M., and BANCHORY at 8·50 P.M., arriving in ABERDEEN about 9·30 P.M.

COACH ARRANGEMENTS.

In connection with the Excursion Train, Mr. MACGREGOR, Invercauld Arms, Ballater, will run an Open Coach from Ballater Station, up the north side of the River Dee by the Bridge of Gairn and Coil-a-Creich to Crathie; returning via Balmoral and the south side of the Dee, affording Passengers a fine view of Abergeldie Castle and the Deer Forest of Birkhall, and arriving at Ballater at 7 p.m.

Fare for the Coach Journey of nearly Twenty Miles, 2/6.

As the number of Coach Passengers will be limited, early application should be made for Tickets, which are obtainable in Aberdeen only.

TICKET ARRANGEMENTS.

Tickets for these Excursions, and for the Coach in connection, may be had, on and after Wednesday of each week, at MURRAY'S TICKET OFFICES, Union Street, Aberdeen, and at the COMPANY'S BOOKING OFFICE, Joint Station.

The Special Excursion Tickets are only available by the Trains named. No Luggage allowed.

Deeside excursion advertisement, 1882 (the train that figured in the lawsuit)

Sir Robert then applied to the Court of Session for an order requiring all trains (other than privately-chartered specials) to call at Crathes unconditionally. The railway company pleaded successfully that the subsidised services were not wholly under its control, and that the Saturday excursion (which had appeared in the time-tables in error) was not available to ordinary fare-paying passengers. The case dragged on, and in 1885 was carried to the Lords, who reversed the judgement so far as the subsidised services were concerned, although the plea for the omission of the stop by the excursion train was allowed. This decision did not affect the only other fast trains on the line, the morning and evening summer residential services, which had always called at Crathes since their introduction in 1880. (See Chapter 9.)

Although the dispute was widely regarded as a 'storm in a teacup' which need never have arisen, it had a deeper significance. The case had not proceeded very far when it became apparent that the Great North considered that traffic in Upper Deeside was increasing to an extent that would soon call for some trains to run non-stop at least between Aberdeen and Banchory. If Crathes did not share in these improvements, Sir Robert Burnett feared that his plans for housing development on part of his estate would be jeopardised. Although the hopes of neither side were ever fully realised, the terms of the feu charter were strictly observed for many years after the lawsuit had ended. In 1914, however, Sir Robert Burnett's successor, Sir Thomas Burnett, agreed to waive his rights, and in the summer of that year certain regular trains began to omit the stop at Crathes.

CHAPTER 9

Crisis and Recovery

GRAVE FINANCIAL DIFFICULTIES

Shortly before the consolidation of the Great North of Scotland Railway in 1866, a financial crisis had arisen in the railway world as the result of over-speculation, largely by contractors. Overend & Gurney's Bank, which had financed many of these schemes, failed, and in the ensuing panic other financial houses collapsed. For the time being, investors lost confidence in railways, and several companies suffered severely.

On the Great North the national crisis aggravated an already difficult situation. The rapid development of the system had overstrained the company's resources, and the traffic on the new lines was, as yet, far from encouraging. Most of the subsidiaries had required additional assistance, and the parent company had entered into commitments far exceeding the amounts originally intended. The prolonged controversy over the junction at Aberdeen had proved extremely costly; the value of the Deeside shares, acquired as a protective measure, was below the amount paid for them; and the company was faced with a heavy outlay for the construction of the Denburn Valley line and the joint station at Aberdeen.

The opening of the Highland Railway had caused a serious drop in revenue. Not only had a considerable amount of traffic been diverted to the new and shorter route to Inverness, but the newcomer had secured the contract for the conveyance of many of the mails which had previously passed through Aberdeen. A clear indication that a difficult period lay ahead was the complete loss of dividend on the ordinary shares in 1865.

That the directors were apprehensive of their policy being called into question when the shareholders became fully aware of this disquieting position is clear from the fact that in 1865 they invited the setting up of a committee to enquire into the company's affairs. This invitation was accepted.

Although a thorough examination of the position appears to

have been undertaken, the report contained little that was constructive beyond a recommendation that the Port Gordon extension of the Banffshire Railway should be postponed. Criticism of the directors was of a mild order, not amounting to censure. For the time being the board remained in office, but some twelve months later, after the consolidation of the system, and the breakdown of the negotiations for amalgamation with the Caledonian Railway, the whole board resigned. Six of the members, including Sir James Elphinstone, the chairman, did not seek re-election.

The new board, which consisted of 13 members instead of 12, met for the first time early in 1867, under the chairmanship of John Duncan. The task confronting the directors was far from enviable. By this time, nearly £300,000 had been oversubscribed to the subsidiary companies; and there were temporary loans, and floating debts, together totalling more than £800,000. Unforeseen difficulties had increased the cost of the Denburn Valley line; and the lease of the Deeside Railway had been agreed on terms by no means favourable to the Great North. Not only was there no immediate prospect of restoring the dividends on the ordinary shares, but even the preference shares were not receiving their full interest. It was at first proposed to raise capital by a further issue of preference shares, but so unsatisfactory was the position that Parliament refused to sanction such a step.

There remained only one course open to the directors—a policy of strict economy in every department. All schemes for the further development of the system had to be postponed. Even the completion of the short extension to Macduff was delayed until 1872, six years after it had been authorised.

On the other hand, the passenger fares were reduced in 1867 to bring them slightly below those in force in the early days. However, these concessions were not permanent; for in 1873, and again in the next year, increases were imposed, which in most cases more than nullified the reductions. At this new high level the fares remained for ten years. Thanks to the agreement of 1866, these increases did not affect the Deeside line (see Chapter 8).

Some years elapsed before there was any improvement in the wretchedly slow and inadequate train services. In the summer of 1871, however, the mid-morning train from Aberdeen was altered to start at 10.15, and accelerated to reach Keith in 2h. 10m. with eight intermediate stops. The earlier arrival in Keith gave a connection with a stopping train on the Highland Railway reaching Inverness at 2.45 p.m. This improvement was short lived, for by the autumn of 1872 the train had been slowed to such an extent that the connection at Keith had been broken. However, despite these handicaps, traffic continued to increase, particularly on the main line, while even the unproductive branches gradually showed signs of improvement. The efforts of the board were thus slowly rewarded.

In 1872, failing health caused John Duncan to relinquish his position as chairman, although he retained his seat on the board, and the chairmanship of the Deeside Railway, until his death three years later. The new chairman was William Leslie, Lord Provost of Aberdeen, a well-known architect and contractor, and a member of the board since 1865. Rigid economy was still the order of the day; but the results of the years of retrenchment were becoming apparent. In 1874 the dividends on the various classes of preference shares were paid in full and for the first time in ten years there was a small dividend on the ordinary shares. By this time, too, most of the extraordinary debts had either been paid off completely or were fast nearing extinction. In the following year the amalgamation with the Deeside Railway still further consolidated the system, and reduced the lines worked to the 18¼ miles of the Morayshire Railway.

Satisfactory as this continued improvement was, it had been made possible only at the expense of progress and efficiency. Save for a few relatively minor additions and improvements, no alterations had been made in the train services for several years. No new locomotives, and very few passenger coaches or goods vehicles, had been constructed since the 1866 crisis; maintenance of stations and track had been reduced to a minimum; and much of the company's plant was in urgent need of renewal.

There is even a suggestion that the maintenance of locomotives had been cut down to a dangerously low level. On 13 September 1878 the boiler of an engine exploded at Nethy Bridge, fortunately without fatal results. At the Board of Trade enquiry the inspector severely criticised the arrangements for the periodical testing of boilers. In his opinion, not only were the tests too infrequent, but were inadequate when carried out with cold water at a pressure only 30 lb. in excess of the normal working pressure (as had been the case with the boiler in question). So strict were the measures of economy then in force that some 16 months elapsed before the damaged engine was reboilered and again placed in service. The recommendation of the Board of Trade inspector for the more efficient testing of boilers was adopted.

TOWARDS BETTER TIMES

The end of the period of recovery was marked by the death of the chairman, and the resignation of the general manager and the secretary, in 1879. The new chairman was William Ferguson, a prominent Aberdeen businessman, who had joined the board at the reconstruction of the company in 1867. He had been elected deputy chairman a year before the death of Leslie.

Ill health occasioned the resignation of both Robert Milne, the general manager, and William B. Ferguson, the secretary. The former remained completely in retirement until his death 12 years later, but Ferguson accepted a seat on the board, although he only survived until the following January. Once again, it was decided to combine the offices of general manager and secretary, and William Moffatt, of the docks department of the North Eastern Railway, was appointed to the dual position.

A few months later the passenger superintendent, Forbes Morrison, resigned, and was succeeded by Alexander Reid, who had received his early training on the London & North Western Railway before joining the North Eastern Railway, where he had been closely associated with the new general manager. William Walker, the goods manager, had resigned at the end of 1877, and had been succeeded by his chief clerk, Alexander Ross.

With the financial position stabilised, the company was able to carry out long-overdue improvements which were to place the Great North among the most progressive and up-to-date systems in the country. Traffic had increased to an extent that called for the doubling of the main line. No additional land was required, as provision for a double line had been made when the railway was built. The first seven miles, from Dyce to Kintore, were opened on 1 June 1880; and the 7½ miles thence to Inveramsay followed on 1 May 1882. Thereafter more than six years elapsed before the widening was extended a further seven miles to Insch on 27 October 1888.

In the meantime much other work was undertaken. Many miles of light iron track, the greater part of it without fishplates, were relaid with heavier steel rails; some single-line sections were shortened by the provision of additional crossing loops; the signalling system was modernised; and the main line, at any rate, made ready for the running of faster trains.

On the Deeside Railway, where no provision for subsequent

LONDON.

TOURIST TICKETS,

Available for Return to 31st December, 1882,

Will be issued from the following Stations

TO LONDON.

FARES:—

	1st CLASS.	2nd CLASS.	3rd CLASS.
From Elgin,	148s. 6d.	104s. 3d.	60s.
„ Keith,	147s. 6d.	103s. 9d.	60s.

Tickets are also issued at

INVERNESS FOR LONDON,

Via ABERDEEN.

FARES:—

FIRST CLASS, **150s.**; SECOND CLASS, **105s.**; THIRD CLASS, **60s.**

No Second Class by Great North of Scotland or Midland Railways.

Advertisement of Cheap Tickets to London, 1882

widening had been made, powers were obtained in 1877 to double the ten miles from Ferryhill Junction to Park; but it was not until an extension of time had been granted that the first 2¾ miles to Cults were completed in the summer of 1884. The remainder of the scheme was then postponed, although the land was acquired.

As a result of heavy expenditure on these works, no dividends were declared on the ordinary shares in 1881 and the two succeeding years. Regular payments were then resumed, but it was not until 1891 that they rose as high as 2½ per cent. Undeterred by this temporary setback, the company took the welcome step in February 1884 of reducing the passenger fares. Thereafter, with the exception of the 'Queens Messenger Trains' on the Deeside Railway, which remained first class only for some years, all trains conveyed first and third class passengers at 2d and 1d a mile respectively.

Scarcely had the era of improvement begun than there occurred the worst accident in the history of the Great North. On 27 November 1882, as the 4 p.m. mixed train from Macduff to Inveramsay was crossing the Inverythan Road Bridge, between Auchterless and Fyvie, the whole structure collapsed. The train was made up of four passenger coaches, marshalled in the rear of five loaded goods wagons and a brakevan. The engine and the first two wagons crossed in safety, although the latter were derailed, but the remaining four goods vehicles and the first two passenger coaches fell 30 ft to the roadway, and were completely destroyed. The third passenger coach hung suspended over the gap, almost undamaged; and the last coach remained on the rails. Five passengers were killed, and 18 others injured. An examination of the wreckage revealed a hidden flaw in one of the cast iron girders of the bridge, which suddenly spread and caused complete collapse under the weight of the train.

THE MORAY FIRTH COAST LINE

The amalgamation with the Morayshire Railway in 1881 completed the consolidation of the system, and coincided with the first steps towards the construction of a route to Elgin *via* the Moray Firth coast. The abandonment of the Port Gordon extension of the Banffshire Railway in 1867 had been a severe blow to the fishing ports west of Portsoy; but several years elapsed before the scheme could be revived. The line projected in 1881 was slightly longer than that previously authorised, and passed at the back of the town of Cullen instead of along the shore at the foot of the cliffs. Although an extension to Elgin was regarded as certain, it was decided to fix the western terminus at Port Gordon for the time being.

This decision evoked strong criticism in the coast towns, where the completion of a through route to the west was strongly urged; and the Highland Railway, taking this objection as its cue, opposed the scheme on the grounds that the district would be better served by a line from Keith running northwards across the hills to Buckie, and thence along the coast at least as far as Cullen. The result was that the bill was rejected.

Next year, both companies promoted railways to serve the district. To overcome the principal objection to the original scheme, the Great North proposed to extend the line beyond Port Gordon to a junction with the Lossiemouth branch near Elgin, 25¼ miles from Portsoy. On the other hand, the Highland Railway sought powers for the branch from Keith to Buckie and Cullen, suggested a year earlier. In the ensuing parliamentary contest, the Great North was successful; but the rival project was cut down to a line from Keith to a junction with the new railway at Portessie. The Highland company was, however, granted running powers along the coast from Portessie—westwards to Buckie, and eastwards to Portsoy. In return, the Great North was granted similar powers between Elgin and Forres. The Acts authorising the railways and conferring the running powers received the Royal Assent on 12 July 1882.

The gradients between Portsoy and Elgin were undulating, and by no means easy. The engineering works included a long viaduct over the Spey at Garmouth, and a series of high embankments and three brick and masonry viaducts across the old sea-town at Cullen. The Spey viaduct, the most impressive feature of the line, was designed to meet the sudden severe floods and considerable changes of bed to which the river is liable near its mouth, and had a central bow-string girder span of 350 ft, and six shorter girder spans of 100 ft each. At Buckie, lines were laid to the harbour, which had been reconstructed some years before.

The 4¼ miles from Portsoy to Tochieneal were opened on 1 April 1884. A new station was provided at Portsoy, a short distance south of the former terminus, retained for goods traffic. There was one intermediate station, at Glassaugh. Some four months later, on 12 August, the 7¾ miles from Lossie Junction (Elgin) to Garmouth, with intermediate stations at Calcots and Urquhart, were brought into use. To serve these two sections of the line, the Portsoy branch trains were extended to Tochieneal, and a local service of about six trains was run between Elgin and Garmouth.

The remaining 13¼ miles from Tochieneal to Garmouth, which included the heavy works at Cullen and the Spey viaduct, were not opened to passengers until 1 May 1886, although goods traffic began on April 5. There were intermediate stations at Cullen, Portknockie, Findochty, Portessie, Buckie, Nether Buckie, Port Gordon, and Fochabers. A more appropriate designation for the last-named would have been Fochabers Road, as the town lay some four miles to the south. It was, however, no worse situated than the station at that time named Fochabers on the Forres-Keith section of the Highland Railway, which was a like distance from the town in the opposite direction. Nether Buckie became Buckpool in the year following the opening of the railway; but it was not until 1918, long after the Highland Railway had opened a branch to the town, that Fochabers was renamed Spey Bay.

To allow trains to run between Aberdeen and the new line without reversing at Grange, a short loop was constructed from the main line to the Banffshire Railway half a mile east of that station, and opened on 1 May 1886. Powers for this loop had not been included in the Act for the line along the coast, but as the necessary land was either already in the possession of the company, or could easily be acquired, its construction was undertaken without parliamentary sanction. Later on, however, it was considered advisable to seek authority for the connection, and relevant clauses were inserted in the company's Act of 19 July 1887.

With the exception of the 1¼ miles from Buckie to Portessie, the railway from Portsoy to Elgin was single track, with crossing loops at the principal stations. This short section of double line was provided to facilitate the movement of fish vans between Buckie harbour and the sidings at Portessie. The single-line sections were controlled by electric tablet, which was soon to supersede the telegraphic crossing orders used on other parts of the system. In May 1889, the tablet-exchange apparatus designed by James Manson, the locomotive superintendent, was installed on the coast route to Elgin, and also on the Fraserburgh line, where it had been given an extensive trial. On 1 January 1893, the Manson apparatus was extended to all the remaining single-line sections, concurrently with the introduction of block working throughout the Great North.

The distance from Aberdeen to Elgin *via* the coast was 87¼ miles, compared with 80¾ *via* Craigellachie. From an operating point of view, however, the longer route, with its less severe gradients, and denser population, had an advantage.

On its completion, the new line was served by four trains in each direction, and by a portion of the fast train leaving Aberdeen at 10.10 a.m., which omitted several stops, and reached Elgin at 12.55 p.m. A similar train was provided in the up direction, leaving Elgin at 1.35 p.m., and reaching Aberdeen in 2¾ hours. Two years later, a second fast train was put on in each direction. The up service left Elgin at 10.10 a.m., and took 2h. 35m. to Aberdeen. The down train started at 7 p.m., and was 5m. slower.

Two mishaps occurred on the new line about 12 months after its completion. The first was at Buckpool on 10 May 1887, when a train was derailed as the result of distortion of the track through expansion caused by the heat of the sun. The train was travelling slowly, and the passengers escaped with a shaking. In his report, the Board of Trade inspector criticised the inadequate ballasting of the track. A similar derailment at Wartle, on the Macduff line, two years earlier suggests that other sections of the Great North were not above such reproach at that period.

The second mishap occurred at Cullen, when a subsidence of an embankment caused the end of the adjoining viaduct to collapse. No train was involved, but the line was closed for a fortnight while temporary repairs were effected. Two spans were replaced by an extension of the embankment, and a third was filled in with concrete.

The branch of the Highland Railway from Keith to Portessie, 13¾ miles of steeply graded single line, had been opened on 1 August 1884. At Portessie, where the Highland trains used the Great North station, the two railways ran side by side for some distance. The junction was immediately east of the station. Although the line formed a direct route between Keith and the coast, the train service was far from lavish. Nor did the Highland exercise any part of its running powers between Buckie and Portsoy. The reciprocal powers granted to the Great North between Elgin and Forres were thus rendered useless, because it was stipulated that neither company should use its powers if the other refrained from so doing.

THE CRUDEN BAY BRANCH

After the completion of the coast route to Elgin, no extension of the system was undertaken until the Cruden Railway was authorised on 24 August 1893, to encourage the development of Cruden Bay and Port Errol, on the Aberdeenshire coast, as seaside resorts. The line, which was 15½ miles long, branched from the Buchan section at Ellon, and reached the coast at Port Errol, whence it turned northwards to the fishing town of Boddam. The engineering works were light, but the gradients were far from easy.

The railway, which was single-track throughout, was opened on 2 August 1897 with intermediate stations at Auchmacoy, Pitlurg, Hatton, Cruden Bay, and Longhaven. In 1899, a halt was opened between Cruden Bay and Longhaven to serve the Bullers o' Buchan, a series of natural cauldrons formed by the sea in the cliffs.

At Cruden Bay, the company acquired a site for a large hotel and an 18-hole golf course. The latter had already been laid out when the branch was opened; but the hotel was not opened until 1 March 1899. Its equipment included an electric generating plant, and a laundry, to which the whole of the company's washing was sent.

The hotel was connected with the railway station, nearly a mile distant, by an electric tramway, opened in June 1899. The tramway was single track, and was laid with bull-head rails to a gauge of 3 ft 6½ in. Current was supplied through an overhead conductor. Coal and stores for the hotel were carried, in addition to passengers. The rolling stock, consisting of two single deck tramcars and three trailer vehicles for goods, was all built at the company's locomotive and carriage works at Kittybrewster.

Trains on the Cruden line stopped at all stations, and were allowed about 40m. between Ellon and Boddam. The number of services never exceeded five in each direction. After the opening of the Cruden Bay Hotel, improved connections were given by the acceleration of trains on the Buchan section.

Through services to and from Aberdeen were inaugurated in the summer of 1899, with a morning train in each direction, running non-stop between Ellon and Aberdeen. The down train was withdrawn in the autumn of 1899 and never reinstated, but the up service survived as a summer-only feature. For some years, a slightly slower through service, leaving Aberdeen early in the afternoon, and returning in the evening, was run daily in the summer. Subsequently, these trains ran on Saturdays only, and later on Wednesdays and Saturdays.

Although efforts were made to popularise the hotel and the golf course, and to develop Port Errol, the results were most disappointing. Nor did the fish traffic from Boddam come up to expectations. Had the railway been extended for three miles to Peterhead, to establish a new and shorter route of 38 miles between that town and Aberdeen, the result might have been different, but such an extension had been opposed when the line was projected. It was all the more unfortunate that some of the company's senior officers had displayed a keen personal interest in the scheme, as the discouraging results evoked criticism of their misplaced confidence and lack of judgement.

CONTINUED PROGRESS

The doubling of the main line was extended for 13¼ miles in 1896—from Insch to Kennethmont on 1 August, to Gartly on 20 September, and to Huntly on 30 November. Although it was stated that the widening was to be carried through to Keith at an early date, it was not until 19 January 1898 that the four miles from Huntly to Avochie signalbox (half a mile east of Rothiemay) were brought into use. Two days earlier, the doubling of the 7¾ miles from Rothiemay to the eastern end of Keith station, and of the loop line between the south and north junctions at Grange, had been completed.

The short section from Avochie to Rothiemay included the masonry bridge over the Deveron, which was only wide enough for a single track. To improve the alignment of the railway, a new double-track lattice girder bridge was built alongside the older structure, which was abandoned, but not demolished. Powers for this deviation were obtained on 12 August 1898; and the new line was opened in the spring of 1900.

On the Deeside line, the widening had been extended from Cults to Murtle on 13 July 1892, and to Culter ten weeks later, on 24 September; but nearly seven more years elapsed before it was completed to Park on 28 August 1899.

In addition to the deviation at Rothiemay, the Act of 12 August 1898 authorised the doubling of the main line from Keith to Keith Town, and from Longmorn to Elgin; of the Moray Firth coast line from Elgin to Lossie Junction; and of the Deeside line from Park to Banchory. Unfortunately, traffic did not increase to the extent then expected, and none of this work was ever undertaken. A similar fate overtook a scheme for the rebuilding of Keith station jointly by the Great North and the Highland companies.

Meantime, the efforts of the general manager and the superintendent had completely revolutionised the train services. The improvements began in May 1880 with a new and faster service in each direction on the Deeside Railway. The up train started from Ballater at 8.8 a.m., and the return service left Aberdeen at 4.30 p.m. One and a half hours were allowed for the journey of 43¼ miles, with stops at Crathes, Banchory, Torphins, and Aboyne. The average speed was barely 30 m.p.h., but the whole line west of Ferryhill Junction was still single, and the gradients between Banchory and Aboyne were far from easy. The trains proved popular, especially with daily travellers to and from Aberdeen, and became a regular feature of the summer timetables.

By 1883, the distinctly liberal schedules of the Deeside expresses had been reduced to 80m. in each direction; and three years later the time for the slightly easier up journey had become 75m. Other services between Aberdeen and Ballater also showed some improvement.

The summer of 1880 also saw a few minor improvements on the main line. Two years later, the Highland Railway restored the connection at Keith to the 11 a.m. train from Aberdeen, to give an arrival in Inverness at 4.20 p.m.; and the connection to the down train leaving at 5 p.m. began to run throughout the year instead of during the summer only. The number of through services between Aberdeen and Inverness thus became four in the down direction, and three in the up.

However, it was not until the summer of 1885 that the first substantial improvements were effected. On 1 July of that year, the down 'Limited Mail', leaving London (Euston) at 8.50 p.m., was superseded by a new passenger train at 8 p.m., and a special postal train half an hour later. These trains were combined at Perth, and reached Aberdeen at 9.55 a.m. To connect with this improved service, the Great North put on a fast train to Elgin, via Craigellachie, leaving Aberdeen at 10.10, and reaching Elgin at 1 p.m., with eight intermediate stops.

A corresponding up service, leaving Elgin at 12.55 p.m. and reaching Aberdeen at 4.20, began in January 1886; and when the Moray Firth coast route was completed, this train was accelerated to leave Elgin at 1.35 via the coast, and at 1.40 via Craigellachie, and maintain its arrival time of 4.20 in Aberdeen.

To facilitate the handling of the mails, a sorting carriage was hired from the Caledonian Railway, and placed in service on 1 January 1886 between Aberdeen and Keith in the 10.10 a.m. train. It returned in the afternoon in the 12.55 from Elgin. When the coast route was opened the carriage, which at that time was hired from the LNWR, began to run to and from Elgin but was only operational between Aberdeen and Buckie. Lineside receiving and delivering apparatus was at eight or possibly more stations on the main and coast lines. The company built two Sorting Carriages and put them into service at the end of 1886. With the accelerated times north of Aberdeen in 1895, 'Postal Trains' were run to Elgin in 1896–97 but the working became the 8.05 a.m. from Aberdeen and the 2.50 p.m. from Elgin via the coast. At the end of May 1916 the service was withdrawn as a wartime economy and never restored.

The accelerations on the main line brought to a head the question of the exchange of traffic with the Highland Railway at Elgin, and the resulting dispute dragged on for more than ten years. Its effects on the policy of the Great North and the development of the train

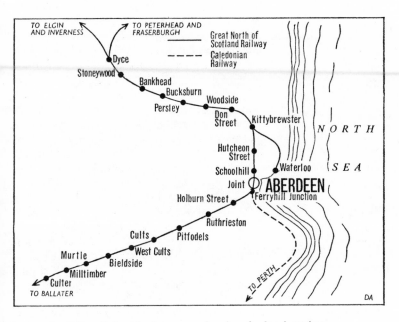

Map of the Aberdeen area showing the local stations

services on the main line are described in detail in the next chapter.

On the Buchan section, the number of trains had been increased to five in each direction by 1885, and the best journey time reduced to 2h. to Peterhead, and 5m. more to Fraserburgh. In the next year, however, the night trains from the south were given a faster connecting service leaving Aberdeen at 10.15 a.m., and reaching Peterhead in 1h. 40m., and Fraserburgh in 1¾h. At the same time, a similar up train, arriving in Aberdeen at 4.25 p.m., was put on. In 1890, this up train was altered to run one hour later; and the departure time of the down train became 9.25 a.m., as the result of improved connections from the south.

By no means the least important of the improvements in the services was the introduction of suburban trains between Aberdeen and Dyce. After a small beginning with one down and two up trains, the number of services was increased in July 1887 to eight in each direction, largely on the recommendation of the general manager. New stations were opened at Bankhead and Stoneywood, and the trains were allowed 20m. for the journey of 6¼ miles, with five intermediate stops.

At that time, the practice was prevalent among railwaymen of naming trains after some outstanding event. As the introduction of the new services almost coincided with Queen Victoria's Golden Jubilee, the trains were promptly dubbed the 'Jubilees'. However, it was the regular travellers who had the last word; to them these suburban trains soon became the 'subbies'.

The new services proved extremely popular, and within six months four additional trains were running in each direction, and new stations had been opened at Hutcheon Street and Don Street. From time to time, extra trains were put on until the number of services became 20 in each direction, at which figure it remained. Although the number of intermediate stops subsequently became nine by the opening of stations at Schoolhill (virtually an extension of Aberdeen Joint station) in 1893, and Persley in 1903, the schedule of 20m. remained unaltered. Not only did its observance demand exceptionally smart station work, but imposed a far from easy task on the locomotives, despite the light weight of the trains.

The success of the suburban services on the main line led to a demand for similar facilities on the Deeside Railway between Aberdeen and Culter, but as the line was still single west of Cults, and the district was purely residential, it was not considered practicable to provide them for the time being. In the summer of 1894, however, by which time double track had been extended to Culter, new stations were opened at Holburn Street, Pitfodels, and West Cults, and a service of ten down and nine up trains was provided. The time allowed for the journey of 7⅜ miles, with seven intermediate stops, was 22m. in the up direction, and one minute less in the down. With minor exceptions, these schedules were never altered. As was the case on the main line, the service proved popular, and the number of trains was subsequently doubled. In 1897, an additional station was opened at Bieldside.

AFTER FIFTY YEARS

By the summer of 1896, when the company reached the fiftieth anniversary of its incorporation, the dispute with the Highland Railway over the Aberdeen-Inverness traffic was nearing its end. Several far from unimportant events had occurred during the latter part of this period, but had tended to be overshadowed by the turmoil of the struggle which had for so long dominated the policy of the Great North.

In 1891, the company acquired the Palace Hotel at Aberdeen, which had been built on the site originally intended for the joint station. Access to the station was by means of hydraulic lifts to a new foot-bridge leading to the north end of the main platform, the roof of which was considerably extended.

After the hotel was acquired, the uniformed porters of other hotels were excluded from the platforms of the station, even for the purpose of collecting passengers' luggage. This arbitrary action was not actively challenged until the summer of 1896, when several proprietors sent their porters on to the platforms to meet incoming trains. After this protest, substantial concessions were granted to the hotels, although their porters were still denied unrestricted access to the platforms.

Shortly after the purchase of the Palace Hotel, the chief offices of the company were transferred from the old Waterloo terminus to more commodious premises in Guild Street, with direct access to the joint station. The new building was completed in 1894, and the offices at Waterloo were then given over entirely to the staff of the goods station.

In the early hours of 29 July 1896, a ballast train proceeding from Rothes to Grange, via the coast, was involved in an unusual accident at Knock. Ordinary traffic had ceased for the night, and the train was being worked without reference to signals. At Knock, it was diverted without warning to the wrong side of the crossing loop, and thence through catch points into a short siding, where it was derailed at the buffer stops. The engine and several wagons were overturned onto the main line; and the driver and fireman, and district permanent way inspector Peter Sleigh, who was also riding on the footplate, were seriously injured. The latter, one of the company's oldest servants, died the next day.

At the enquiry, an ambiguity in the wording of the traffic circular was revealed, as it was by no means clear whether the train was to reach Grange *via* Keith or *via* the coast. The stationmaster at Knock, not realising that the train would pass his station, had not altered the points after the passing of the last down train.

Towards the end of 1897, the directors invited the whole of the staff in turn to a series of four evening receptions in Aberdeen. The receptions were held in the following January and March, for about one quarter of the staff, and their wives or friends, on each occasion. The evening's entertainment included an exhibition of cinema films (at that time a great novelty), a concert, and a display by a detachment of the Gordon Highlanders, followed by supper and dancing. Shortly after midnight, special trains were run to all parts of the system to take the guests to their homes.

These highly successful and enjoyable social functions, the like of which had never been held elsewhere, did much to strengthen the already cordial relations between the directors and the staff. Most appropriately, they marked the conclusion of the struggle with the Highland Railway, and thus closed a chapter in the history of the Great North on a particularly happy note.

CHAPTER 10

The Road to Inverness

ENTERPRISE LEADS TO WARFARE

The progressive policy of the Great North after the years of financial stringency soon led the company to press for the improvement of the through services between Aberdeen and Inverness, and to seek a revision of the agreement of 1865 for the exchange of traffic with the Highland Railway at Keith. This problem was complicated by the fact that the Highland Railway had the shortest route between Keith and Elgin, but the two Great North lines (and especially the coast route) served more populous districts.

That the Highland would be entitled to some recompense for loss of revenue if Elgin became the point of exchange was not questioned; but that company persisted in regarding the line from Forres to Keith as a branch, whose trains were arranged to connect with those on the Perth-Inverness line, frequently to the detriment of the Aberdeen services. It was hoped that an improvement would result when the Great North was able to exercise running powers between Elgin and Forres, but this concession was nullified by the failure of the Highland Railway to use its reciprocal powers between Buckie and Portsoy. However, before this impasse arose, a direct attack had been made on Inverness from another direction.

It had long been recognised that eventually the main line from Inverness to Perth would have to be shortened by the elimination of the detour through Forres, but the Highland Company was naturally reluctant to build a more direct route through mountainous and sparsely-inhabited country, and on its completion be obliged to lower its fares. In 1883, an independent company promoted the Glasgow & North Western Railway, from the North British Railway at Maryhill, in the northern suburbs of Glasgow, to Inverness, *via* the east side of Loch Lomond, Rannoch Moor, Glencoe, Ballachulish, and Fort William. The distance from Glasgow to Inverness was about 165 miles, compared with 207 miles by the Caledonian and Highland Railways.

The bill was rejected by Parliament in June 1883, but only after the Highland had undertaken to seek powers in the next session to shorten its line. At this juncture, the Great North began to press a claim for an entry into Inverness, first with a proposal for joint ownership of the new railway, and when this was declined, with a rival bill for a jointly-owned line.

The line projected by the Great North branched from the Strathspey line west of Nethy Bridge, and crossing under the Highland main line, to which there was to be a connecting spur, passed through Carr Bridge and Moy to join the Highland Railway in the outskirts of Inverness. The distance from Aberdeen to Inverness—130 miles—compared unfavourably with the 108 miles of the route *via* Keith and the Highland Railway.

Local landowners then promoted the Strathspey, Strathdon & Deeside Junction Railway, from Nethy Bridge to the Deeside Railway near Cambus o' May, through the mountainous and desolate country of Glen Avon and Upper Strathdon. This line, which was about 40 miles long, was remarkable for its extremely severe gradients, and summit level of 1,500 ft. The engineering works included a tunnel nearly two miles long, and several big bridges. The distance from Aberdeen to Nethy Bridge was 82 miles, and to Inverness, *via* the line proposed by the Great North, 115 miles. The company was independent of the Great North, although the latter was willing to work the line.

The direct line to Inverness promoted by the Highland company differed but little from that proposed by the Great North, save that it left the existing route at Aviemore, five miles south of Boat of Garten. The engineering works were heavy, but the gradients, although steep, were somewhat less severe than those on the rival route.

When the bills for the two lines to Inverness were submitted to Parliament in 1884, the Great North was defeated, but the Highland received its Act on 28 July. The bill for the Strathspey, Strathdon & Deeside Junction Railway was also rejected, and the promoters decided to wind up the undertaking.

Although defeated in Parliament, the Great North had demonstrated the need for improved services between Aberdeen and Inverness. Clauses for the regulation of this traffic were inserted in the Highland Act for the shortened route to the south, and into an Act for other purposes, which the Great North obtained on the same day. Facilities were to be provided for the exchange of traffic at *any* junction (i.e. at Keith or at Elgin); unrestricted through bookings were to be granted; services for passengers and goods were to be conveniently arranged, and to include a reasonable number of through coaches and wagons; unnecessary delays were to be avoided; and both companies were to deal with the traffic 'as if it were traffic that they wished to cultivate'.

How slender were the chances of this compromise proving satisfactory became apparent in July 1885, when the night trains from the south were accelerated, and the Great North put on the improved service leaving Aberdeen at 10.10 a.m., and reaching Keith at 11.50 a.m., and Elgin at 1 p.m. The through coaches were sent *via* Keith, but the alteration gave passengers the option of joining the connecting train for Inverness at Elgin. No sooner had this timetable come into force than the Highland train was altered to leave Keith 20m. earlier, and the connection at Elgin was severed, although the arrival time at Inverness (2.45 p.m.) remained unaltered. However, by October, after the 10.10 a.m. from Aberdeen had been slightly altered to reach Keith at 11.46 a.m., the Highland justified its action by starting the connecting train at 11.50, and reaching Inverness at 1.30 p.m.

A SEVEN-YEAR TRAFFIC AGREEMENT

Although the services between Aberdeen and Inverness had been improved, the Great North had undoubtedly suffered a defeat, because the Highland was obviously determined to retain Keith as the point of exchange for through traffic. The prospects of developing the new line from Portsoy to Elgin as a route to Inverness were far from rosy, and the Great North petitioned the Board of Trade for an order providing for two connections in each direction at Elgin. The board approached the matter with reluctance and diffidence, and temporised with an order which, although it provided for traffic passing to and from the Great North at Elgin, still left Keith as the point of exchange for the through coaches between Aberdeen and Inverness.

The Great North was not satisfied with this result, and immediately applied for the case to be reheard. Permission was granted; but before the rehearing could be held, the companies reached a compromise in the spring of 1886, and entered into a working agreement for the conduct of the through traffic. The agreement, which was to remain in force for seven years, provided not only for the arrangement of the services, but also for the pooling of receipts from the through traffic as between Grange and Elgin, irrespective

1st JULY, 1890,

AND UNTIL FURTHER NOTICE.

TIME TABLES

OF THE

GREAT NORTH OF SCOTLAND RAILWAY.

The
only Time Tables
published

By
authority of the
Company.

Passengers, Carriages, Horses, &c., are booked Through from London, Edinburgh, Glasgow, &c., to Inverness and the North at same Through Fares and Rates via Aberdeen as via Dunkeld.

ALL PREVIOUS TIME TABLES WITHDRAWN.

PRINTED BY

G. CORNWALL AND SONS, PRINTERS, ABERDEEN.

GRATUITOUS COPY.

(1,850.)

Front cover of GNSR Public Timetable for July 1890

of the route by which the trains travelled. Disputes were to be referred to an independent arbiter.

As a result of the agreement, a number of alterations and additions were made to the services in the summer of 1886. The Highland midday train from Keith was altered to start 20m. later, and to make connection at Keith and at Elgin with the 10.10 a.m. from Aberdeen. Inverness was reached at 2.15 p.m., a deceleration of 45m. In the opposite direction, a train left Inverness at midday to connect with the improved service (established by the Great North six months earlier) leaving Elgin at 1.35 *via* the coast, and at 1.40 *via* Craigellachie, and reaching Aberdeen at 4.20. Through coaches between Aberdeen and Inverness were run in these trains by the then recently-completed coast route. There was also a new early morning down service *via* Keith, leaving Aberdeen at 3.35, and reaching Inverness in 4½h.

Less than two years after the agreement came into force, the arbiter, James Grierson, general manager of the Great Western Railway, died, and was succeeded by Henry Tennant, general manager of the North Eastern Railway. Whether William Moffatt was in any way responsible for the appointment of his former chief must remain an open question; but it is significant that relations between the two companies thereafter steadily deteriorated, and the number of disputes referred to the arbiter increased.

In August 1888, a second improved service in each direction was provided on the main line. The up train left Elgin at 10.10 a.m., *via* the coast, and reached Aberdeen in 2h. 35m., with six regular and seven conditional stops. It ran non-stop from Huntly to Aberdeen in 68m., the longest non-stop run so far attempted on the Great North. The down train, which left Aberdeen at 7 p.m., and served only the coast route, was 5m. slower, but made no less than 15 regular and four conditional stops. Both trains included through coaches between Glasgow and Elgin *via* Perth and Aberdeen, but despite strong protests by the Great North, the Highland refused to provide connections to and from Inverness. On the other hand, the journey time from Inverness to Aberdeen was brought below 4h. for the first time by the acceleration of the 3 p.m. train by 10m. east of Keith.

In March 1890, the opening of the Forth Bridge gave the North British Railway the shortest route by 29 miles between Edinburgh and Aberdeen, and, in conjunction with its English partners, the Great Northern and the North Eastern, by 17 miles between London and Aberdeen. Although no attempt was then made to exploit this advantage to its fullest extent, the journey times of the through services between Aberdeen and the south by both the East Coast and West Coast routes were substantially reduced.

On the Great North, the 10.10 a.m. from Aberdeen was retimed to start 40m. earlier in the summer of 1890. The Highland train was altered to leave Keith correspondingly earlier. The connections were maintained at Elgin from the Craigellachie line and the Moray Firth coast route. However, by the time these alterations came into force, a major development had occurred in the dispute between the Great North and the Highland Railway.

THE LONG STRUGGLE CONTINUES

Anxious to take full advantage of the improvements south of Aberdeen, the Great North sought powers in 1890 for a line from Elgin to Inverness, running more or less parallel to the Highland Railway. There was to be a branch from Elgin to Burghead, and another in the Black Isle, on the north side of the Beauly Firth, from the Highland Railway at Muir of Ord to Fortrose. The latter was to be approached by running powers over the Highland Railway from Inverness. The opposition of the Highland company on the grounds that the traffic agreement rendered the proposed line unnecessary secured the rejection of the bill; but it was obvious that the Great North would renew its efforts to gain direct access to Inverness.

A favourable opportunity soon arose. To revive the west-coast fishing trade, a company had obtained powers in 1890 for a railway to connect Ullapool, in Wester Ross, with the Dingwall & Skye section of the Highland Railway at Garve, some 30 miles north of Inverness. Much of the intervening country was uninhabited; and the engineering works were far from light. The Highland company had expressed its willingness to work the line, but was unable to offer financial assistance.

The Ullapool company was unable to raise sufficient capital, and the scheme was shelved until, in 1892, the Great North offered to assist with the construction, and to work the line, provided it could secure running powers between Elgin and Garve. Such powers would, of course, have included access to Inverness. Needless to say, the Highland company strongly opposed this threatened invasion of its territory, and although still unable to help the local undertaking, secured the rejection of the Great North's bill. Shortly afterwards the Garve & Ullapool company was wound up.

A similar line to connect Gairloch and Aultbea, on the Ross-shire coast, with the Highland Railway at Achnasheen was promoted in 1893. The Great North offered to assist the company financially and to work the line, subject to the granting of running powers for its trains between Elgin and Achnasheen. Once again, the opposition was able to defeat what was in reality a thinly-veiled attempt to secure access to Inverness.

Although frustrated in its attempts to reach Inverness, the Great North had at least succeeded in securing further improvements in the through services. In the summer of 1890, the afternoon up train was altered to leave Inverness at 12.30 (subsequently 12.40) and Elgin at 2.25, by both Great North routes, and to reach Aberdeen at 5.15. The schedule was slightly eased, but the connection to the south was much improved. Two years later, as the result of an appeal to the arbiter, a new through service in each direction was provided, *via* Elgin and the coast. The up train left Inverness at 9 a.m., to connect with the morning fast train from Elgin, which was retimed to start at 10.20, and slightly accelerated to maintain its arrival time of 12.55 in Aberdeen. In the opposite direction, the evening fast train was altered to leave Aberdeen at 6.40, and to reach Elgin at 9.20. The Highland Railway had at last agreed to provide a connection from Elgin, due in Inverness at 10.40.

The improvements did not last long; for when the traffic agreement was terminated in 1893, at the instigation of the Highland Railway, that company withdrew the Inverness connections to the 10.20 a.m. from Elgin and the 6.40 from Aberdeen, on the grounds that they were not paying. These retrograde steps were taken at the start of the summer holiday season, and aroused a storm of protest, but an appeal to the Railway & Canal Commissioners was necessary before a compromise was reached. In January 1894, the 9 a.m. from Inverness re-appeared as a stopping train, starting at 8.45. At Elgin, connection was made with the fast train *via* the coast, but passengers for Aberdeen could also travel *via* Keith. The Inverness connection to the 6.40 p.m. from Aberdeen was not reinstated.

In the absence of a traffic agreement, relations between the two companies deteriorated, and passed from crisis to crisis. So far as passengers were concerned, the frequent disputes and continued lack of facilities betokened only pettiness. Thus, in the summer of 1894, when the Great North put on a new up fast morning service, reaching Aberdeen at 9.55 a.m., to connect with the principal day trains to the south, the departure time from Keith (8.25 a.m.) exactly coincided with the arrival of the early train from Inverness.

THE

MORAY FIRTH COAST LINE.

THIS new Railway forms part of the Company's Main System between Aberdeen and Elgin and affords direct access to the fishing towns of Buckie, Cullen, Findochty, Port-Gordon and to Fochabers-on-Spey, Garmouth, and other places along the Moray Firth.

It also opens up a convenient and attractive Coast Route to and from the North of Scotland **via ABERDEEN.**

SPECIAL NOTICE.

Passengers with Ordinary Return or Tourist Tickets between Inverness *or any place on the Highland Railway North or West of (but not including) Elgin,* and Aberdeen *or any place South of Aberdeen, or any local Station South of Grange,* have the option of travelling in either direction by one of the following Routes, viz. :—

(1). **By the Moray Firth Coast Line** *via* **Grange, Cullen, Buckie, and Fochabers-on-Spey.**

(2). *Via* **Keith, Dufftown, Craigellachie, and Rothes. By this Route Passengers obtain views of the Valleys of the Fiddoch and Spey.**

(3). *Via* **Mulben.**

NOTES.

1. Passengers holding Ordinary Return or Tourist Tickets between the Elgin Station of the Great North Railway, and Stations south of Grange or south of Aberdeen (*via* Aberdeen), have the option of travelling *via* Keith and Craigellachie; or *via* Grange, Portsoy, and the Moray Firth Coast Line—Return Tickets being available to go *via* Moray Firth Coast Line, and return *via* Craigellachie and Keith, or *vice versa.*

2. Holders of Through Tickets between Stations in England and Stations on the Moray Firth Coast Railway, Elgin (G.N.S.), or Stations on Highland Railway West of Elgin, *via* ABERDEEN, may also travel as an alternative route from Inveramsay *via* Turriff to Banff Bridge or Macduff, and resume the journey from Banff Harbour Station travelling by the Moray Firth Coast Line *via* Portsoy and Elgin or *vice versa.*

July, 1890. W. MOFFATT, General Manager.

☞ ASK FOR TICKETS VIA ABERDEEN.

Moray Firth Coast Line Notice—from GNSR Public Timetable of July 1890

Several months elapsed before the easily-timed Highland train was accelerated to make the connection, and for the time being through passengers had to use a long-established slow train from Keith, which did not reach Aberdeen until 10.55 a.m.

The summer of 1894 was also marked by other improvements on the main line, and for the first time bookings of 40 m.p.h. and upwards appeared in the timetables. The most notable feature was the retiming of the 10.20 a.m. from Elgin, which had its non-stop run from Huntly to Aberdeen broken by a conditional stop at Dyce, and a ticket stop at Schoolhill, although the schedule for the 40¾ miles was reduced to 63m.

In contrast to these creditable efforts was the leisurely speed of several of the connections on the Highland Railway; and this, together with the refusal of the Highland to exchange more through coaches at Elgin, caused great dissatisfaction in Aberdeen. Three out of the six up through services gave a connection at Elgin; but in the opposite direction only one did so. Convinced that improved services would bring a substantial increase in traffic, the Great North promoted another bill for running powers to Inverness in 1895.

In support of the application, it was urged that the unprogressive policy adopted in Inverness had resulted in an inadequate service; that chronic unpunctuality on the Highland Railway caused serious delays to the Aberdeen trains; and that that company had been obstructive at Elgin by refusing to accept through coaches from the Craigellachie line, and only one set from the coast route.

The Highland company retorted that the traffic between Aberdeen and Inverness was insufficient to warrant any substantial improvement or the entire separation of all these services from those on the main line to Perth. Moreover, even if the Great North was prepared to run separate trains, the capacity of the line between Forres and Inverness, nearly all of which was single track, would be overtaxed, and the unpunctuality to which the Highland Railway had always been prone would reach chaotic proportions.

To avoid the expense of a parliamentary contest, the Great North withdrew its bill, and the two companies agreed to seek a settlement of their differences, either within the framework of the facility clauses of the Acts of 1884, or by means of a new agreement. However, when it became clear that neither side was prepared to make substantial concessions, the matter was referred to the Board of Trade, who nominated the Railway & Canal Commissioners to act as arbiters. After a full investigation of the dispute, the commissioners retired for a prolonged consideration of their verdict, doubtless hoping that the contestants would solve the problem for themselves. But the chances of an amicable settlement had become even more remote as the result of developments south of Aberdeen.

AFTER THE RACE TO ABERDEEN

In August 1895, competition between the East Coast and West Coast companies for the Anglo-Scottish traffic culminated in the 'Race to Aberdeen' by the night trains leaving London at 8 p.m. The story of the contest is well known, and it will suffice to say that after several nights of spectacular, but wasteful, racing, wiser counsels prevailed, and both trains were timed to reach Aberdeen by 6.30 a.m.—an improvement of nearly 2½h. on the schedules previously in force.

This acceleration enabled passengers to catch the stopping train on the Great North leaving Aberdeen at 6.50 a.m. This train connected at Keith, but not at Elgin, with a Highland train, which joined the mail from Perth at Forres, and reached Inverness at 11.5 a.m. The Great North was thus able, without alteration to its own services, to compete for through traffic to Inverness on level terms (as regards time) with the Highland Railway. However, only a few passengers availed themselves of the longer route, possibly because of the inconvenience of changing trains in Aberdeen at such an early hour.

In September, a new train was put on, leaving Aberdeen at 6.45 a.m., and reaching Elgin by both routes at 9.15, in ample time to connect with the Highland train. This 2½h. schedule was the fastest so far attempted. Only 65m. were allowed for the 40¾ miles from Aberdeen to Huntly, with two regular and six conditional stops; and five regular and four conditional stops were included in the 80m. schedule for the 40 miles from Huntly to Elgin *via* the steeply-graded Craigellachie line. However, it was seldom that anything like all these conditional calls had to be made. The rear portion of the train, detached at Huntly, was allowed 75m. for the 46½ miles thence to Elgin, *via* the coast, with five regular stops. Although the load was light, this was distinctly smart work over a far from easy road.

A corresponding evening up train was put on, leaving Elgin at 7.30 *via* the coast, and 2m. later *via* Craigellachie, to reach Aberdeen at 10 p.m. with 11 regular stops. A Highland train, leaving Inverness at 6 p.m., connected with this service at Elgin and Keith.

SIGNALLING

(36) Keith Up Home, a splitting signal with a telegraph arm on one post.

(37) Pitcaple signal box. This design was to be found all over the system, in some places without the roof overhang at the sides and ends.

(38) Inverurie, in 1989. Example of a large, wooden box with more ornamentation to the design.

THE LATTER YEARS OF STEAM

(39)   6847 piloting 6849 on special train at Elgin in 1934. Both class D40, earlier class F. The line on which the train is standing had no platform and was only normally used by goods trains.

(40)   Former GER 2-4-0T 67164 of class F4 at St Combs in 1951. The cowcatcher was fitted for working this Light Railway. The first two vehicles were built from the steam railcar bodies.

(41)   Class B1 61349 at Cairnie Junction running the wrong way on the up line, 1951.

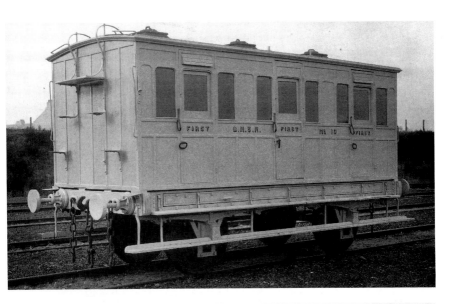

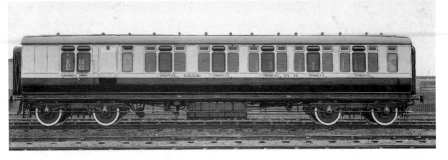

ROLLING STOCK

(42) Four-wheeled first no 10. This vehicle dated from the 1850s and was typical of the earliest stock. Built by Brown Marshall, which became part of Metropolitan Railway Carriage and Wagon Co.

(43) Composite 66, showing the corridor side. It had 12 first and 24 third seats, plus lavatory and guards compartment. Built 1908 and withdrawn in the 1950s.

(44) Steam railcar no 29, one of the pair built in 1905. They were not successful and were withdrawn in 1907, suffering the same problems as most railcars of the time.

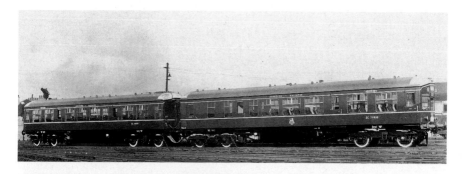

DIESEL RAILCARS

(45)   *Two car battery electric railcar, based on Derby lightweight vehicles, introduced on the Deeside line in March 1958. It was in service until August 1962, was then in departmental use and is now preserved.*

(46)   *Diesel railbus on a trial trip at Aberlour in September 1958. These vehicles were useful on the Speyside line, where four additional stops were provided, but gave a rough ride.*

In the summer of 1896, the night trains from London to Inverness and the special postal train for the north of Scotland were considerably accelerated, with the result that the Highland Railway was able to bring its mail train from Perth into Inverness by 10.15 a.m. The connecting train was therefore altered to leave Keith at 8.20, and call at Elgin at 8.53.

To maintain the connections at both Keith and Elgin, the Great North accelerated the 6.45 from Aberdeen to reach Keith in 1h. 22m., and Elgin *via* the coast, in 2h. 3m. The train ran non-stop from Aberdeen to Huntly in 45m., at 54.3 m.p.h.; and the remainder of the journey was scheduled in 73m., with four stops. At Huntly, 5m. were allowed for dividing the train, and for the engine to take water. Approximately one half of the journey was over single track, but the Manson tablet-exchange apparatus permitted high speed through the crossing loops.

The run from Aberdeen to Huntly ranked among the fastest in the country; and the high speeds between stops, and the smart station work that had characterised the train since its introduction, a year earlier, were fully maintained along the Moray Firth coast. A high record of punctuality was achieved, and instances of time lost by a late start being regained were by no means unknown. On the other hand, the load seldom exceeded 105 tons from Aberdeen to Huntly, and 75 tons thence to Elgin; and the number of passengers joining or leaving the train at the intermediate stations was very small. The back portion of the train went forward from Huntly at 7.41, and reached Keith at 8.7, and Elgin, *via* Craigellachie, at 8.58.

The train soon lost much of its usefulness, as the schedules of the competing services from London to Aberdeen were eased by nearly an hour in the autumn, and the Great North could no longer provide a connection reaching Inverness at the same time as the Highland mail. The derailment of the West Coast train at Preston in the previous August, as the result of excessive speed round a sharp curve, has been suggested as the cause of this drastic deceleration. However, as the alteration came into force some considerable time after the accident, it would appear more likely that the companies agreed to slow their trains for reasons of economy.

Meantime, a notable change had occurred at Inverness: Andrew Dougall, secretary and general manager of the Highland Railway and its constituents since their inception, had retired in February 1896, and had been succeeded by Charles Steel, the assistant superintendent of the North Eastern Railway. There can be little doubt that Dougall had been over-zealous in the interests of his company, and had not only exercised considerable influence with the board, but had introduced into the dispute an element of personal animosity. On the other hand, the new general manager came to Inverness with the expressed intention of cultivating better relations with the Great North; but there were to be further skirmishes, and one more Parliamentary contest, before the hatchet was finally buried.

The summer of 1896 saw the two companies involved in litigation regarding alleged overcrowding of the through coaches from Inverness to Aberdeen by local passengers on the Highland Railway. Protests from Aberdeen met with no success, and in July the Great North claimed the right, under the facility clauses in the Acts of 1884, to assist with the regulation of the traffic by sending a uniformed inspector to Inverness station to prevent the indiscriminate use of the through coaches. Not unnaturally, the Highland took strong exception to such interference within the very gates of its citadel, and immediately applied to the Court of Session for an interdict.

Negotiations for a settlement had begun by the time the case came into court; and before the hearing was completed, a compromise was reached. The Great North undertook to withdraw the inspector from Inverness; and the Highland to exercise better supervision of the through traffic. It was, however, agreed that the Great North should provide a travelling attendant on certain trains to ensure that the through coaches were not monopolised by local passengers.

THE FEUD IS ENDED

Scarcely had the Inverness station dispute been settled than further trouble arose over the exchange of through coaches at Elgin. It had been agreed that one through service in each direction should use the Moray Firth Coast route, and the Great North now desired that the down train should be the accelerated 6.45 a.m. from Aberdeen. But as the interval between the arrival of the Great North train and the departure of the connection for the Inverness train was only 5m., the Highland would not guarantee to take the coaches from Elgin, and pressed for Keith as the point of exchange. However, the Great North insisted on sending the coaches *via* Elgin, although a through service was by no means assured.

With no prospect of a lasting settlement by negotiation in sight, and while still awaiting the arbitration of the Railway & Canal

Commissioners, the Great North prepared to make another application to Parliament in 1897 for running powers from Elgin to Inverness. The only new feature of the proposals was an offer by the Great North to bear the expense of doubling the line to enable it to accommodate the extra traffic. This decision appears to have hastened the commissioners in their task; for their findings were made known before the bill was considered by Parliament.

Although strictly impartial, the arbitration was a determined effort to achieve a final settlement of the dispute. Keith and Elgin were each to be the point of exchange for an equal number of services in both directions; services exchanged at Elgin were to include through coaches to and from both Great North routes, if necessary; and if called upon to do so, each company was to maintain the average speed of a train after it had been handed over at Keith or Elgin. The timetable was to be drawn up by the companies, and submitted to the commissioners for approval.

The official recognition of Elgin as a point of exchange for through traffic was regarded 'in Aberdeen as strengthening the Great North's case in applying for running powers to Inverness, and the company approached the committee stage of the bill with considerable confidence. For the moment, it appeared likely that these arguments would prove convincing; but after the general manager of the Highland Railway had given an undertaking that his company would faithfully observe the commissioner's arbitration, the tide turned in favour of the opposition, and the bill was rejected.

The refusal of Parliament to sanction anything beyond the findings of the Railway & Canal Commissioners ended the feud between the two companies. Although the efforts of the Great North to gain direct access to Inverness had failed, Elgin had been placed on a parity with Keith for the exchange of traffic. On the other hand, the Highland was now secured from further attacks on Inverness; and had besides the satisfaction of retaining Keith as the point of exchange for some of the through trains.

The 'Commissioners' Service', as the revised timetable was popularly called, came into force on 1 April 1897. Between Aberdeen and Inverness there were eight through services, four by each route. With one exception, the down trains using the Highland Railway from Keith were slow, and required 4½ to 5h. for the 108-mile journey. The trains exchanged at Elgin were faster, and were remarkable for their smart point-to-point schedules, some of which included a number of conditional stops. Through Inverness coaches by both Great North routes were run in these trains. The portions for the Craigellachie line did not call at Keith, but stopped at the more conveniently-situated station of Earlsmill, which was renamed Keith Town in 1897.

The best time (3½h.) was made by the two trains leaving Aberdeen at 6.45 a.m. and p.m. The former had been slowed by the inclusion of extra stops, and now required 2¼h. to reach Elgin, both via the coast and Craigellachie. On the completion of the Highland Railway's shortened route to the south in November 1898, its departure time became 6 a.m., to enable the connections at Inverness to be maintained. The 9.45 a.m. and the 2.20 p.m. reached Elgin in 2h. 20m., and Inverness in 3h. 40m. The latter was an entirely new service. On the Highland Railway, the improvements were maintained by the omission of several stops between Elgin and Inverness.

There was also the connection to the night and special postal trains from the south. This now left Aberdeen at 8.5 a.m., with through coaches for Elgin by both Great North routes, but not for Inverness. The Craigellachie portion reached Elgin at 10.25, where it overtook the stopping train for Inverness, via Keith, leaving Aberdeen at 7.5 a.m.

In the up direction, there were four trains via Keith, and three via Elgin. As was the case with the down services, the latter took through coaches for both Great North routes, and did not call at Keith. The fastest one, the 1.40 p.m. from Inverness, reached Aberdeen in 3½h. It ran from Elgin to Aberdeen in 2h. 20m. Of the services via Keith, the 3 p.m. from Inverness, reaching Aberdeen in 3h. 5m., secured pride of place as the fastest train ever run between the two towns with steam traction.

For the time being, trains serving both the coast and Craigellachie lines were divided or joined at Huntly; but in the summer of 1898, an exchange platform, named Cairnie Junction, was opened at Grange South Junction. This alteration not only effected an economy in engine mileage, and facilitated the handling of the traffic, but also enabled additional connections to be given between Keith and the Moray Firth coast.

CHAPTER 11

Light Railways and Bus Routes

The settlement of the long-standing dispute with its Highland neighbour left the Great North free to consider several schemes for new lines within its own territory. Without exception, these railways were to serve rural districts, where traffic was not likely to be heavy, and it was proposed to take advantage of the then recently-passed Light Railways Act, of which high hopes were entertained.

One of the first schemes to be considered was for a line running westwards from Aberdeen to Skene and Echt, through the fertile and fairly well-populated country lying between the rivers Don and Dee. In 1896, an independent company promoted the Aberdeenshire Light Railway from Aberdeen to Echt, a distance of 17 miles. The line was to be of standard gauge, and to have its own roadbed between Echt and the western outskirts of Aberdeen, but the connection thence to the harbour and the existing railways was to be laid along the public roads. The cost was estimated at £6,000 a mile.

The Great North then proposed the Echt Light Railway on the same route, but using the Aberdeen street tramways to reach the city and the main railway system. It was even proposed that the railway company should acquire the tramways, which were then privately owned. Objections were lodged against the laying of additional tracks along the streets in fast-developing residential areas, and to the use of the tramways for goods traffic. This opposition caused the promoters of the Aberdeenshire Light Railway to abandon their scheme, although it failed to discourage the Great North. In April 1897, the Light Railway Commissioners approved the line between Echt and the outskirts of the city, but the objection to the use of the tramways was upheld, despite an undertaking by the company to use special goods wagons, and engines that consumed their own smoke.

The Great North then proposed to extend the railway northwards on its own roadbed for three miles to join the main line at Kitty-brewster, and a light railway order for the whole scheme was made in January 1898. By that time, however, it had become clear that extravagant requirements by the local authorities in regard to the width of overbridges, and the high price demanded for some of the land, would increase the cost of the Kittybrewster extension far beyond the estimate. The powers for the whole line were therefore allowed to lapse.

The provision of a railway for the district was next considered by the Aberdeenshire County Council; and in 1904, a 3-ft. gauge electrified line, laid beside the public roads, was projected from Echt to the city boundary. The tramways had recently been acquired by the Aberdeen Corporation, and it was hoped that arrangements could be made for the through working of passenger and goods vehicles. However, the cost of laying mixed gauge on these tracks proved an insurmountable obstacle, and the scheme for the light railway was dropped and never revived.

Shortly after the promotion of the Echt Light Railway in 1896, the Great North projected a similar line northwards from Aberdeen to Newburgh, a distance of 15 miles. Beyond the city boundary, at Bridge of Don, the route presented no great difficulty, but access to the harbour and the main-line railways could be secured at a reasonable cost only by making use of the street tramways. Once again, no satisfactory solution to this problem was forthcoming, and the scheme was shelved indefinitely.

Concurrently with the lines in the neighbourhood of Aberdeen came a suggestion for a light railway, about 20 miles long, from the main line at Dufftown to Tomintoul. The country was moun-tainous, but there were no serious engineering difficulties. The route was, in fact, almost the same as that suggested in 1846 for the Banffshire Extension Railway. Although the scheme was supported by the Great North and the Banffshire County Council, the esti-mated traffic receipts were considered insufficient, and no applica-tion was made to the Light Railway Commissioners.

THE ST COMBS BRANCH

A far more promising line was projected in 1897 from Fraser-burgh to the fishing village of St Combs, five miles to the east. The scheme was promoted by local interests to cater for the rapid expansion of the herring fishing industry that followed the intro-duction of steam drifters based on Fraserburgh; but the Great North assumed full responsibility for the undertaking, and received the order authorising the railway on 8 September 1899.

The estimated cost of the works was £16,444, towards which the Treasury contributed £5,000. The order did not require the railway to be fenced. Instead, it was stipulated that engines in regular use on the line were to be fitted with cowcatchers in front, and at both ends if no turntables were provided. An unusual feature was a clause authorising the use of electric traction. Had advantage been taken of these powers, the line would have been an example, unique in Great Britain, of a type of rural electric railway that became common on the Continent. However, steam traction was chosen.

For the most part, the railway was laid on the surface of the ground, across sandy links of little value. For about half a mile from Fraserburgh, it ran parallel to the existing line. As the branch was to be worked by one engine in steam, no signals or crossing loops were provided, apart from a run round for engines at St. Combs.

A considerable time elapsed before construction was begun, and it was not until 1 July 1903 that the railway was opened. There was an intermediate station at Inverallochy (renamed Cairnbulg within a few weeks) and a halt at Philorth Bridge. Some twelve months later, a second halt was opened at Kirkton Bridge, in the outskirts of Fraserburgh. Six trains were run in each direction on weekdays only, but the service was soon slightly increased. At first, 17m. were allowed for the five-mile journey, but this schedule was increased to 20m., to allow for ticket collection.

In November 1905, a steam railcar was introduced, to run ten trips daily. This experiment was unsuccessful, and lasted only for a few months. The service was then reduced to seven trains in each direction, with additional trains at weekends, to take the crews of drifters to and from their homes.

MORE FRUITLESS SCHEMES

In 1908 a light railway was projected westwards along the coast for 4½ miles from Fraserburgh to Rosehearty, and thence inland for a like distance to New Aberdour. A railway from Fraserburgh to Rosehearty was no new proposal. Indeed, more than 20 years earlier, on 28 July 1884, the Great North had obtained an Act for such a line, but these powers were never exercised.

The promoters of the light railway obtained the promise of a

Treasury grant of £7,000, and made arrangements for the Great North to work the line; but then the obstacle which had wrecked the Echt and Newburgh schemes was encountered. The only feasible route to the Great North station, on the east side of the town, was through the streets, some of which were narrow and congested. This difficulty, which had not arisen with the St Combs line, proved insurmountable, and the scheme was abandoned.

After the failure of the Rosehearty line, no proposals for new railways in north-east Scotland were made for some years. Early in 1914, however, the Scottish Light Railways & Development Syndicate promoted the West Buchan Light Railway to connect the Buchan section of the Great North at Maud with the Macduff branch at Turriff. The line was about 12 miles long, and passed through a rich agricultural district. The engineering works were light, as the route followed a natural trench, the remains of an ancient river valley. A working agreement was sought with the Great North, and application was made for a Treasury grant. Negotiations with the Light Railway Commissioners, and with the Board of Agriculture for Scotland, had reached an advanced stage when the outbreak of war caused the scheme to be shelved.

Two other light railway schemes shared the same fate in 1914. The first was for the completion of the Deeside Railway to Braemar; and the other for the extension of the Alford branch for 19 miles to Bellabeg, in Upper Strathdon. There were good prospects that a Treasury grant would be forthcoming for the Braemar extension; but the Board of Agriculture for Scotland decided not to recommend State assistance for the Strathdon line, because public funds had been expended on the reconstruction of the road through the valley. The Great North had already established motor bus services on both routes; but it was assumed that these would be withdrawn, and that the company would undertake to work the railways.

During the 18 years preceding the outbreak of war in 1914, more than 100 miles of light railway were projected in north-east Scotland; but with the sole exception of the branch to St. Combs, none of the lines was built. Local opposition and the high prices demanded for land caused most of these schemes to fail. After the opening of the St Combs line, the Great North was not directly concerned in the promotion of light railways. Far more successful results were achieved by the company's motor bus services, which could be established, modified, or even abandoned without difficulty, and with the minimum of capital expenditure, because they made use of existing roads.

PIONEER BUS SERVICES

The Great North was one of the pioneers among British railway companies in introducing motor bus services. In almost every case, independently-owned horse-drawn coaches were already operating on the routes selected; and light railways to serve the districts had been proposed or were subsequently projected. The introduction of motor vehicles resulted in a substantial saving of time, despite the severe speed restrictions then in force. No service was scheduled at more than 11 m.p.h. The fares were higher than the standard third class railway rates, averaging more than 1½d per mile.

The four earliest vehicles were supplied complete, except for the tyres, by Milnes-Daimler but thereafter the usual GNSR practice was to purchase the chassis from outside suppliers and fit them with bodies built by the company's locomotive and carriage works at Inverurie. Before 1914, Milnes-Daimler products were favoured, with fifteen chassis purchased, but Durkopp (of Germany) and Maudslay provided six each and Straker-Squire three. Most of the buses were single-deckers, with seats for eighteen passengers and space on the roof for 15 cwt of luggage. During the first five years of road-motor operation, vehicle bodies were deliberately designed to be demountable and the Great North built several extra bodies, of charabanc and lorry type, which were used interchangeably, according to season and traffic needs, on some of the Milnes-Daimler and Straker-Squire chassis. Two double-decked bus bodies with rear-platform staircase to the top deck, were built in 1905 but weight restrictions then in force obliged the company to remove the upper deck seats and use the buses in traditional manner, although their staircases were retained. Two years later, another two double-decked cars, seating twelve passengers above and sixteen below and carrying 10 cwt of luggage, entered service and continued in use for almost twenty years, although they were restricted to one route for most of that time. All the vehicles had petrol engines and were fitted with solid rubber tyres on the basis of an annual mileage contract, since wear and tear on tyres was a major problem due to the condition of the roads at that time. Part of the old locomotive works at Kittybrewster was converted into a workshop for light repairs to road motors, but heavy repairs were carried out at Inverurie.

The first service began on 2 May 1904 between Ballater and Braemar. Once a sufficient number of vehicles had been delivered, a pattern of working was established whereby the cars made five

MOTOR OMNIBUS SERVICE BETWEEN BALLATER AND BRAEMAR.

BALLATER TO BRAEMAR.

		A.M.	P.M.	P.M.	
BY TRAIN.	Aberdeen, depart,	8 5	12 20	5 35	...
	Culter, ,,	8 19	12 34	5 48	...
	Banchory, ,,	8 43	1 0	6 11	..
	Torphins, ,,	9 0	1 15	6 26	...
	Aboyne, ,,	9 20	1 35	6 46	...
	Ballater, arrive,	9 45	2 0	7 10	...

		A.M.	P.M.	P.M.	
BY OMNIBUS.	Ballater Station, depart,	10 5	2 15	7 20	...
	Bridge of Gairn,				
	Abergeldie,	*	*	*	...
	Crathie,				
	Inver,				
	Bridge of Dee,				
	Braemar (Invercauld Arms Hotel), arrive,	11 30	3 40	8 45	...
	Braemar (Fife Arms Hotel), ,,	11 35	3 45	8 50	...

BRAEMAR TO BALLATER.

		A.M.	P.M.	P.M.	
BY OMNIBUS.	Braemar (Fife Arms Hotel), depart,	8 5	1 45	4 5	...
	Braemar (Invercauld Arms Hotel), depart,	8 10	1 50	4 10	...
	Bridge of Dee,				
	Inver,				
	Crathie,	*	*	*	...
	Abergeldie,				
	Bridge of Gairn,				
	Ballater Station, arrive,	9 40	3 20	5 40	...

		A.M.	P.M.	P.M.	
BY TRAIN.	Ballater, depart,	9 55	3 35	6 0	...
	Aboyne, arrive,	10 16	3 56	6 21	...
	Torphins, ,,	10 35	4 16	6 41	...
	Banchory, ,,	10 47	4 28	6 53	...
	Culter, ,,	11 10	4 53	7 15	...
	Aberdeen, ,,	11 30	5 15	7 35	...

* Provided seats are available, Passengers may join the Omnibus for or at any intermediate place on payment of Fares to be ascertained from the Conductor.

FARE.—BALLATER to BRAEMAR, or *vice versa*, 2/6.

TICKETS are issued on the Omnibus and should be retained until completion of the journey. Through tickets from Aberdeen to Braemar and *vice versa* are issued at the Booking Office at these places only.

SEATS may be booked beforehand on application at any of the Company's Stations and at the Booking Office, Braemar ; and to prevent disappointment early intimation should be given.

PASSENGERS' LUGGAGE.—Small hand luggage, under the Passenger's own care, carried free ; other luggage, not exceeding 1 cwt. each package, which can be conveyed without inconvenience, charged according to distance, size, and weight.

PARCELS.—Small parcels and packages charged according to distance, size, and weight.

BICYCLES, which can be carried without inconvenience, charged 1/- each.

N.B.—*The Company give notice that they do not undertake that the Omnibuses shall start or arrive at the times above specified ; nor will they be responsible for any loss, damage, or inconvenience which may arise from delay or detention.*

For further information apply to the Booking Clerks at Ballater and Braemar; to any of the Company's Stations ; or to Mr. W. DEUCHAR, Passenger Superintendent, Aberdeen.

Timetable of motor bus service between Ballater and Braemar, winter 1904 trips in each direction on weekdays during July, August and September, in connection with trains to and from Aberdeen. The journey time allowed was 1½ hours for the 16½-miles trip. During May and October the service was reduced to three journeys each way, while for the remaining months of the year only two journeys were provided. Not until 1908 was a Sunday service introduced and then the principal reason for operation, begun on 1 November, was the daily conveyance of mails; in 1909 one of the original Milnes-Daimlers was converted to a 9-seater mail car specially to accommodate this service. Mechanical breakdowns and unsuitable tyres caused considerable trouble at first, but once these defects had been remedied, the service became increasingly popular. The tourist traffic frequently called for the provision of relief cars.

The winter months imposed a hard test on the reliability of the service. At Braemar the road reached a height of 1,100 ft, and snowdrifts and severe frost frequently impeded traffic. To minimise the risk of delay to the connecting trains, it was arranged that when the roads were heavily snowbound the cars running to Ballater should start 15m. in advance of their scheduled times. This rule was subsequently applied to other routes. A high standard of reliability, if not of punctuality, was achieved, which earned universal appreciation.

On 15 November 1904 another bus service was started, between Udny station and Methlick via Tarves and Keithfield, a distance of 10¼ miles. The district was wholly agricultural, without an influx of visitors during the summer months. Initially two journeys in each direction were provided on weekdays, but receipts proved disappointing. In an effort to improve the situation, from 1 August 1905, three return journeys were introduced with a slightly different route between Methlick and Tarves adopted for each. However, from 1 October 1906 the cars reverted to two trips in each direction until the end of the year when the service was discontinued; this was the only such failure the Great North encountered with its road motors in the years preceding World War I.

ROUTE MILEAGE TREBLED

In 1905 another two omnibus routes were opened by the company; on 1 May between Huntly and Aberchirder (11¾ miles) and on 1 June between Culter and Midmar (Tillybirloch) via Echt (12½ miles). Although each service worked as a 'feeder' for the trains at the respective railheads, the Huntly cars ran to and from the town square, since the station lay on the town's outskirts. Again, the basic omnibus services on weekdays consisted of two return journeys each day through the year, but extra workings were scheduled according to the traffic potential of the route, the season and the day of the week. At Cutler, a new development was initiated when a petrol lorry was based there to provide a delivery and collection service for goods in the outlying districts. These pioneer routes were established without parliamentary sanction, but in 1906 the company obtained wide powers to operate road motor vehicles for the carriage of passengers, goods and mails. Not only did this regularise the Great North's road operations, but also it served to strengthen the company's position when dealing with local highway authorities who sought compensation for wear and tear on roads used by the GNSR motors.

During the next two years the route mileage operated by the railway's road motors was trebled. In 1906 all-year services began between Alford and Bellabeg, in Strathdon (19½ miles) on 1 May; between Aberdeen and Cluny via Skene (16½ miles) on 1 September; and between Aberdeen and Midmar via Echt (17 miles) on 1 November. The Midmar service was in effect a diversion of the existing one, based on Culter but was discontinued between there and Cairnie. The number of journeys on these new routes varied between two and five in each direction, according to the route and the day of the week. The terminus in Aberdeen for passenger road services was at Schoolhill station and the routes thence to Cluny and Midmar were remarkable as the first that did not directly 'feed' the railway. So successful were these passenger service experiments that the company started a separate service for goods, when, in December 1906, it bought over the business and steam lorry belonging to Smith, the carrier, of Echt. To complement Smith's 5–ton Yorkshire Steam Wagon Co vehicle, the Great North bought a second, similar machine that same month and operated them initially from the carriers' quarters in The Green. Later, however, the company's goods motors were transferred to work out of Guild Street goods station, adjoining Aberdeen Joint passenger station.

TOURIST SERVICES

The spring and summer of 1907 saw the introduction of one regular and two seasonal tourist services. The former came into operation on 1 April between Aberdeen (Schoolhill) and Newburgh, a distance of 15¼ miles by the original routing but soon reduced by a half-mile when an alternative approach to Newburgh was adopted. Two, and subsequently three journeys were made in each direction on weekdays, and a separate service was provided for goods. Although Durkopp and Maudslay cars were used at times on this route, it soon became the permanent home of the two double-decked Milnes-Daimlers.

The seasonal routes were introduced on 1 July between Ballater and Bellabeg, via Dinnet (20¾ miles) and Ballindalloch and Tomintoul (15¾ miles). At Bellabeg the former connected with the already established omnibus service from Alford, which was extended now during the summer months for a further 8¼ miles to Corgarff, at the head of the strath. The mountainous road thence to Tomintoul, which reaches a height of more than 2,000 feet at the Lecht Pass, was then considered too rough and steep for motor vehicles, although it was used by a privately owned horse-drawn coach. These services together formed part of the 'Three Rivers Tours', a series of circular trips by rail and road from Aberdeen through Deeside, Donside and Speyside. Those tours which included crossing the Lecht took two days to complete, with an overnight stay at Tomintoul in either direction, but the third tour traversing Deeside and Donside only was accomplished in one day. Five petrol motors fitted with open-sided, charabanc bodies were used for this tourist traffic. After an interval of three years, the Great North decided to provide a regular, but still seasonal, omnibus service on the Tomintoul route and this began on 1 July 1910. Intermediate passengers were then catered for and not just through tourist traffic, although seats for the former were offered only on an 'as available' basis.

Only one other GNSR bus service came to be provided before the outbreak of war in 1914; on 18 November 1912 the Great North took over the business and vehicle – a second-hand de Dietrich – of Simpson who operated between Fraserburgh, Rosehearty and New Aberdour. The service represented a substitute for the light railway which had been unsuccessfully promoted some years earlier; between Fraserburgh and Rosehearty a more frequent service was provided than on any other route. The fares were somewhat lower than on the company's other buses, although they did not compare favourably with those on the neighbouring light railway to St Combs.

Meantime, road services for goods traffic had been developed considerably. To supplement the three petrol-engined chassis which could be fitted with 2-ton lorry bodies, and the two 5-ton Yorkshire steam wagon lorries, the Great North purchased in mid-1907 a Foden 5-ton steam lorry. Some three months later, in November, the Company bought over the business of Smart, 'Royal Deeside Carrier', of Ballater and thus acquired three standard model Sentinel 5-ton steam lorries from Alley and McLellan of Glasgow. Unlike the petrol motors all the GNSR steam lorries were capable of hauling a 3-ton trailer, and therefore were considered superior for collection and delivery work in country districts. Regular services were run between Alford and Strathdon, and Ballindalloch and Tomintoul, in addition to the Echt and Newburgh services; but other vehicles were moved from district to district to deal with seasonal traffic. Loaded lorries were also taken by rail to stations for the start of the delivery round.

SERVICES DURING THE WAR

In the summer of 1914, the road fleet comprised thirty-four passenger vehicles and 11 lorries. All the former were petrol-engined and all were single-decker buses except seven charabancs and two double-deck buses. Included among the charabancs were two brand-new 28-seater vehicles purchased complete from Coventry Daimler; these cars during World War I served to convey soldiers who were sent home to convalesce in the North-East. The lorry fleet consisted of eight steam wagons and three petrol lorries. The regular route mileage was 150, or nearly half the company's railway mileage. Save on the service between Udny and Methlick, the traffic returns had been satisfactory, although the margin of profit had never been large. The official view was that the road services were developing the rural areas and constituted extensions of the railway.

During the war years, the tourist routes were suspended and other services were modified, to meet restrictions imposed by the Government. Sufficient supplies of motor spirit were allocated to the company to maintain a basic motor omnibus service on all routes but following the outbreak of war, three of the four Maudslay chassis bought new in 1913 were requisitioned by the War Department. The Great North retained the bus bodies from these vehicles and a year later, in 1915, was permitted to purchase three replacement 'Caledon' chassis from the Scottish Commercial Car Co Ltd for use with these bodies. Fewer restrictions were applied to the use of the steam lorries. Permission was given in 1915 and 1916 for the replacement of five of the old lorries, for which the same number of new Fodens was purchased. In 1917 the omnibus fares were subjected by official order to the 50% increase which was applied then to the railway.

After the war had ended, the tourist cars were reinstated for normal use, and other services strengthened. Only one additional route was attempted, at the end of May 1921 when a limited service of buses was introduced between Aberchirder and Turriff but this service was withdrawn a mere five months later. During 1916, three Thornycroft 'J' type chassis were released to the Great North as replacements for worn out bus chassis. So satisfactory did these new machines prove to be that after the war no fewer than thirteen more of this type were purchased for the same purpose. The six chassis which arrived in 1919 received GNS-built single-deck bus bodies of the usual 18-seat type, but in 1920 the company obtained complete two 32-seater buses; one of 'Lothian' type with body and chassis produced by Scottish Motor Traction (SMT) and the other with an SMT-body on a Thornycroft chassis. For the Great North, the 'Lothian' vehicle was quite unusual since it had a full-front, wholly enclosed body within which the driver sat beside, and not behind, the engine. The following year, another six Thornycroft chassis were purchased and for these the company built its own 32-seater bus bodies.

But already an altogether different climate of competition between transport modes had begun to manifest itself, compared with pre-war times, and as evidence of this the Great North withdrew on 28 February 1922 its bus services to Echt and Midmar and to Newburgh in favour of local private operators.

THE 1918 COMMITTEE

In February 1918, the Secretary of State for Scotland appointed a committee to report on the rural areas in which the development of local industries depended on improved transport facilities. The enquiry was to embrace proposals for new railways, and a programme of road construction and improvement. For the most part, the railway schemes examined had been promoted previously. In Aberdeenshire and Banffshire, all the light railways projected since 1896 were reconsidered, although only four—the Ballater & Braemar, the Alford & Strathdon, the West Buchan, and the Fraserburgh, Rosehearty & New Aberdour—were recommended for construction.

In view of the virtual impossibility of carrying lines to Echt and Newburgh through the suburbs of Aberdeen, the committee recommended the provision of a special concrete road beyond the city boundary for the existing road motor services. This novel expedient was designed, not only to permit of an accelerated service, but to overcome the objections of the County Council regarding undue wear and tear of the roads by heavy vehicles.

The findings of the committee were published before the war had ended, and it was not then possible to carry out any of the recommendations. The cessation of hostilities was followed by an enormous rise in wages and the cost of materials, and it was not deemed practicable to embark on the construction of any new lines. Nevertheless, it was generally assumed, so far as north-east Scotland was concerned, that the railways would eventually be built; and as late as 1921 the possibility of the work being undertaken by the grouped company of which the Great North was to form part was discussed.

Banchory Station. The year is 1914. Deeside basks in midsummer sunshine as a trim 4-4-0 of the Great North of Scotland Railway's latest class V pauses at one of the station's two through platforms with an afternoon train en route from Ballater to Aberdeen. Before long, the concourse of the substantial Victorian station will bustle with city merchants and workers homeward bound off one of the suburban trains which the GNSR worked to and from a bay platform by the fence behind the waiting motor cars.

Rail service began at Banchory in 1853, but growth of the town in the 1880s and 1890s prompted the GNSR to rebuild the station in 1902/3 with the result shown in the painting by David White.

D40 62242 shunting in the yard at Craigellachie with a freight for Aviemore
Built as GNSR class V no 113 in 1899, this locomotive was

Inverurie in 1988. A down passenger, consisting of a mixture of mark I and II coaches, departs behind a class 47 while an up freight, hauled by a class 37, waits for the road. (K. Fenwick)

The 'Northern Belle' excursion to Dufftown on the branch in 1984, hauled by 47524. The train includes mark II firsts from one of the overnight Anglo-Scottish trains plus a catering vehicle. (A. Mitchell)

Years of Maturity

MODERNISATION CONTINUED

In expectation of a substantial increase of traffic after the introduction of the 'Commissioners' Service' on the main line in the
spring of 1897, the directors of the Great North embarked on
another programme of improvements. The most pressing need was
for an extension of the cramped and inadequate locomotive works
at Kittybrewster. Largely on the advice of William Pickersgill, the
locomotive superintendent, who had come to Aberdeen from the
Great Eastern Railway in 1894, it was decided to move the works
to a new site at Inverurie. Tenders were invited in the autumn of
1898, and construction began by the end of the year.

The works covered an area of 4½ acres, or about one-fifth of the
land acquired, and were fully equipped on the most up-to-date
lines. Apart from a few machines moved from Kittybrewster, the
whole of the plant was new. On the recommendation of Pickersgill,
electricity, generated on the premises, was used for lighting and for
power. The first block of buildings was occupied by the carriage
and wagon department in 1901. The locomotive department followed in 1902, and the office staff a year later. The change was
completed in 1905 by the arrival of the permanent way department.

To provide accommodation for the staff, the company built a
large number of houses, all of which were lit by the electric
generating plant at the works. Additional land was acquired for
allotment gardens and a park. Technical classes were organised for
the engineers and apprentices, and social activities were encouraged
by the provision of recreation rooms and a hall for the staff
dramatic and musical societies.

The small and old-fashioned passenger station at Inverurie, at the
south end of the town, was replaced on 10 February 1902 by a new
station, near the works, half a mile farther north. The Old Meldrum
branch, which ran parallel to the main line for some distance, was
shortened by this amount, and accommodation was provided for

the branch trains at the outer face of the up platform of the new station. Traffic on the main line and the approaches to the works was controlled from a new signalbox with 96 levers, the second largest on the system.

A far more formidable undertaking, authorised in 1899, although not completed until many years later, was the rebuilding of Aberdeen joint station. Although the layout had been criticised as unduly lavish in 1867, traffic had increased so rapidly that within 15 years the capacity of the station became overtaxed at busy periods. In 1883, plans for enlarging the station to provide accommodation for the North British trains were considered, but abandoned on the grounds of expense. Subsequently, the situation at the north end was slightly eased by the provision of an additional bay platform; and limited alterations to the booking and other offices were undertaken.

The congestion became worse; and many complaints were received, not only of delayed trains, but of the dangerous state of the rather low platforms when rendered slippery by slime from large quantities of fish traffic. Dissatisfaction was also expressed because the platforms were open to the weather for a considerable portion of their length. Although the companies reached agreement on the question of completely rebuilding the station, the Caledonian was not prepared to bear the whole cost of widening the line southwards to Ferryhill Junction. The delay which ensued while a settlement was being negotiated was widely misconstrued as indicating a refusal by the Caledonian to consider any scheme for substantial improvement.

To permit the extension of the passenger station, the adjoining goods stations were rebuilt on a new site farther to the east. This alteration involved the companies in a dispute, first with the harbour commissioners, and then with the town council, regarding the rearrangement of the connections to the lines laid along the quays. A long delay occurred before this matter was finally settled. Unexpected difficulties and delays were also encountered with the widening of the railway to Ferryhill.

Meantime, at the other end of the main line, the antiquated station at Elgin had been rebuilt. Intended as a temporary measure in 1862, but never superseded by more permanent premises, the station had been aptly described some 30 years later as 'a miserable collection of dilapidated wooden sheds, bordering a large bare platform space completely open to the weather'. In 1897, it was hoped that the Highland would collaborate in the provision of a joint station; but after detailed plans had been prepared, that company decided not to proceed with the scheme. The Great North therefore undertook the reconstruction of its own station, and the work was completed in 1902.

The layout, which was similar to that of the joint station at Aberdeen, remained unaltered; but the level of the platforms was raised, and ample protection was afforded from the weather. The station buildings were entirely renewed in an imposing design, and on a scale befitting a traffic centre of far greater importance. Through trains between Aberdeen and Inverness in both directions were accommodated at a single long platform, an extension of which led to the adjoining Highland station. At the eastern end of the station were three terminal bays. Lossiemouth or Moray Firth Coast trains could enter or leave these bays without conflicting with trains on the Craigellachie line.

ENTERPRISE ILL-REWARDED

Unfortunately, less than two years experience showed clearly that the improved services were too lavish, and that traffic was not developing to the extent that had been forecast. After some adjustments necessitated by the opening of the Highland Railway's shortened route to the south in November 1898, an extensive revision of the main-line timetables began in the next year, and the number of through services between Aberdeen and Inverness was reduced to six in each direction, with an extra down train daily in summer, and once a week in winter.

In the down direction, the 9.45 a.m. fast service was replaced by a stopping train running *via* Craigellachie only, and the midday stopping train was suspended. The 6 a.m. from Aberdeen ran *via* the coast only, and was withdrawn during the winter. After 1902, however, it ran throughout the winter on Mondays only, although the Inverness coaches were exchanged at Keith. Throughout the year, the 2.20 p.m. served the Craigellachie line only; and in winter the 6.45 p.m. ran *via* the coast only.

In the up direction, the most drastic alteration was the replacement of the fast service leaving Inverness at 3 p.m. by a stopping train connecting at Keith with an existing train, which was slightly accelerated to reach Aberdeen at 7.25. The 4.15 stopping train was also withdrawn on the Highland Railway, although it still ran between Elgin and Aberdeen, *via* Craigellachie, during the summer only.

The schedules of several other trains in both directions were slightly eased, particularly on the steeply-graded Craigellachie line. The best time between Aberdeen and Elgin thus became 2h. 20m. (by one up and two down trains), although the other fast trains in both directions were only slightly slower. The journey time to and from Inverness varied between 3h. 35m. and 4h. 20m.

On the Buchan section, the connection to the night trains from the south had been altered to leave at 8.10 a.m., although its schedule remained unchanged, and its place at 9.25 had been taken by a new and slightly slower train. There was also a new early morning down train running in advance of the 8.10. The service thus became unbalanced, with six down trains and five up.

.·. If this pass is not used it is requested that it be returned and not destroyed

Great North of Scotland Railway.

No. 27

Pass *Mr. MacBey* ....*First*............ CLASS CARRIAGE.

Between *Elgin or Keith* ......and...... *Aberdeen*

on ....day of.................. *June* 1899

Why granted *Highland Railway*

J.F. Moffatt,

Aberdeen, 10th May 1899 .....per *W. Dunbar*

☞ This pass must be delivered up to the Guard or Ticket Collector when demanded, and is available only for One Journey. It is granted under the condition that the party holding it, or his representatives, shall have no claim for compensation in case of accident.

Free pass—Elgin to Aberdeen, issued in 1899

In the summer of 1898, the afternoon down train was altered to start at 4.40, run non-stop to Ellon in 30m., and reach Peterhead at 6.15, and Fraserburgh 10m. later. With slight variations, this timing was in force during subsequent summers, although the train reverted to its former schedule during the winter months. On the other hand, an acceleration of the second morning up train in the summer of 1899 lasted for one season only.

By the end of the century, the summer expresses on the Deeside line were allowed 75m. in the down direction, and 5m. less in the up. The remaining trains—six each way in summer, and one less in winter—required 95 to 100m. in both directions between Aberdeen and Ballater. The economy measures introduced in 1899 had little or no effect on these services, which continued almost unaltered for several years.

The disappointing traffic returns were reflected in reduced dividends. In 1898, the ordinary stock had been subdivided into preferred and deferred classes. Thanks to the economies effected, the dividends on the former were speedily restored to the 3 per cent level established in the early 1890s, but the holders of the deferred shares never received more than 1½ per cent.

THE HIGHLAND AMALGAMATION SCHEME

Although the settlement of 1897 had failed to bring increased prosperity to either company, it had resulted in far more cordial relations between the Great North and the Highland. So completely had the former antagonists composed their differences that proposals for a joint working agreement speedily followed. For the moment, however, financial difficulties and opposition, especially among the more conservative sections of the Highland shareholders, caused the scheme to be shelved. Nevertheless, the new locomotive works at Inverurie were envisaged to meet the needs of both railways.

The question of a working agreement was reopened early in 1905, and within a few months a scheme for complete amalgamation was put forward. It was proposed that the combined system should be known as the Highland & North of Scotland Railway, with headquarters in Aberdeen, and the locomotive, carriage and wagon works at Inverurie. A bill to authorise the fusion as from 1 January 1907 was drafted towards the end of 1905. The scheme was opposed by some of the Scottish and English railways, and in Inverness, where it was feared that the removal of the Highland administrative offices and locomotive works would result in unemployment and a serious loss of trade.

The terms of the amalgamation were accepted without serious opposition by the Great North shareholders early in 1906; but it was otherwise when the vote of the Highland shareholders was taken. Although there was a majority in favour of the fusion, not only was the opposition quite considerable, but a large number of shareholders displayed complete indifference and did not vote. In view of this unsatisfactory and by no means representative result, the directors of the Highland Railway felt compelled to press for the bill not to be lodged with Parliament, a step to which the board of the Great North reluctantly agreed.

The amalgamation scheme was never revived; but in 1908 it was agreed that certain trains between Aberdeen and Inverness should be worked throughout by the engine of one company. Over the years this arrangement was modified from time to time, but from late 1914 until, at least, the autumn of 1916 the GNSR worked all the trains with the Highland paying its share of the cost. Late in 1914 arrangements were made to repair Highland Railway locomotives at Inverurie.

LONG-DISTANCE EXCURSIONS

In 1905 and '06, while the amalgamation proposals were under consideration, the train services showed signs of recovering from the 'economy blight'. On the main line, the improvements started on 10 June 1905, with the introduction of a half-day excursion from Aberdeen to Boat of Garten, on Wednesdays and Saturdays, during the summer months. The train ran non-stop from Aberdeen to Craigellachie in 85m., and reached Boat of Garten in 2½h. Not only was the non-stop run of 68 miles to Craigellachie the longest ever scheduled on the Great North, but the average speed of 48 m.p.h. was at that time the highest on any part of the system, and came near to equalling the record set up by the 6.45 a.m. between Aberdeen and Huntly in 1896. By no means the least remarkable feature of the trip was the fare of half-a-crown (12½p) for the journey of 101¼ miles in each direction.

The train continued every summer and in 1908 was extended over the Highland Railway for 17 miles from Boat of Garten to Kingussie. This innovation did not prove popular, and lasted for one season only. Also in that year, the non-stop run from Aberdeen was shortened to one of 64 miles (for which 81m. were allowed) by the inclusion of an additional stop at Dufftown. A subsequent development was a service of cold luncheons on the outward journey. As the company had no restaurant cars, passengers had to place their orders in advance to enable food to be provided from the Palace Hotel, and served in saloon carriages fitted with tables. Teas were served on the return journey.

So successful was the Strathspey excursion that from 1906 a similar train was run to Elgin *via* the Moray Firth coast. The 58 miles from Aberdeen to Tillynaught were timed non-stop in 75m., and Elgin was reached in 2h. 10m. with four more stops. As was the case with the Strathspey excursion, none of the regular trains equalled these timings.

On the Deeside line, a half-day excursion to Ballater had been a regular summer Saturday feature for many years, and had, in fact, been one of the points at issue in the lawsuit brought by Sir Robert Burnett in 1883. From June 1905, this train also ran on Wednesdays, and the trip was extended to Braemar by means of the then recently-established motor bus service.

BREAKS WITH THE PAST

Meantime, several changes had occurred among the directors and chief officers. In September 1904, the chairman died at the age of 81. Throughout his long term of office, Ferguson had spared neither time nor effort on behalf of the company. Cordial relations between the directors and the staff had always been his personal concern, and such was the affectionate regard in which he was held that he was commonly referred to by his patronymic, Kinmundy, an expression of esteem that he deeply appreciated.[1] An activity of a completely different nature, for which his extensive knowledge of north-east Scotland well fitted him, was the compilation of a guide book to the districts served by the Great North—*The Great North of Scotland Railway: A Guide*, published by David Douglas, Edinburgh, in 1881.

The new chairman was Sir David Stewart, a member of the board since 1891. One of Aberdeen's most prominent business men, he had twice been elected Lord Provost, and had been knighted by Queen Victoria at Balmoral in 1896.

Alexander Reid, the passenger superintendent, had already resigned in February 1900, to go to Ireland as general manager of the Dublin, Wicklow & Wexford Railway, and had been succeeded by William Deuchar. The son of an Aberdeenshire farmer, Deuchar had entered the company's service in 1871, at the age of 21, and after gaining outdoor experience, had been appointed to the passenger superintendent's office. In 1893 he became chief clerk to the general manager.

In 1906, the general manager resigned, after more than half a century of railway life, of which 26 years had been spent with the Great North. Moffatt had proved himself an able manager, and had energetically pursued the bold and progressive policy that had revolutionised the system. In the contests with the Highland Railway, he appears to have adopted a far from conciliatory attitude when replying to acrimonious correspondence from Inverness; but once the long-standing dispute had been settled, he used his con-

[1] His family seat was Kinmundy House, near Mintlaw, Aberdeenshire.

siderable influence to bring about a closer understanding between the two companies. Although he remained in office until he was nearly 70, Moffatt enjoyed more than 20 years of retirement, and had reached the age of 92 when he died in September 1929.

Moffatt was followed as general manager by George Davidson, who had joined the solicitor's department in 1881, and became the company's solicitor in 1905. To enable him to continue with his former duties, Thomas Macintosh, chief clerk to the general manager, was appointed secretary.

At the end of 1906, one of the few remaining links with the early days was broken by the resignation of the engineer, Patrick Barnett, who had entered the company's service in 1857. His successor, James Parker, was a newcomer to the Great North. For several years before his appointment, he had been an assistant engineer on the South Eastern & Chatham Railway.

Alexander Ross, goods manager since 1878, and the last survivor of the old regime, retired in 1909, after nearly 50 years with the company, and was succeeded by his assistant, Simon Willox, who held office until the grouping of 1923.

The first task awaiting the new engineer was the preparation of the final plans for the reconstruction of the joint station at Aberdeen. Nearly eight years had elapsed since the work had been authorised; but apart from the widening of the line to Ferryhill Junction, little had been done to alleviate the serious congestion in the passenger station. In 1907, however, the construction of additional platforms for through traffic on the west side of the station was begun. These were opened in the next year, and used for local and excursion trains. As part of the scheme for enlarging and improving the station, the company acquired the adjoining Station Hotel in 1910.

The foundations of the new station were laid on 28 May 1913; and the work of dismantling the old roof was begun three months later. By the end of July 1914, all the new platforms were in use, and the greater part of the station buildings occupied. The last portions of the old station were demolished a few weeks later. Wartime difficulties then brought work to a standstill, and the new station was not fully completed until 1920.

The general layout of the old station, with its through platforms and adjoining terminal bays was retained; but the platforms were raised and lengthened, and the number of bays was increased to five at the south end, and four at the north. On the west side of the station were a long island platform, and a shorter platform, which

UP TRAINS.   Deeside Section.

STATIONS	1	2	3	4	5	6	7	8	9	10	11	12	13	14	15	16	17	18	19
	Pass.	Pass.	Pass.	Pass.	Pass.	Exp. Pass.	Pass.				Pass.	Pass.		Pass.	Goods	Pass.	Pass.	Pass.	Pass.
Leave	a.m.	a.m.	a.m.	a.m.	a.m.	a.m.	a.m.				a.m.	a.m.		p.m.	a.m.	p.m.	p.m.	p.m.	p.m.
BALLATER			6 50			8 30					9 55								
Camb. O'May			6 57								10 2								
Dinnet			7 3		a						10 8								
Aboyne			7 11			8 45					10 16								
Dess			7 17								10 22								
Lumphanan			7 23								10 28								
Torphins			7 30			9 0					10 35								
Glassel			7 35								10 40								
Banchory ar.			7 42			9h9					10 47								
Do. de			7 48		8 45	9 12					10 52				11 45			2 35	
Crathes			7 54		8 51						10 58				12p10			2 41	
Park			8 1		8 57						11 5				12 25			2 47	
Drum			8 4		9 0						11 8				12 35			2 50	
Culter ar.											11 13				12 43				
Do. de	6 0	7 0	8 9		9 5	9 25	9 30				11 13	11 25		12 33	1 0	2 0	2 38	2 55	3 20
Miltimber	6 2	7 2			8 23		9 8					11 27		12 35	1 10	2 3	2 40		3 22
Murtle		7 4			8 25		9 11					11 29		12 37	1 20	2 5	2 42		3 24
Bieldside	6 6	7 6			8 27		9 13					11 31		12 39		2 7	2 44		3 26
West Cults		7 8			8 29		9 15					11 33		12 41		2 9	2 46		3 28
Cults	6 10	7 10	8 18		8 32		9 18					11 35		12 43	1 30	2 12	2 48		3 30
Pitfodels					8 34		9 42					11 37		12 45		2 14	2 50		3 32
Ruthrieston	6 15	7 15			8 37		9 45					11 40		12 48		2 17	2 53		3 35
Holburn St.	6 18	7 18	t		8 40		9 48					11 43		12 51		2 20	2 56	t	3 38
ABERDEEN *arrive*	6 22	7 22	8 30		8 44	9 30	9 37		9 52		11 30	11 47		12 55	1 50	2 24	3 0	3 10	3 42

	a.m.	a.m.			a.m.	a.m.						p.m.				p.m.	p.m.	p.m.	p.m.
Aberdeen de.	6 50					10 0						12 43							4 35
Peterhead ar.	8 46					12 0						2 40							6 15
Fraserb'gh ,,	8 56					12 10						2 50							6 25
Aberdeen de.	7 3	8 5			9 45	9 52								1 20		2 30	3 30	3 45	
Alford ar.	8 33					11 10									2 10			5 2	
Inverurie	7 49	8 31				10 37											4 25	5 10	
Oldmeldrum	8 15					11 0										3 35		6 20	
Macduff		9 50				12 15													
Buckie		10 30			12 58												6 31		
Keith	9 10				11 55												5 35		
Keith Town		9 39			12 8											3 58	5 43		
Elgin v.Craig.		10 35			1 10											4 52	6 55		
Do. v. Buckie		11 8			1 35												7 10		
Inverness		11 55			2 15											6 21	9 8		

ALPHABETICAL, &c., NOTES FOR PAGES 28 AND 29.

a On Fridays calls at Dinnet to lift Passengers for Aberdeen and beyond.

c Passing time, does not stop.

e On Saturdays will be due to leave Aboyne at 1·58, Dess 2·13, and arrive Lumphanan at 2·21 p.m.

g Due to arrive Aboyne at 1·43 p.m. and Torphins at 2·49 p.m.

h Examine and collect Aberdeen Tickets at Banchory. The collected Tickets to be sent to Holburn Street by following Train.

k Stops at Murtle to put off Live Stock when required.

t Stops at Holburn Street for Collection and Examination of Tickets.

Passengers for Holburn Street may be booked to that Station by all Trains which are shown in the Working Time Tables to stop there for the collection of tickets.   P. 95/2645.

Train Crossing Stations—UP TRAINS—*continued.*

No. 11 Up 9·55 a.m. Train crosses 8·5 a.m. Down Train at Ballater, 10·10 a.m. Down Train at Banchory, and 9·5 a.m. Down Goods Train at Crathes.

No. 22 Up 3·35 p.m. Train crosses 3·20 p.m. Down Train at Torphins, 2·50 p.m..Down Goods Train at Banchory, and passes 1·0 p.m. Up Goods Train at Culter.

No. 24 Up 1·0 p.m. Goods Train crosses 10·30 a.m. Down Goods Train at Aboyne, 1·40 p.m. Down Saturday only Train at Lumphanan, 3·20 p.m. Down Train at Banchory, 2·50 p.m. Down Train at Crathes, and shunts at Culter to allow 3·35 p.m. Up Train to pass and go before it.

No. 29 Up 6·25 p.m. Train in September crosses 2·50 p.m. Down Train at Dinnet, 6·15 p.m. Down Train at Torphins, and 6·50 p.m. Down Train at Crathes.

No. 32 Up 7·25 p.m. Train during July and August crosses 2·50 p.m. Down Train at Ballater and 6·15 p.m. Down Train at Dinnet.

Page from Working Timetable for July 1921

had been opened before the reconstruction of the old station wa
begun. Cross-over roads for engine release were provided in botl
directions at the middle of the three main through platforms, eacl
of which was long enough to accommodate two trains.

The main through platform was 1,596 ft long; and the tota
length of the platform faces (11,340 ft) ranked second only to tha
at Edinburgh (Waverley), the longest in Scotland. The platform
were connected by two footbridges, one at either end of th
station. That at the northern end led directly to an entrance to th
short suburban platform from Bridge Street. The over-all roof of th
old station was replaced by a roof of unusual design, with a mai
span covering the circulating area, and separate umbrella roofs fo
each platform. Another notable feature was the provision of stean
heating apparatus for warming trains standing at the platforms
Traffic was controlled from three signalboxes of which the one a
the northern end, with 127 levers, was the largest on the Grea
North.

TRAIN SERVICE DEVELOPMENTS

The years immediately before the first world war did not se
many changes in the train services. Such alterations as there wer
mainly tended towards slightly easier timings, especially on th
main line. In the summer of 1911, co-operation with the Nortl
British Railway resulted in the introduction of a through coacl
between Edinburgh and Elgin. On the Deeside line and the Buchaı
section, improvements introduced in the summer of 1906 had beer
short-lived, apart from a new evening fast train from Fraserburgl
and Peterhead. The services on the branches remained almosı
unchanged, save that the number of mixed trains was considerably
reduced, particularly during the summer holiday season. Many oı
the branch trains averaged barely 25 m.p.h.

In June 1914, the services on the Deeside line were strengthenec
and improved. Sir Thomas Burnett had recently waived his righı
to have all trains stopped at Crathes, and the down evening express
was accelerated to reach Ballater in 65m. The train ran non-stop tc
Torphins (23¾ miles) in 33m., and covered the 19½ miles thence tc
Ballater in 32m., with a stop at Aboyne. Banchory (16¾ miles) was
served by a slip-coach in 24m. from Aberdeen. The morning up
train called additionally at Banchory, and was allowed 66m. for
the rather easier eastbound journey.

The slip-coach service to Banchory was unique on the Great
North, and was also remarkable as the only one ever operated on

a standard-gauge single line. The service was cut short by the war. It lasted for one summer only, and was never revived.

The early years of the new century had seen the over-optimistic policy of the previous 20 years tempered with caution. The branch to St Combs had been the only addition to the system, which now totalled 336 miles, but road motor services, with a combined route mileage of 150, had been established. Traffic returns had not always been encouraging, but careful management had maintained the dividends on the ordinary stocks, without impairing the high standards of efficiency which had for so long characterised the Great North.

THE GREAT NORTH AT WAR

Although the Great North did not have to undertake a task comparable with that of its Highland neighbour in carrying vast quantities of coal and stores for the Navy over a steeply-graded and largely single-track line, its achievements during the first world war were of no mean order for so small a system.

At Peterhead, the harbour was used for bunkering minesweepers and other small craft, and by the spring of 1919, nearly 40,000 tons of coal had been carried over the Buchan line for this purpose. Inland from Peterhead, at Lenabo, near Longside, the Admiralty established an airship base, to which a contractor constructed a branch. More than 32,000 tons of materials and stores were despatched by rail to these hangars.

The increased traffic overtaxed the capacity of the railway north of Dyce, all of which was single track. Powers to double the 13¼ miles from Dyce to Ellon, which included the steep gradients on either side of the summit at Newmachar, were obtained on 24 June 1915, but wartime difficulties delayed the start of the work until long after hostilities had ended, and the special traffic had declined. The 1½ miles from Parkhill to a new signalbox at Elrick were brought into use on 31 May 1920, but the remainder of the work was not undertaken. The double track from Parkhill to Elrick remained in use until October 1921, and then during the herring seasons until 1925. Single-line working was then resumed, and the additional track and signals were dismantled.

To meet the demands for railway sleepers and pit props, large areas in the north of Scotland were completely cleared of timber. Most of this work was undertaken by the Canadian Forestry Corps, but German prisoners of war were also employed. On the Great

North, forestry camps were established at Kemnay, Knockando and Nethy Bridge. The railway company laid in the necessary sidings, and was responsible for the carriage of the timber.

Considerable relief was afforded to the seriously congested main line of the Highland Railway from Perth to Inverness by the diversion of traffic *via* Keith and Aberdeen. Although this arrangement was mostly confined to goods traffic, special passenger trains (including naval ambulance trains) were run as required. An appreciable measure of relief was also afforded by the locomotives of the Great North, which ran more than 500,000 miles over the Highland Railway during the war years.

Soon after the outbreak of the war, a number of vehicles were hastily converted at Inverurie for use as a naval ambulance train. Later, two passenger-train vans were equipped for similar work. These were frequently used by the Red Cross Society to move wounded men from hospitals to convalescent homes in north-east Scotland. Although not called upon to send rolling stock overseas while active hostilities were in progress, the Great North provided 31 coaches for use in France during the period of demobilisation, early in 1919.

Of the 609 members of the staff who served with the forces during the war, 93 either fell in action or died of wounds. A memorial tablet was placed in the offices at Aberdeen, and a sum of £2,000 was voted by the directors and invested, to provide assistance for the dependants of the fallen. Arrangements were made for these funds ultimately to be used to assist employees who had met with accidents in the course of their work.

The only notable staff change during the war years was the retirement of the passenger superintendent in April 1918. For several years, Deuchar had been a prominent member of the superintendents' conference at the Railway Clearing House, and had been elected to the chair in 1913. He had also been appointed chairman of the Scottish superintendents' conference. The new superintendent was William Johnston, who had entered the service of the company in 1881, and after gaining both outdoor and indoor experience in several departments, had been appointed chief clerk to the general manager.

As was the case on most other railways, train services on the Great North were maintained without serious reductions until the war had entered its third year, when the need for releasing staff for service with the forces made drastic alterations inevitable. By the summer of 1918, the services on the main line had been reduced, and the fastest time between Aberdeen and Elgin had become 2h. 42m., by one up train *via* Craigellachie. The best down train also used this route, and took 3h. The morning and evening Deeside summer express had survived, with timings of 72m. down and 67m. up, in each case with three intermediate stops. On the branches, the number of trains had been reduced, but there were no instances on the Great North (as there were on so many other railways) of closure as a measure of economy.

THE LAST YEARS OF INDEPENDENCE

During the war, the financial position of the railways deteriorated seriously. Higher wages, the introduction of the eight-hour working day, increased prices for coal and materials, and heavier taxation more than doubled the working expenses, and it became obvious that extensive reorganisation, including large-scale amalgamations, would be necessary. At first, it was proposed that the railways of Scotland should form one group, entirely independent of the English lines, but this was found to be unworkable because of the relatively weaker financial position of the Scottish companies compared with the larger English undertakings. A revised scheme was embodied into the Railways Act, which received the Royal Assent on 19 August 1921, four days after the government had relinquished the wartime control of the railways.

The Act provided for four groups: a North Western & Midland; an Eastern & North Eastern; a Western; and a Southern. The Scottish railways were allocated to the two northern systems: to the North Western Group, the Caledonian, the Glasgow & South Western, and the Highland; to the Eastern Group, the North British, and the Great North of Scotland. The title chosen for the latter was the London & North Eastern Railway. With a route mileage of more than 6,700, it was the second largest of the new undertakings.

On the Great North, two notable changes in the directorate occurred while the negotiations for the grouping were proceeding. In October 1919, the chairman, Sir David Stewart, died at the age of 84, and was succeeded by Andrew Bain, a leading Glasgow steel merchant, who had joined the board in 1899, and become deputy chairman in 1906. Bain resigned in February 1922, and the last months of the company's independence were passed under the chairmanship of Alexander Duffus, an Aberdeen lawyer, and a member of the board since 1915.

Improvement of the train services began soon after the war had ended, and by the summer of 1919, all the fast trains had been restored to the main line, except the 6 a.m. from Aberdeen, which was never reinstated. In some cases, however, the timings were easier than in 1914. A pre-war feature that did not re-appear on the mail trains was the sorting carriage, which had been withdrawn at the end of May 1916. On the Highland Railway, the after-effects of the war were more severe, and not all the connections to and from Inverness attained the standards of the Great North.

The Deeside expresses remained unaltered, with a schedule of 72m. in the down direction and 5m. less in the up. On the Buchan line there was an improvement on the 1914 timings by the acceleration of the 8.30 a.m. from Aberdeen to reach Peterhead in 86m. and Fraserburgh in 95m. The timetables showed no outstanding changes on the shorter branches.

Post-war difficulties in replacing older engines withdrawn from service and scrapped led to a shortage of motive power, which was overcome, to a limited extent, by the loan of five old 4—4—0

THROUGH RESTAURANT CAR SERVICE.

A Restaurant Car Service is provided Daily on the following Trains:—

					A.M.						P.M.
Aberdeen, dep.	.	.	.	.	8 5	Inverness, dep.	.	.	.	.	12 50
Elgin, arr.	.	.	.	.	10 35	Nairn ,,	.	.	.	.	1 16
Forres ,,	.	.	.	.	11 7	Forres ,,	.	.	.	.	1 38
Nairn ,,	.	.	.	.	11 28	Elgin ,,	.	.	.	.	2 25
Inverness ,,	.	.	.	.	11 55	Aberdeen, arr.	.	.	.	.	5 14

Meals are served at the undermentioned Charges:—

Breakfast, - - - - - - -	3s.
Luncheon, - - - - - - -	3s.
Tea, - - - - - - -	1s.

The Car is available for both FIRST and THIRD CLASS Passengers.

Part page from Public Timetable for October 1922, showing restaurant car working tender engines from the Great Central Railway in June 1920. Although they were by no means suited to the traffic, they remained on the Great North until the autumn. New locomotives then began to come into service, but the next two years saw a tendency towards the easing of schedules.

The only outstanding development during this period was the hire of a restaurant car from the North Eastern Railway in the autumn of 1922. The car worked in the 8.5 a.m. train from Aberdeen, and returned from Inverness at 12.50 p.m. The through coaches between Edinburgh and Elgin were resumed in October 1921, but the older Glasgow-Elgin service was not restored. Both workings had been withdrawn in the autumn of 1914.

The grouping came into force on 1 January 1923. The Great North, with its route mileage of 333½,[1] was the smallest constituent of the London & North Eastern Railway, but it was the only one that came to the group without the complication of subsidiary undertakings. On the other hand, 38 miles of running powers over London, Midland & Scottish (former Caledonian) tracks, from Kinnaber Junction, near Montrose, to Aberdeen, separated the lines of the Great North from the remainder of the system. This gap was one of the greatest anomalies of the grouping, and one that was incapable of adjustment.

The final dividend on the preferred ordinary stock was 3 per cent, the rate maintained without a break since the turn of the century. The deferred ordinary stock received 1½ per cent, which was slightly above the average for the past 20 years. Great North debentures and stocks were then exchanged for equivalent holdings in the new company. The chairman was elected to the amalgamated board; and the officers and staff entered the service of the London & North Eastern Railway, for the most part in the Northern Scottish Area, which embraced the lines of the Great North.

Thus did the Great North of Scotland Railway lose its identity, more than 76 years after the formation of the company. Financial difficulties had figured largely in its early history, and had twice prevented an amalgamation that would have opened the way to wider fields. Recovery, progress and a measure of prosperity had followed before the aftermath of war had sounded the death-knell of the old regime. An unprecedented situation had arisen, and disaster had been averted only by amalgamations on a scale never previously contemplated.

[1] The Great North owned 333 miles 40 chains and exercised running powers continuously over 3 miles 51 chains.

CHAPTER 13

Locomotives and Rolling Stock

DANIEL KINNEAR CLARK: 1853—1855

In October 1853, Daniel Kinnear Clark was appointed superintendent of the locomotive works at Kittybrewster, then under construction. Born in Edinburgh in 1822, Clark had served an apprenticeship with Thomas Edington & Son, at the Phoenix Ironworks, Glasgow, and had subsequently gained experience with another private firm, and with the North British Railway, before setting up in practice as a consulting engineer in London at the early age of 30.

For the opening of the railway to Huntly, Clark designed, and William Fairbairn & Sons, of Manchester, constructed, twelve 2—4—0 tender engines, with outside cylinders 15 in. diameter by 20 in. stroke. The heating surface was 749 sq. ft. in the first seven and 808 sq. ft. in Nos 8 to 12. The fireboxes were raised, and were surmounted by large brass domes, with inverted bell mouths. Spring safety valves of the Salter type were mounted on the domes. The chimneys were fitted with copper caps. The design was characterised by its simplicity, and the engines were not provided with sanding gear, nor was any protection from the weather afforded to the driver and fireman. The weight in working order was 23¼ tons.

Nos. 1 to 7 were intended for passenger traffic, and had 3 ft 6 in. leading wheels, and 5 ft 6 in. coupled wheels. The remaining five, described as goods engines, were generally similar, but had 5 ft driving wheels. They had originally been designed as six-coupled engines, but had been altered to 2—4—0s, to enable them to undertake mixed-traffic duties.

The tenders of both classes ran on four wheels, with outside bearings, and were of rather small capacity. They were fitted with the only brake power available on the engines—wooden blocks, operated by a hand wheel.

Although the makers were repeatedly urged to deliver the locomotives in good time, only Nos. 1 to 5 had arrived by October 1854; and it was with this inadequate stock that the line to Huntly

LOCOMOTIVES—1

(47) *Class 1, no 4A, built 1854 by Fairbairn to design of D K Clark. Shown here as rebuilt 1888. Withdrawn 1897.*

(48) *Cowan 2-4-0 no 25, class B, built Stephenson 1861, rebuilt as shown here August 1882 and withdrawn April 1907.*

(49) *Rebuilt Cowan 4-4-0 of class H at Banff Harbour. The smallest of four classes of 4-4-0s designed by Cowan, particularly suited to the smaller branch lines.*

LOCOMOTIVES—2

(50) *Manson 0-6-0T no 41 of class E, later J91. Built Kitson June 1885 and withdrawn June 1934. Rebuilt in Aug 1908 as seen here. There were nine locos in this class, the only six-coupled type owned by the GNSR.*

(51) *Johnson 0-4-4T no 92 of class R, later G10. Built Neilson December 1893 and withdrawn May 1939. These locomotives were the mainstay of the Aberdeen 'Subbies'.*

(52) *Manning Wardle 0-4-2T 68190 of class X (Z4). Originally numbered 116, the GNSR altered it to 43. One of four engines of two very similar classes which were introduced in 1915 for shunting the quays at Aberdeen.*

LOCOMOTIVES—3

(53) Rebuilt Cowan class M (D45) no 40. Entered service October 1878 and
       withdrawn June 1932.
(54) Johnson 4-4-0 no 80, class S (D41). Entered service December 1893 and
       withdrawn in March 1951.
(55) Pickersgill 4-4-0 no 100 of class T (D41). Built Neilson, entered service
       February 1896 and withdrawn July 1947.

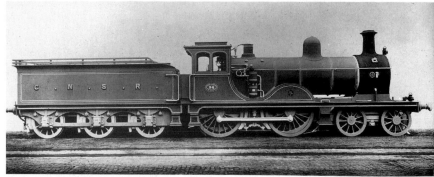

LOCOMOTIVES—4

(56) *Pickersgill 4-4-0 no 29, class V (D40). Entered traffic July 1909 and withdrawn August 1956.*

(57) *Heywood 4-4-0 no 54, later named Southesk, of class F. Similar to class V, with which they shared the LNER classification D40. Built October 1920 and withdrawn in January 1947, the first of the class to go.*

(58) *The swansong of GNSR steam – preserved class F no 49 'Gordon Highlander' on its penultimate outing at Bathgate in October 1965.*

was opened. Within a few days, one engine had been severely damaged in the collision at Kittybrewster, and another had developed a mechanical defect. For the time being, the remaining three engines had to handle all traffic, both passenger and goods. Nos. 6 and 7 had been delivered by the end of the year; but the goods engines (Nos. 8 to 12) were not completed until the summer of 1855.

By 1860, these locomotives had been provided with sandboxes, and front and rear weather boards. They were also fitted with Clark's smoke prevention system, a series of holes in the firebox for the admission of air, which was kept in circulation by means of steam jets. The use of this apparatus was continued on the Great North for many years.

Both classes were rebuilt, for the most part with small rounded cabs, of the Stirling pattern, in place of the front weather boards, in the early 1880s[1], and were withdrawn from service some ten years later. Latterly they made way for new engines by having the letter A added to their numbers.

When new, these early engines were painted a medium shade of green, with black borders and bands, but without any lining. The buffer beams were painted red; and the numbers were painted on the splashers of the front pair of driving wheels.

Soon after the opening of the line to Huntly, Clark became involved in a dispute with the company. Residence in Aberdeen had been one of the conditions of his appointment, but he had never shown any intention of fulfilling this obligation. When the directors pressed the point, Clark replied that supervision at Kittybrewster could be carried out by a whole-time assistant, and that residence in the north of Scotland 'would be inimical to his advancement in his profession'. This refusal to observe his contract led to his resignation in March 1855.

Clark's subsequent career as a consulting engineer was distinguished, and included several public appointments. He is also widely known as the author of The Steam Engine, and Railway Machinery. At the time of its publication in 1855, the latter was the most comprehensive work that had appeared on the subject.

JOHN FOLDS RUTHVEN: 1855—1857

Clark was succeeded at Kittybrewster by his works foreman, John Folds Ruthven. The new superintendent did not make any

---

[1] These cabs were designed by James Manson, who had served his apprenticeship at Kilmarnock under Patrick Stirling

departures from his predecessor's practice, and the first two locomotives delivered after he had taken office had been designed by
Clark.

The approaching completion of the steeply-graded extension from
Kittybrewster to the Waterloo Quay called for the provision of
banking engines; and an order was placed with Beyer Peacock &
Co., of Manchester, in the summer of 1855 for two small 0—4—0
tank engines, which were delivered in the next year, and numbered
13 and 14. They had 15 in. by 24 in. outside cylinders, 4 ft 6 in.
wheels, and well tanks fixed between the frames, under the boilers.
The raised fireboxes were fitted with Clark's smoke prevention
apparatus, and were surmounted by brass domes with Salter-type
safety valves. The weight in working order was 24 tons. At first,
the footplates were unprotected, but weather boards were provided
a few years later, and cabs were added when the engines were
reboilered in 1887. The domes were then moved forward to the
middle of the boilers.

In the course of nearly 60 years, these little engines did a vast
amount of banking and shunting work at Aberdeen and elsewhere.
They were placed on the A list in 1890, when new engines bearing
the same numbers appeared, and were eventually sold in 1916 to
James Barclay of Glasgow who hired them to the government and
they may have been used in building the line from Longside to
Lenabo. Later No. 14 went to the National Shell Filling Factory at
Chilwell but there is no further trace of No. 13. No. 14, however, was
at Tareni Colliery, Glamorgan, as late as 1943.

Four more 2—4—0s, with 5 ft 6 in. coupled wheels, were ordered
from Fairbairn & Sons in 1856, and numbered 15 to 18. The fireboxes were equipped with Clark's smoke prevention apparatus.
They were delivered in April and May 1857 and originally had
eccentric crankpins giving 22 in. stroke. These proved troublesome
and were later removed, the stroke becoming 20 in.

In common with the earlier series, these engines were provided
with sanding gear and weather boards a few years after their
construction, and were rebuilt, in most cases with the addition of
cabs, between 1880 and 1885. Shortly afterwards, they were placed
on the A list, and all had been withdrawn from service by the end
of the century.

In May 1857, Ruthven resigned from the service of the company
to re-enter private practice, where he was for many years closely
associated with D. K. Clark.

WILLIAM COWAN: 1857—1883

William Cowan, was appointed locomotive superintendent of the Great North shortly after Ruthven's resignation. Born in Edinburgh in 1823, Cowan had entered the locomotive department of the Arbroath & Forfar Railway in 1839, and had subsequently spent several years with the Edinburgh & Glasgow and the Great Northern Railway. In September 1854, he joined the locomotive department of the Great North.

The first locomotives designed by Cowan were nine 2—4—0s, built by Robert Stephenson & Co. They were generally similar to the so-called goods engines of 1854, with 5 ft 1 in. coupled wheels, but had 16 in. by 20 in. outside cylinders, and were provided with Clark's smoke prevention apparatus, weather boards, and sanding gear from the first. They were the last 2—4—0s constructed for the Great North. The first six, numbered 19 to 24, were delivered in 1860, and the remainder (Nos. 25 to 27) in the next year.

The whole series was rebuilt, with cabs in place of weather boards, between 1880 and 1883; and with the exception of No. 27, which retained its original number, had been transferred to the A list by the end of the century. No. 20 was withdrawn from service in 1900, and most of the others followed a few years later. No. 27 survived until 1909, by which time it had become the last 2—4—0 owned by the company.

To provide additional locomotives for the rapidly expanding system, Cowan designed, and Robert Stephenson & Co. constructed, a series of nine 4—4—0 tender engines, with 16 in. by 22 in. outside cylinders, and 5 ft 1 in. coupled wheels. They were among the earliest of this type in the country; and their wheel arrangement appears to have been determined by the sharp curves on the lines west of Keith. Originally, the leading wheels had outside bearings and springs, which gave them an unusual appearance. These engines were delivered as follows: Nos. 28 to 30 in 1862; Nos. 31 to 34 in 1863; and Nos. 35 and 36 in 1864.

The boilers were 11 ft 4½ in. long by 3 ft 9¾ in. diameter. The heating surface was 956½ sq. ft, and the grate area 10½ sq. ft. Large bell-mouthed brass domes, and Salter-type safety valves, set to a pressure of 140 lb. per sq. in., were mounted on the raised fireboxes. The weight of the engines in working order was 32½ tons when new, 34½ tons after rebuilding, and of the four-wheel tenders 15½ tons.

The whole class was rebuilt between 1880 and 1883, with cab: and with bogies of more usual design. Nos. 29 and 31 were with drawn in 1905; and by 1917 all save Nos. 34 and 35 had passed to the scrap heap. These two veterans survived until 1920, and came near to equalling the record for long service set up by the 0—4—0 tank engines. They had been transferred to the A list a few years earlier.

Six outside cylinder 4—4—0s were built by Neilson & Co., of Glasgow, in 1866, and numbered 43 to 48. Although similar in appearance to the earlier class, they had larger boilers, and generally increased dimensions. The cylinders were 16 in. by 24 in., and the coupled wheels 5 ft 6½ in. The bogies had inside springs and bearings, and were centrally pivoted in a cast iron cup. They were among the earliest in which provision was made for lateral play The engines weighed 36 tons in working order, and the four-wheel tenders 15¼ tons.

All save two of these engines were provided with six-wheel tenders of increased capacity when the whole series was rebuilt with the addition of cabs, between 1889 and 1891 and slightly larger boilers were fitted. The brass domes and Salter-type safety valves were retained, but were moved from the fireboxes to the middle of the boilers.

For longevity this class rivalled the earlier 4—4—0s and the 0—4—0 tank engines. Nos. 43 and 46 were withdrawn in 1921, after completing 55 years service. No. 47 went in the next year, but the remaining three passed to the London & North Eastern Railway at the grouping. Shortly before it was scrapped, No. 45, the last survivor, hauled a train of old Great North coaches at the railway centenary pageant at Darlington in July 1925. Nos. 45 to 48 had been relegated to the A list in 1920.

The delivery of the second series of 4—4—0s coincided with the financial crisis of 1866. So rigid were the economies imposed that no locomotive construction was sanctioned for the next ten years, while even then the position did not permit the complete relaxation of the emergency measures. Maintenance of locomotives was cut down to a minimum, with disastrous results at Nethybridge in September 1878, when the boiler of No. 31 (one of the 4—4—0s built in 1863) burst along its bottom seam while the engine was standing in the station.

Two years before this mishap occurred, the provision of additional locomotives had become imperative, and six 4—4—0s, generally similar to, but somewhat larger than, those already in service, had been ordered from Neilson & Co. These were delivered in 1876, and were numbered 49, 50, and 54 to 57. In the next year, No. 57 was renumbered 52, taking the number of one of the former Deeside Railway engines withdrawn from service at that time.

The new class had 17 in. by 24 in. outside cylinders, and 5 ft 6½ in. coupled wheels. The boilers had a heating surface of 1,107 sq. ft, and a grate area of 14 sq. ft. The working pressure was 140 lb. per sq. in. The engines weighed 39 tons, of which 25¼ tons was available for adhesion. These engines were the first on the Great North to be fitted with cabs at the time of their construction. The six-wheel tenders had outside springs, and weighed 27 tons.

These additions to the locomotive stock did not by any means meet the needs of the steadily increasing traffic; and a further nine 4—4—0s were built by Neilson & Co. in 1878. They were numbered 40, 51, 53 and 57 to 62. The boilers and fireboxes were similar to those of the preceeding class, but the working pressure was raised to 150 lb. per sq. in., and the size of the cylinders was increased to 17½ in. by 26 in. The diameter of the coupled wheels was 5 ft 7 in. Some modifications were introduced into the design of the cabs, and for the first time, rounded splashers were fitted to the rear driving wheels. The weight of the engines in working order was 39½ tons. The tenders, which ran on six wheels, had inside springs, and weighed 29 tons.

In 1879, three more locomotives of this type, but with 6 ft 1 in. driving wheels, were built by Neilson & Co. They were numbered 1, 2 and 3; and the older engines bearing these numbers were then relegated to the A list.

The whole of this series of 18 engines was rebuilt between 1896 and 1904 with larger boilers, and other minor alterations, which increased the weight of each class by some 3 tons. The old-fashioned bell-mouth brass domes were replaced by round-top domes, mounted on the centre of the boilers, and the Salter-type safety valves by enclosed Ramsbottom valves on the fireboxes. The appearance of the engines was further altered by the substitution of a newer and plainer design of chimney for the original copper-capped type.

No. 52, which had been damaged in the derailment of a ballast train at Knock in July 1896, was rebuilt in the next year, with a square cab, with two side windows and a raised roof. This innovation became standard for all new engines two years later. Although relegated to secondary duties, all these engines survived until after the grouping. In 1920 Nos. 49 to 54 had passed on to the A list.

During Cowan's last four years at Kittybrewster no new locomotives were required. In October 1883, he retired from the service of the company at the comparatively early age of 60. He continued to reside in Aberdeen until his death in March 1898.

For some time after his appointment, Cowan made almost no alteration in the painting of the locomotives, although a somewhat lighter shade of green was soon introduced. By 1866, however, more elaborate livery had been adopted. The locomotives were painted grass green, picked out with black bands, edged with red lines. The buffer beams and lamps were red. The large domes, the wide bands at each end of the boiler, and the beading round the splashers of the driving wheels, all of which were of polished brass, together with the copper-capped chimney, gave the engines a distinctly smart appearance.

In 1876, oval number plates, with raised letters and figures, appeared on the sides of the cabs in place of the numbers painted on the splashers. For the time being they were used only on new engines, but were gradually fitted to the older types.

Between 1863 and 1866, the Great North took over the working of the Morayshire, the Banffshire and the Deeside Railways, all of which had locomotives of their own.

THE MORAYSHIRE RAILWAY

Some years before the opening of the Morayshire Railway, James Samuel, the company's locomotive superintendent and engineer, had patented a design for a steam railcar, or light engine, with a vertical boiler, for use on lines where traffic was by no means heavy. The inventor claimed not only that these cars could be cheaply constructed, but that their use would reduce operating expenses, and wear and tear of the track to a minimum. By 1849, at least two had been constructed by William Bridges Adams, at the Fairfield Works, Bow, for the Eastern Counties Railway, of which Samuel was also engineer.

On the Morayshire Railway, Samuel's designs were adopted in a modified form, and two 2—2—0 light engines were constructed by Neilson & Co. in readiness for the opening of the line in August 1852. They were numbered 1 and 2, and are said to have been named *Elgin* and *Lossiemouth* respectively. As the Morayshire Railway was then completely isolated, they had to be delivered by sea at Lossiemouth harbour.

Far from complete details of these locomotives have survived, but they appear to have differed from the original design in that the engine was not permanently attached to a coach. The boilers carried a working pressure of 120 lb. per sq. in., and the vertical cylinders were 10 in. by 16 in. The diameter of the driving wheels was 5 ft, and of the carrying wheels 3 ft. The weight in working order was about 14 tons.

Whatever the success of Samuel's engines elsewhere, they proved far from satisfactory on the Morayshire Railway. On the day of the official opening, the failure of the engine of the special train threatened to turn the proceedings into a fiasco; and on several subsequent occasions difficulty was experienced in maintaining a reliable service. The climax was reached in 1858, when continued unpunctuality and engine failures led to the Inverness & Aberdeen Junction company taking over the working of all traffic between Elgin and Orton.

Neither of the original locomotives remained in service long enough to be taken over by the Great North. One was withdrawn in 1859, or early in the next year, and the other in 1863, when the Morayshire company ceased to work its own traffic. Latterly, the survivor appears to have worked between Elgin and Lossiemouth only.

In 1854, Samuel was succeeded by Joseph Taylor, of the Scottish Central Railway, who coped with the shortcomings of the loco-motives until he was killed in an accident. On the evening of 23 April 1857, after the last train had reached Lossiemouth, the engine was returning towards Elgin, propelling a wagon to a lineside ballast pit, when it met the other engine running light, and bunker fore-most, in the opposite direction. In the ensuing collision, the flimsy cab of the light engine was crushed, and Taylor, who was riding on the footplate, was killed.

It transpired that the light engine had been under repair at Elgin, and Taylor had taken it for a trial run, under the mistaken im-pression that all traffic had ceased for the night. The Board of Trade inspector commented sharply on this serious breach of the rules for working single lines. The engine propelling the wagon was not severely damaged, and there was no interruption of traffic.

Taylor was succeeded first by Robert Blackwood, and then by George Golightly, two shadowy figures of whom little appears to have been recorded. The latter held office until the Great North took over the working of the line in 1863.

Needless to say, Samuel's designs were not perpetuated when

additional locomotives were required. In June 1859, Neilson & Co. delivered the first of two small 2—4—0 engines with saddle and side tanks; the second followed some 18 months later. They were numbered and named 3, *Glen Grant*, and 4, *Lesmurdie*, respectively. These engines appear to have been designed by the makers. Cylinder and coupled wheel sizes were 12 in. by 18 in. and 4 ft 10 in. for No. 3 and 14 in. by 18 in. and 4 ft 9½ in. for No. 4. The weight in working order was about 25 tons. The boiler of No. 3 was domeless with the safety valve enclosed in a brass column, similar to those subsequently adopted by Samuel Johnson on the Midland Railway, but No. 4 had a centrally placed dome with a Salter safety valve on top. The chimneys were fitted with copper caps. The sides of the tanks were carried back to form side wings to the footplate. The cabs were of sheet iron, made in one piece and bent to shape.

Both engines were taken over by the Great North in 1863, and were renumbered 41 and 42, and had their nameplates removed. One of them worked between Orton and Rothes until that line was closed in 1866. Subsequently, one was employed on the Lossiemouth line, and on station pilot duties at Elgin, and the other on the Old Meldrum branch. No. 42 was withdrawn from service in 1883, and No. 41 early in 1885.

The Morayshire engines were painted green, of a shade similar to that used on the Great North, with very little lining.

THE BANFFSHIRE RAILWAY

The Banff, Portsoy & Strathisla company started business in August 1859 with two 0—4—2 tank engines, built by Hawthorn & Co., of Leith, and numbered and named, 1, *Banff*, and 2, *Portsoy*. They were designed by the makers, and had 13 in. by 18 in. inside cylinders, 5 ft coupled wheels, and 3 ft trailing wheels. The weight in working order was 20 tons. The fireboxes were raised, and were surmounted by the domes, on which Salter-type safety valves were fitted. The footplates were protected by front weather boards, placed in front of the domes, and by rear boards, mounted on the bunkers.

In 1859 the company bought an 0—4—2 tender engine from Hawthorn after inspecting its sister at work on the Deeside Railway. The engine weighed 28 tons and probably had cylinders 15¼ in. by 24 in. with 4ft 6in. diameter driving wheels, while the four-wheel tender weighed 16 tons. Named 'Keith' it was No. 3. Another locomotive ordered from Hawthorn in October 1860 and delivered in

July 1861 became No. 4 'Strathisla'. The specification had required that it should be 'no less powerful than No. 3 and fitted with Clark's patent smoke consuming apparatus.'

When the Great North took over the working of the Banffshire Railway in 1863, the four engines were renumbered 37, 38, 39 and 40 respectively, and the nameplates were removed. In the next year No. 39 was sold to the Deeside Railway, while No. 40 was hired to that company in 1865. On the other hand, the two tank engines continued to work between Grange and Banff and Portsoy for many years. Both were withdrawn from service at the end of 1884, or early in 1885, and sold to a contractor.

During the company's brief independent existence, the head-quarters of the locomotive department were at Banff. The company painted its locomotives green, but details of the lining and lettering have not survived. The shade of green is said to have differed some-what from that adopted on the Great North, and to have more closely resembled the dark green used by the Inverness & Aberdeen Junction Railway.

THE DEESIDE RAILWAY

When the Deeside company decided to work its own traffic, an order was placed with Hawthorn & Co. for two 0—4—2 tank engines. These were delivered in February and August 1854, and were numbered 1 and 2 respectively. As was the case with all other Deeside locomotives, they were not named. From the incomplete information that has survived, it appears that these engines were similar to, although slightly smaller than, those supplied by Haw-thorn & Co. to the Banff, Portsoy & Strathisla Railway five years later.

No. 1 was withdrawn from service in 1865, as it had become too light for the increasing traffic; but No. 2 survived for another 18 years, and probably was repaired with parts recovered from No. 1. For some time, No. 2 worked the Royal specials. While engaged in this duty, it is said to have had a panel representing the Royal Stewart tartan painted on each of the tanks, but authentic inform-ation about this unique feature appears to be lacking.

In the autumn of 1854, a 0—4—2 tender engine was obtained from Dodds & Son, of Rotherham, and numbered 3. The details of its design are obscure, but it appears to have had 5 ft coupled wheels, and to have weighed, together with the tender, about 35 tons. Mechanical defects delayed the delivery of the engine, and caused endless trouble after it had been placed in service. So unsatisfactory was its performance that an order for a similar engine was cancelled. Although No. 3 remained on the stock lists for fourteen years, it appears to have done very little work.

In 1857, Hawthorn & Co. delivered the first of a series of four 0—4—2 tender engines, of similar dimensions to B.P&S Nos. 3 and 4. The safety valves were of the Salter type, and were fixed on the domes, which were mounted on the fireboxes. Front weather boards formed the only protection for the enginemen. With one exception, the tenders ran on four wheels, and weighed 16 tons.

These engines were numbered and delivered as follows:

No.	Date New
4	1857
5	1859
6	1860
8	1866

No. 5 was completed in time for the opening of the Aboyne extension and No. 8 was delivered in readiness for the completion of the line to Ballater. To enable it to work the Royal specials non-stop between Aberdeen and the new terminus, it was provided with a larger tender, running on six wheels, and weighing about 24 tons.

An additional locomotive of this type had been built by Hawthorn & Co. in 1859 for the Banff, Portsoy and Strathisla Railway. Four years later it passed into the hands of the Great North but was acquired by the Deeside Company becoming their No. 7. As locomotives were not permitted to pass over the harbour lines at Aberdeen under their own power, it had to be hauled by horses from Waterloo to Guild Street. It is, however, alleged to have had sufficient steam in the boiler to assist the horses. For many years, similar stories were current about other transfers, and of new locomotives delivered to the Great North from manufacturers before the opening of the Denburn Valley line in 1867.

In September 1866, the Great North leased the Deeside Railway and Nos. 2 and 4 to 8 were renumbered 39 and 49 to 53 respectively. The Dodds engine, No. 3, was given a nil valuation as 'being partly broken up and unserviceable' and was not renumbered. It was removed from the GNSR stock list during the first half of 1868 but was not finally written off until March 1871. In 1878 Nos. 40 and 53 may have been renumbered 63 and 64 respectively pending their withdrawal a year later.

Compared with their contemporaries on the Great North, the Deeside locomotives did not have long lives. The considerable overhang at the leading end is said to have made the tender engines unsteady, a fault that became more pronounced as the speed of the trains increased with the gradual improvement of the services. They passed to the scrap heap in the following order:

Deeside No.		Date Withdrawn
3	.....	1868 (or 1871)
4	.....	1875
5	.....	1876
7	.....	1877
6	.....	1879
8	.....	1879
2	.....	1883

The locomotive sheds and repair shops of the Deeside Railway were at Banchory. Until 1864, John Willet, the company's engineer, acted as locomotive superintendent. Both departments were then taken over by William B. Ferguson, the secretary and general manager.

Until they were taken over by the Great North in 1866, the Deeside locomotives were painted dark blue, with black lining. The title Deeside Railway, surmounted by the engine number, appeared in gilt letters, within a gilt border, surrounded by a broad border of black, on the side wings of the footplates.

JAMES MANSON: 1883—1890

James Manson, manager at the Kilmarnock Works of the Glasgow & South Western Railway, was chosen to succeed Cowan on the Great North. Born in Ayrshire in 1846, Manson had served his apprenticeship at Kilmarnock, under Patrick Stirling, but had subsequently spent some years in marine engineering. He returned to the Glasgow & South Western in 1878, and became successively locomotive inspector and works manager.

The locomotives designed by Manson for the Great North differed considerably from those of his predecessors, particularly in external appearance. Without exception, they had inside cylinders. The display of polished brass disappeared from the boilers and splashers of the driving wheels. Round-topped cast iron domes, mounted on the centre of the boilers, were substituted for the bell-mouthed brass domes; and the Salter safety valves were replaced by open Ramsbottom valves on the fireboxes. Copper-capped chimneys were abandoned in favour of chimneys similar to those used by Patrick Stirling on the Great Northern Railway. For the greater comfort of the enginemen, side doors were fitted to the cabs, an improvement that was subsequently extended to many of the older locomotives. Clark's smoke prevention apparatus was retained in a modified form, without steam jets.

The first locomotives embodying these alterations were six 4—4—0s, built by Kitson & Co., of Leeds, in 1884, and numbered 63 to 68. These engines were slightly smaller than the final classes designed by Cowan. They had 17½ in. by 26 in. cylinders, and the diameter of the driving wheels was 6 ft. The heating surface was 1,036 sq. ft, and the working pressure 140 lb. per sq. in. The weight of the engines in working order was 37 tons 2 cwt. The tenders weighed 29 tons and had a capacity of 2,000 gallons of water and 3 tons of coal. In 1885, three more locomotives of this type, but with driving wheels reduced to 5 ft 6 in., were built by Kitson & Co. They were intended for mixed traffic duties, and were numbered 69 to 71.

Although it had frequently been suggested that the company should build its own locomotives, it was realised that it was out of the question to attempt construction on a large scale in the small repair shops at Kittybrewster. In 1887, however, it was decided to undertake the construction of two locomotives. These engines were similar to Manson's mixed traffic class, but the diameter of the driving wheels was 1 in. more. They were numbered 5 and 6, and named *Kinmundy* and *Thomas Adam*, in honour of the chairman and deputy chairman respectively.[1] These names, which were painted in a curve above the works plate on the driving wheel splashers, were removed some twenty years later.

Nos. 63 to 68 and 69 to 71 were rebuilt between 1905 and 1917 with larger boilers working at a pressure of 150 lb per sq. in. in the cases of Nos. 63 to 71. While Nos. 5 and 6 were similarly rebuilt, their boiler pressure was raised to 165 lb per sq. in. All three series were fitted with new chimneys and boiler mountings as well as various other alterations. In this form they survived until withdrawn between 1924 and 1936.

To meet the needs of the steadily increasing traffic and faster trains, Manson designed a further nine 4—4—0 locomotives, which were built by Kitson & Co. in 1888, and numbered 4, 7, 9, 10, 17, 18, 72, 73 and 74. Outstanding features were the slide valves placed on top of the cylinders, and actuated by rocking shafts, and swing-

[1] Kinmundy was the chairman's patronymic. See footnote on page 132

link bogies, with double pins. The cylinders were 18 in. diameter by 26 in. stroke. The boilers, which were 4 ft 4 in. in diameter, carried a working pressure of 150 lb. per sq. in., and had a total heating surface of 1,193·7 sq. ft. The diameter of the driving wheels was 6 ft 0½ in., and of the bogie wheels 3 ft 9½ in. The weight of the engines in working order was 42 tons, of which 28 tons 18 cwt rested on the driving wheels. The tenders weighed 29 tons.

Six more locomotives of this type were built by Robert Stephenson & Co., in 1890, and numbered 12 to 14 and 75 to 77. The latter three had 6 ft 6½ in. driving wheels, the largest ever used on the Great North. The tenders were of increased capacity and weighed 38 tons. They ran on eight wheels and were of most unusual design. The leading ends were carried on four-wheel bogies, and the trailing ends on fixed axles, with outside bearings. They were specially notable as the first eight-wheel tenders used on a British railway.

In October 1913 No. 77 was rebuilt with a boiler similar in size to the original but fitted with a Schmidt superheater and working at 160 lb per sq. in. In May 1914 No. 76 was rebuilt but with a non-superheated 165 lb per sq. in. boiler. After comparative trials between the two, the remainder of the three classes were reboilered between 1916 and 1920. No. 74 received a Schmidt superheater (replaced with a Robinson type by the LNER). Of the others Nos. 17, 18, 72, 73, 12, 14 and 75 were given Robinson superheaters and worked at 165 lb per sq. in. while the remainder had saturated 165 lb boilers.

After rebuilding, those fitted with superheaters weighed 47 tons, and the others 46 tons. In most cases, the eight-wheel tenders were replaced by tenders of standard design. Nos. 76 and 77 were rebuilt with an extended roof to the cab, supported on side pillars, but No. 75 retained its original cab.

Shortly after his arrival at Kittybrewster, Manson designed, and Kitson & Co. built, a series of nine 0—6—0 side tank engines—the only six-coupled type ever owned by the Great North. They were also remarkable as the first tank engines in the country to have cabs fitted with side doors. The first six, numbered 8, 11, 15, 16, 39 and 42, appeared in 1884. The remainder were delivered in the next year, and were numbered 37, 38 and 41. They had 16 in. by 24 in. cylinders, and 4 ft 6in. wheels. The heating surface was 756 sq. ft, and the working pressure 140 lb. per sq. in. The earlier set weighed 37½ tons in working order, but those completed in 1885 were slightly larger, and weighed 1 ton more.

Although primarily intended for shunting and banking duties, for several years these engines did yeoman service on the smartly-timed Aberdeen suburban services. They also worked short-distance passenger and goods trains on the main line, and on the Alford branch. In 1903, No. 8 was fitted with front and rear cowcatchers, and sent to Fraserburgh to work the unfenced light railway to St. Combs. The whole series was rebuilt between 1907 and 1911, and given larger boilers, with a heating surface of 846 sq. ft. and working to a pressure of 150 lb. per sq. in., and new chimneys and boiler mountings. These alterations increased the weight by 4½ tons.

Manson continued the style of painting introduced by his predecessor with only minor alterations, although the initials GNSR appeared for the first time on the tenders. The six-coupled tank engines had their oval number plates fixed on the sides of the tanks, and did not display the company's initials.

In September 1890, Manson relinquished his position with the Great North to return to the Glasgow & South Western Railway as locomotive superintendent. He remained at Kilmarnock until his retirement in 1912. During his seven years at Kittybrewster, he had designed 35 locomotives for the Great North, all of which passed to the London & North Eastern Railway in 1923.

Manson is remembered as the inventor of the automatic tablet exchange apparatus, which made possible the running of fast trains on single lines, without risk of injury to the enginemen. This device was first used on the Great North, and was evolved after experiments with a modified form of the apparatus used to pick up and deliver mail bags had proved unsuccessful.

The tablet apparatus consisted of two pairs of spring-loaded steel forks, placed back to back, parallel to the track. One pair of forks was mounted on a steel frame beside the track, and the other on a hinged bracket inside the cab of the engine. The forks beside the line could be moved forward by a hand lever to come directly under those on the engine. When not in use, the latter were swung back inside the cab.

The tablets were placed in leather pouches fitted with a strong looped handle. The one for the single-line section ahead was placed in the forward fork of the frame on the ground, and picked up by the corresponding fork on the engine. Similarly, the tablet for the section in rear was delivered and picked up by the forks facing in the opposite direction.

The apparatus proved successful, and was installed throughout the single-line sections on the Great North. To encourage its use by other companies for the protection of their enginemen, Manson generously refrained from patenting his invention, although strongly urged to do so.

JAMES JOHNSON: 1890—1894

Manson's successor at Kittybrewster was James Johnson, who had received his training under his father, Samuel Johnson, the locomotive superintendent of the Midland Railway, and had remained at Derby as an assistant. Three years elapsed before any locomotives designed by the new superintendent made their appearance, but in 1893 Neilson & Co. delivered six 4—4—0s, numbered 78 to 83.

These engines were more powerful than any previously owned by the Great North, and had 18 in. by 26 in. inside cylinders, with valves actuated by direct motion in place of the rocking shafts introduced by Manson. The driving wheels were 6 ft 1 in. diameter, and the bogie wheels 3 ft 9½ in. The boilers had a heating surface of 1,207 sq. ft, and carried a working pressure of 165 lb. per sq. in. The fireboxes were not fitted with Clark's smoke prevention apparatus, the use of which was then abandoned. The weight of the engine in working order was 43 tons 18 cwt, of which 30 tons was available for adhesion. The tenders were slightly smaller than those designed by Manson. They weighed 35 tons, and ran on six wheels.

Distinguished by their capacity for rapid acceleration and sustained high speed, these engines worked the principal main-line services with outstanding success for several years. Five of the six were reboilered between 1918 and 1921 and No. 80 in 1924. services with outstanding success for several years. Nos. 80 and 82 remained in their original condition until the grouping, but the others were rebuilt between 1915 and 1919.

Neilson & Co. also built nine 0—4—4 side-tank engines for the Great North in 1893. Numbered 84 to 92, they had been designed by Manson, but their construction had been deferred. Johnson introduced modifications, to make the boilers, fireboxes and valve gear identical with those of his 4—4—0s, but the cylinders were slightly smaller—17½ in. by 26 in. The coupled wheels were 5 ft diameter, and the trailing wheels 3 ft 0½ in. The weight in working order was 53¾ tons. Unlike the 0—6—0 tank engines, the 0—4—4s were not provided with the standard oval number plates, but had their numbers painted on the coal bunkers, and displayed the company's initials on the sides of the tanks.

These engines were intended for working the Deeside line, and for several years were almost wholly confined to that section, although one was allocated to the Cruden Railway when that branch was opened in 1897. By about 1900, however, most of them had been transferred to the Aberdeen suburban services, on which they worked for many years. The whole series was rebuilt between 1916 and 1922.

The locomotives designed by Johnson were characterised by their neat appearance, and pronounced Midland Railway features. This resemblance extended from the chimneys and the contour of the smokeboxes to the safety valves encased in a brass column on the fireboxes, and to the frames of the tenders, all of which were of unmistakable origin. Johnson further adhered to Midland practice by fitting a second set of safety valves on the domes, but without the Salter spring balances, which were for so long a feature of locomotives built at Derby. His successor, William Pickersgill, removed these valves, and substituted enclosed Ramsbottom valves for those mounted on the fireboxes.

In August 1894, Johnson resigned from the Great North to join a firm of engineers in the west of England. During his short term of office, he had placed 15 new locomotives in service, the whole of which passed to the London & North Eastern Railway at the grouping.

WILLIAM PICKERSGILL : 1894—1914

William Pickersgill, the new locomotive superintendent at Kitty-brewster, had gained the whole of his experience on the Great Eastern Railway. He had entered Stratford Works as an apprentice, at the age of 15, and subsequently occupied a number of positions with the company.

At the time of Pickersgill's appointment, the dispute with the Highland Railway was at its height. In anticipation of a successful application to Parliament for running powers to Inverness, and of a substantial increase in traffic, additional 4—4—0 locomotives were ordered from Neilson & Co. Their principal dimensions and general appearance were identical with those of Johnson's engines; but the safety valves on the domes were dispensed with, and the brass columns on the fireboxes were replaced by enclosed Rams-bottom valves, similar to those used on the Great Eastern Railway.

Twenty-six locomotives of this type were built between 1895 and 1898—Nos. 93 to 99 in 1895; Nos. 19 to 24, and 100 in 1896; Nos. 101 to 106 in 1897; and Nos. 107 to 112 in 1898.[1]

[1] In 1897, the makers became Neilson Reid & Co. by amalgamation

The last 12 appeared after the introduction of the 'Commissioners' Service' in April 1897. They had tenders of increased capacity, fitted with coal rails, and weighing 37 tons 2 cwt.

Ten more 4—4—0 locomotives were ordered from Neilson Reid & Co. in 1899. They were generally similar to those already in service, but had square cabs, fitted with side windows, and a raised ventilator in the roof. The first five were delivered, and numbered 25, 26, and 113 to 115; but it was then decided that the others were not required, as the increase in traffic had fallen short of expectations. They were sold to the South Eastern & Chatham Railway, where they became Nos. 676 to 680.

When the first of Pickersgill's locomotives was rebuilt, some of the earlier locomotives, designed by Manson, already had been given superheated boilers, but the experiment was not extended to any of the later types. Eleven of the locomotives designed by Pickersgill—Nos. 19, 21, 93, 97, 98, 100, 108 and 112 to 115—were rebuilt between 1916 and 1921. No. 110 was fitted with Weir feed water pumps in 1920, but the results were not successful, and the apparatus was removed two years later.

In 1898, the removal of the works from Kittybrewster to the northern outskirts of Inverurie was authorised. Pickersgill's advice was frequently sought while the works were being planned and equipped, and it was on his recommendation that plant to generate electricity for lighting and power was installed. The workshops and offices for both the locomotive and carriage departments were completed between 1901 and 1903; and accommodation for the permanent way department was added two years later.

Long before the move from Kittybrewster had been completed it had become obvious that the number of locomotives already in service would be sufficient to meet the needs of the traffic for a considerable time, and that the new works had been planned on a scale that was not justified. However, the work of repairing locomotives and rolling stock was greatly facilitated, and the construction of a limited number of passenger coaches and goods wagons was undertaken.

In 1905, two experimental steam railcars were placed in service. They ran on eight wheels, and had vertical dome-topped boilers, supplied by Cochran & Co., of Annan. These boilers were the first of their kind to be used for railway work. They were 9 ft 6 in. high by 6 ft diameter, and carried a working pressure of 150 lb. per sq. in. The heating surface was 500 sq. ft, and the grate area 9 sq. ft. The engines were built by Andrew Barclay Sons & Co., of

Kilmarnock, and had two horizontal 10 in. by 16 in. outside cylinders, fitted with Walschaerts valve gear. The cylinders were at the footplate end, and drove the leading wheels of the bogies, which were not coupled to the trailing pair. The diameter of the driving and carrying wheels was 3 ft 7 in. The coal bunkers had a capacity of 15 cwt, and 600 gal. of water were carried in a tank under the body of the car.

Saloon-type bodies, with seats for 45 passengers, were built for the cars at Inverurie. The only entrance and exit for passengers was at the end of the car, through a small guard's compartment, which was fitted with duplicate engine and brake controls, used by the driver when the car was travelling with the engine in the rear. The overall length of the vehicle was 50 ft and the weight in working order 47 tons.

The cars were given locomotive numbers 29 and 31. They were tried first of all on the Aberdeen suburban services; but one was soon sent to the Lossiemouth branch, and the other to the St. Combs light railway. They failed completely to justify claims made for them; for not only were they noisy and uncomfortable while in motion, but the boilers were incapable of maintaining an adequate head of steam. Within two years, both had been withdrawn from service, and broken down into their component parts. The coaches were converted into third class saloons, and the engines adapted for shunting duties at Inverurie works. The latter did not long survive in this form, although the boilers were used for stationary work for several years.

Apart from the railcars, no additions had been made to the locomotive stock since 1899. However, in 1909, two 4—4—0 tender engines were constructed at Inverurie. They were similar to those built ten years earlier, and were numbered 27 and 29. In the course of the next six years, six more locomotives of this type were built at Inverurie, in the following order:

Nos.			Year Built
31 and 36	...		1910
28 and 33	...		1913
35	...	...	1914
34	...	...	1915

The last two were not completed until after Pickersgill had left the Great North. A mishap during construction appears to have delayed the completion of No. 34 until after No. 35 had been placed in service.

In May 1914, Pickersgill was appointed to succeed John Mac-Intosh as locomotive superintendent on the Caledonian Railway. During his 20 years with the Great North, he had designed 39 new locomotives, all of which survived until long after the grouping, and had undertaken extensive reconstruction among the older types.

THOMAS HEYWOOD: 1914—1922

Thomas Heywood, chief assistant locomotive superintendent on the Taff Vale Railway, was chosen to succeed Pickersgill at Inverurie. Heywood had entered the locomotive department of the Taff Vale Railway as an apprentice in 1896, and had subsequently spent several years abroad, in the service of the Burma Railways, before returning to South Wales.

The outbreak of war three months after Heywood's appointment caused further locomotive building at Inverurie to be postponed, although the two 4—4—0 tender engines already under construction were completed. On the other hand, the rebuilding of several locomotives was carried out during the next four years, in addition to repair work, and a number of government contracts. The only new locomotives placed in service were four small 0—4—2 tank engines, which were purchased in 1915 for shunting on the Aberdeen harbour lines.

These engines were designed and built by Manning Wardle & Co., of Leeds, and were delivered in pairs. The first two had 14 in. by 20 in. outside cylinders, 4 ft coupled wheels, and 2 ft 9 in. trailing wheels. The working pressure was 160 lb. per sq. in. When new, they were numbered 116 and 117, but in August 1915 their numbers were changed to 30 and 32. The second pair were also Nos. 116 and 117 at first but in April 1916 they were re-numbered 43 and 44. They were slightly smaller, with 13 in. by 20 in. outside cylinders, and 3 ft 6 in. coupled wheels. In common with the six-coupled tank engines, these locomotives had their numberplates on the sides of the tanks, and did not carry the company's initials.

After the war had ended, nearly two years elapsed before the first locomotive designed by Heywood appeared. These were of the 4—4—0 type, and differed but little from the class introduced by Pickersgill 20 years earlier, save that they were fitted with Robinson superheaters. The weight in working order was 48 tons 13 cwt, of which 33¼ tons rested on the driving wheels. The tenders ran on six wheels, and weighed 37 tons 8 cwt.

Six engines of this type were built by the North British Locomotive Co. in the autumn of 1920.[1] Contrary to the usual practice, they bore both numbers and names as follows:

No.		Name
47	...	Sir David Stewart
48	...	Andrew Bain
49	...	Gordon Highlander
50	...	Hatton Castle
52	...	Glen Grant
54	...	Southesk

For some time after it appeared, No. 54 was unnamed. During the miners' strike in the spring of 1921, No. 49 was adapted for burning oil fuel, but the apparatus was removed after coal supplies again became normal.

Later in the same year, two similar engines were built at Inverurie. They were numbered and named 45, George Davidson, and 46, Benachie. The latter was the final addition to the locomotive stock of the Great North, and the tenth, and last, engine to be built at Inverurie.

Shortly after Heywood came to the Great North, the style of painting was modified, and the wheels of the engines and tenders appeared in black, without any lining. In 1917, however, an entirely new livery was adopted. The engines were painted black, lined with yellow and red. The last series of eight 4—4—0 engines displayed the company's coat of arms on the splashers of the front driving wheels below the nameplates, which were of brass and curved to fit the top of the splashers.

On 31 December 1922, the Great North owned 100 tender engines and 22 tank engines, the whole of which passed to the London & North Eastern Railway, although the oldest types did not long survive the grouping. A complete system of renumbering was introduced by which 6,800 was added to the existing numbers, and green once more became the colour for almost all the tender engines. In 1928, however, the LNER adopted a black livery for all except its most modern and powerful passenger classes.

The complete absence of six-coupled tender engines had always been a remarkable feature of the locomotive stock, but in the interests of economy, all locomotives were designed to undertake mixed traffic duties. This policy was also partly responsible for the

[1] The North British Locomotive Co. was formed in 1903 by the amalgamation of Neilson Reid & Co., Sharp Stewart & Co., and Dübs & Co.

small number of tank engines, although the length of some of the branches restricted their use.

The rolling stock required for the opening of the railway to Huntly was built by Brown, Marshall & Co., of Birmingham, to designs approved by D. K. Clark. As was the case with the locomotives, deliveries fell behind schedule, and little more than half the passenger coaches had arrived when public services were begun in September 1854. Whether it had been intended to provide any second class coaches is not clear. If so, this part of the order was cancelled, as none ever appeared.

In the goods department, the position was even worse. Half the open and closed wagons were still undelivered; of the 60 cattle trucks ordered, only one had arrived; and there were no horseboxes or special wagons for sheep. The resulting loss of traffic was sufficiently serious to call for mention at the meeting of the shareholders held in November. By that time, however, the makers had made good the deficiencies, after a sharply-worded complaint from the company had elicited the naïve reply : 'We did not expect you to open the line so soon. Our experience has been that there is a delay of at least two months between the proposed and actual dates of opening' (!)

The passenger coaches ran on four wheels, and were 21 ft 9 in. long over the buffers, and weighed 9 tons. They were equipped with Newall's chain brake, and wood-covered spring buffers. A seat fitted with a hand rail and a footboard was provided for the guard on the roof. Contrary to subsequent practice, the doors were hung with the hinges on the right and the handles on the left. The external finish was dark brown, with yellow lining and lettering. With modifications from time to time, this remained the standard livery on the Great North for more than 40 years.

The first class coaches had upholstered seats and arm rests, and were divided into three compartments, each seating six passengers. Two oil lamps, hung from the roof in recesses in the partitions between the compartments, provided illumination at night. The third class coaches accommodated 40 passengers, and were divided into four compartments by one full-height, and two quarter-height partitions. The seats were plain wooden benches, entirely devoid of upholstery, and a single oil lamp in the centre of the roof was the only illumination.

During the next 12 years, the growth of the system called for a large number of additional coaches, most of which were built by outside contractors. They were generally similar to those already in use, save that the guard's seat on the roof, and the outside luggage rails in the case of some of the mail and guard's vans, soon disappeared. Towards the end of this period, a few somewhat larger vehicles, running on six wheels, appeared, although they did not become at all common until several years later. The standard of comfort afforded to passengers showed practically no improvement until after Manson had taken charge of the locomotive and carriage departments in 1883.

By this time, the Board of Trade was strongly urging the provision of continuous automatic brakes on passenger trains throughout the country. On the Great North, a number of trains were equipped with the Westinghouse brake, and so satisfactory were the results that it was adopted as standard in 1891. This decision brought the Great North into line with its southern neighbours, the Caledonian and North British Railways. On the other hand, the adoption of the automatic vacuum brake on the Highland Railway necessitated the provision of dual-fitted rolling stock for the through services between Aberdeen and Inverness.

The first corridor coaches were designed by Pickersgill, and built in 1896. They were 36 ft long, and ran on six wheels. They were not vestibuled, and the end compartments ran the full width of the coaches. The first class coaches had four compartments, and the third class and composite coaches five. Lavatories were provided for both classes. These coaches were the first on the Great North to be lighted by electricity. Stone's system, with a separate generator and accumulators for each coach, was adopted. They were also remarkable as the first corridor coaches in Scotland, other than those used on the through Anglo-Scottish services.

A new style of painting was introduced at this time. The lower parts of the coaches were finished in purple lake, and the upper panels in cream, with gold lining and lettering. These colours remained standard until the grouping.

Eight-wheel bogie corridor coaches appeared on the main-line services in 1898. They were 48 ft long, and weighed 25 tons. Provision was made for vestibule connections, although by no means all of them were so equipped at the time of their construction. Some years later, the final development of this design included small lights above the windows, and higher elliptical roofs. In the early years of the twentieth century, chain communication between the passengers and the guard, and steam heating were introduced.

For secondary services, similar, but shorter, non-corridor coaches were adopted. The earlier types ran on six wheels, but subsequently eight-wheel bogies were used.

The early bogie coaches were followed by a saloon which included royalty among its passengers. It ran on eight wheels, and was 48 ft long, and was distinguished by its clerestory roof. Electric light and steam heating were installed. The interior was divided into two saloons, a first class compartment, and a small compartment for an attendant. The saloon in the centre of the coach could be converted for night use. Refreshments could be prepared on a small stove in the attendant's compartment.

The goods rolling stock included a number of fish trucks fitted with continuous brakes, which could either be formed into separate special trains, or attached to passenger trains.

On 31 December 1922, the Great North owned 766 coaching vehicles, 3,603 goods wagons, and 124 service vehicles. For the most part, this stock continued to work in northern Scotland, and was not widely dispersed. The distinctive colours of the coaching stock gave place to the varnished teak adopted as standard for the London & North Eastern Railway.

CHAPTER 14

Under LNER Aegis

AFTER THE GROUPING

On the formation of the LNER, a board of directors was established to guide the new company in its development. Twenty-six directors were nominated from the constituent companies, in numbers which reflected approximately the size and importance of each company. As the smallest member of the group, the Great North of Scotland Railway provided only one director, Alexander Duffus. The chairman of the new board was William Whitelaw, a Scottish landowner who had been chairman of first the Highland Railway then later the North British Railway. From the outset the board adopted a relatively devolved form of management based on three principal areas—Southern, North-Eastern and Scottish—with a chief general manager in overall charge. The Scottish Area was sub-divided into a Southern Scottish (ex-NBR) and a Northern Scottish (ex-GNSR) Area, although a general manager (Scotland) was appointed to oversee the two divisions. Ralph (later Sir Ralph) Lewis Wedgwood, who had been the North Eastern Railway's general manager, became LNER chief general manager while the post of general manager (Scotland) was filled by James Calder, former general manager of the NBR. George Davidson, the last general manager and solicitor of the GNSR, went to Edinburgh to become legal adviser (Scotland) for the LNER.

In the North-East of Scotland, the Grouping was followed at first by innovations rather than changes. The summer of 1923 saw the introduction of a sleeping car between London (King's Cross) and Lossiemouth. From Aberdeen, the car was attached to a new seasonal express for Inverness, leaving at 7.45 a.m. and running non-stop to Huntly in 58 m. Elgin was reached, via Craigellachie, at 9.56 a.m. and Lossiemouth at 10.20 a.m. The then recently-introduced breakfast car was transferred to this train, but reverted to the 8.05 a.m. from Aberdeen at the end of the summer. A second bogie corridor composite, restaurant car of North Eastern Railway origin was transferred from the Southern Scottish Area in December 1923 to operate on the Aberdeen and Inverness route; later both cars were used also on excursion services.

The sleeping car returned from Lossiemouth at 4.05 p.m., and leaving Elgin at 4.30 p.m., reached Aberdeen at 7.04 p.m. to connect with the night train to London. This through working of 610 miles was exceeded on the British railway system only by the train from Elgin to Penzance in 1984. It continued as a regular feature of the summer timetables until the beginning of World War II in September 1939.

Another facility for holiday-makers in the summer of 1923 was a through coach on Fridays from Edinburgh (Waverley) to Cruden Bay. North of Aberdeen, the coach was attached to the late afternoon fast train to the Buchan line, and a quick connection for Cruden Bay was provided at Ellon. The return working on Monday mornings was not advertised as a through-coach service. This experiment was not repeated, although the accelerated service from Aberdeen to Cruden Bay lasted for one more summer. Traffic on the branch had always been disappointing, and the hotel at Cruden Bay had never been justified. Shortly before the Grouping, an attempt by local residents to revive the scheme for extending the railway from Boddam to Peterhead had failed to secure support.

Halts to serve distilleries were opened on the main line between Auchindachy and Drummuir in 1924 at Towiemore, and on Speyside between Aberlour and Carron in 1933 at Dailuaine; the former was not advertised publicly until 1937, however. These were the only additions made by the LNER to the provision of stations on the former Great North. Two private stations had existed on the GNSR for many years and continued into LNER days; these were Philorth outside Fraserburgh, on the Buchan section, and Knockando House (up to 1905 the name was just Knockando) on the Strathspey section. Philorth first appeared in 'Bradshaw' in 1924 and two years later became a public stopping-place, on request. Knockando House platform remained private and was not advertised to the public.

SUNDAY SERVICES

Apart from the subsidised services on the Deeside line, run during the visits of the Royal Family to Balmoral, Sunday trains had been unknown on the Great North since the mail trains were withdrawn in 1864. The LNER broke with this tradition by introducing long-distance trains during the summer, and Aberdeen suburban services throughout the year. By 1928, there were two Sunday trains in each direction, between Aberdeen and Elgin, calling at principal stations via the coast. Subsequently, one of the trains was altered to run to and from Inverness, via Keith, and the other was extended from Elgin to Lossiemouth.

A through Sunday service from Aberdeen to Strathspey, begun in the summer of 1929, was extended three years later over the former Highland Railway from Boat of Garten to Kingussie, but this experiment lasted only for two seasons. The Strathspey train had been withdrawn by 1936, but survived as a Saturday excursion. Refreshment cars were run in all these long-distance trains, and day excursion tickets were issued on a generous basis.

There was also a Sunday service to Ballater, and by 1938, to Macduff. The Deeside line had a few additional Sunday trains to and from Banchory, which ran non-stop between Aberdeen and Culter. All the Sunday services, and the Strathspey Saturday train, were withdrawn at the start of World War II and were never restored.

In the Aberdeen suburban area, Sunday services at hourly intervals throughout the afternoon and evening were introduced in June 1928, to Dyce, on the main line, and to Culter, on the Deeside line. The trains were continued through the winter, and in the summer of 1929 the services to Culter were increased to half-hourly frequency by a Sentinel-Cammell steam railcar. However, by the autumn of 1930 bus competition had become so serious that all the Sunday suburban trains were withdrawn. The services on the main line were never restored; but after an interval of nearly four years, in June 1934, an hourly afternoon and evening service was resumed between Aberdeen and Culter. These trains ran during the summer only and were finally withdrawn in September 1936. A few months later, the weekday suburban services also had succumbed to bus competition.

ROAD SERVICES AND COMPETITION

The bus and lorry services inherited from the Great North were continued by the LNER virtually without change at first. Their financial state was scrutinised carefully by the new owners, since despite their high scale of charges, these railway-owned services had never yielded more than a small profit. Most of the vehicles were equipped with solid tyres and the buses mostly seated eighteen passengers; thus they were restricted in operation to a maximum legal speed of 12 m.p.h. When, in the early '20s, legislative restrictions were eased to allow pneumatic-tyred buses, seating at most fourteen persons, to operate at up to 20 m.p.h., the LNER (NSA) vehicles became distinctly disadvantaged. Not until 1925 were any new buses purchased to redress this balance. Then, only three Karrier machines, meeting the up-dated specification, were provided.

On 1 June 1925 the Aberdeen, Dunecht and Cluny service was extended a short distance to Millbank, but it reverted to the original terminus some months later, before it ceased altogether at the end of the year. The summer-only operations of buses between Balindalloch and Tomintoul, and of charabancs between Ballater and Strathdon ceased, as usual, at the end of the tourist season, but were never restarted. Also terminated during the year were the lorry services on the Tomintoul and the Strathdon routes.

Decline continued in 1926 when no fewer than thirteen passenger road-motors were withdrawn, including two charabancs and the only two double-decked buses the GNSR, and the LNER (NSA), ever had.

However, four new Thornycroft twenty-seater buses, along with two lorries of the same make, were introduced. The former were placed on the Ballater and Braemar service while the latter went to Huntly on 15 November to inaugurate a goods service between there and Aberchirder. Preceding that date, the remaining summer-only bus service, between Strathdon and Cockbridge, ceased for the season, also never to restart again.

Throughout this time, competitive services were developing quite extensively and not always under conditions that were economic. The railway was not alone in sustaining loss of business; electric street tramways suffered also from the predatory actions of unregulated bus competitors. On 9 June 1927, the Aberdeen Suburban Tramways Co. ceased to operate its separate Mannofield to Bieldside and Woodside to Bankhead lines. Since 1904 these had been worked virtually as extensions of the connecting Aberdeen Corporation Tramways, and as such had competed strongly with the Culter and Dyce suburban train services respectively. However, the end of these tramway services did not lessen competitive pressures on the LNER, because in place of the trams buses appeared in the name of the Aberdeen Suburban Transport Co.—as the company retitled itself.

Further road-motor retrenchment resulted in 1927 when the Fraserburgh, Rosehearty and New Aberdour service was handed over to a local operator on 10 July. During the year, six more buses were withdrawn, including one of the Karrier vehicles which had been delivered only two years earlier. To offset some of these losses, three more Thornycrofts, two buses and a lorry, were acquired. Later in the year, on 1 October, prospects appeared to brighten when green and cream liveried LNER buses began to work between Aberdeen and Inverurie, via Blackburn and Kintore. More encouraging still was the appearance in the next year of another four new Thornycroft buses, of which two were 32-seaters. On 1 June 1928 further advances were made, when the Huntly and Aberchirder bus route was extended to Banff, via Alvah. However, the preceding month had seen the demise of the Huntly-based lorry service, started only some eighteen months earlier.

On 3 August 1928, the LNER (together with the other British mainline railway companies) obtained comprehensive, statutory powers to provide and work road services. The Railways (Road Transport) Acts opened the way to further expansion in, among other places, the Northern Scottish Area of the LNER and in 1929 no fewer than twenty-four new buses were added to the railway's fleet in North-East Scotland. From 8 April, the Alford and Strathdon service commenced operation to and from Aberdeen, in conjunction with the Aberdeen and Inverurie service. This latter was strengthened the next month when the service and six vehicles belonging to J. S. Mitchell of Inverurie were purchased by the LNER and integrated, from 15 May, into the railway's road operations. Just a month later, a completely new set of bus services was inaugurated from 17 June, along the Moray Firth coast between Elgin and Macduff, an area where particularly strong competition from private buses had seriously depleted railway revenues. Additional short workings were provided between Portgordon and Cullen, but from the outset these operations along the coast incurred losses, unlike the Aberdeen-based services.

Finally, from 1 July came the most ambitious development, when LNER buses commenced through road service the length of Deeside, between Aberdeen, Banchory, Ballater and Braemar. Coupled with this, an hourly service was provided on the section between Aberdeen and Banchory. Even more intensive working ensued from 7 October between Aberdeen and Culter, where for almost a decade the suburban trains had been subjected to severe competition from private buses.

THE ROYAL COMMISSION ON TRANSPORT

Even as the tempo of change in North-East transport quickened, influences were at work in the wider context of road and rail interaction in Britain as a whole. Between 1928 and 1931 a Royal

Commission on Transport reviewed the structure and functions of the different modes of conveyance. Three Reports were issued and among the many recommendations made were several for systems which would regulate more closely than hitherto the burgeoning road transport industry. Indeed, regulation became a feature of public policy for transport during the '30s and for nearly fifty years thereafter.

The Road Traffic Act, 1930 ended an existing, relatively loose system for local authorities (counties and municipalities) to license bus operators, and substituted a more comprehensive and rigorous system, for individual licensing of vehicles, of operating staff and of services operated. In use the road-service licensing came to be applied in a discriminatory manner, which tended to favour established operators over new ones, and large organisations over small ones. It was against this background that discussions were opened in early 1929 between the Scottish Motor Traction Co Ltd of Edinburgh and the LMSR and LNER companies jointly. SMT had been founded in 1905 and had grown to become a premier bus operator in Scotland. However, as well as developing its own services directly, in the post-war period it had embarked on indirect involvement in other bus companies by taking shareholdings in them, one such company was W. Alexander and Sons Ltd of Falkirk.

The outcome of the discussions was that the two railway companies were offered the opportunity to acquire jointly a 50% financial stake in a restructured SMT Company which in effect would be the holding company for a substantial group of bus companies, currently in direct competition with the railways. In return, the railways were asked to divest themselves of their bus services in Scotland to their new associates. Day-to-day responsibility for bus operation under the new arrangement would remain in the hands of SMT and its associated companies' managers. The railway companies agreed and on 15 August 1929 the new SMT Co Ltd was established. Meanwhile, SMT had continued to consolidate its position as a holding company by purchasing, from the Balfour Beatty consortium, the Scottish General Omnibus Co Ltd group of bus operators, among which was Scottish General (Northern) Omnibus Co Ltd of Elgin.

From 16 February 1930, the LNER relinquished the Elgin-Macduff services to SG(N)O Co Ltd but did not hand over any vehicles. However, soon thereafter the remaining LNER (NSA) bus operations were transferred to W. Alexander and Sons Ltd such that all direct involvement by the railway ceased after 15 August. The transfer involved four principal sets of services, operated over 312 miles of routes; along with thirty-four buses, four lorries, thirty motormen and twelve conductresses. In addition, several of the outlying garages, which did not constitute an integral part of any railway buildings, were handed over. The nominal separation of the Moray Firth coast services from the other ex-LNER ones did not last long, since SG(N)O Co Ltd was incorporated into W. Alexander and Sons Ltd the following year.

The regulation of road haulage developed more slowly and to a lesser extent than did that for road passenger undertakings. The Royal Commission proposed a generally similar system of control based on the licensing of vehicles but powers of control were less comprehensive, particularly with operators who carried only their own goods or who provided dedicated service for a manufacturer or trader. Since a large part of the haulage industry operated under these exclusive terms, the railway companies found only limited scope to become involved, in the manner of the Scottish arrangement with SMT for passenger transport. Several of the large, ply-for-hire road hauliers, like Pickfords and Carter Paterson, did pass into railway control about this time, however. The Road and Rail Traffic Act, 1933 did establish road-haulage licensing but, more importantly for the railways, it did not provide for any direct regulation of road-haulage charges while still retaining existing statutory restrictions on the railways' ability to offer more competitive rates for carrying goods.

In North-East Scotland, the remaining railway-owned road services for public conveyance of freight continued only a little longer than did those for passengers. On 3 November 1930 the Aberdeen–Newburgh service was withdrawn, to be followed on 30 June 1931 by that of the Aberdeen, Cluny and Midmar route. Thereafter, LNER(NSA) goods road motors operated only for collection and delivery service, as part of primarily railway conveyance of freight.

ECONOMIC DEPRESSION AND RECOVERY

The Wall Street Crash of October 1929 produced world-wide economic repercussions. In Britain these served to accentuate a recession in economic activities which had begun to take effect earlier. In July 1928, the Big Four railway companies has advised the railway unions that labour costs had to be reduced as a matter of urgency since revenues had fallen while costs continued to rise. Cuts in wages, salaries and directors' fees were implemented in August

1930 and remained in effect for several years, with additional cuts applied to the incomes of high earners for a couple of years from May 1931. During this time, the LNER was severely affected by declining revenues, with nearly a 50% reduction in income recorded between 1929 and 1932.

In the Northern Scottish Area, as elsewhere, economy measures were introduced. Several stations were down-graded to the status of unmanned halts; at a larger number of stations the post of station-master was abolished and groups of adjoining stations were placed under the charge of a single station-master, usually for pairs of stations. Various clerical and administrative posts were down-graded, but a proposal to abolish the Area basis of organisation in favour of a District one was opposed by 'Aberdeen interests', backed by the one, locally-based, director on the LNER Board, Alexander Gray. Other measures adopted to try to reduce operating costs included the introduction, at certain times of the day, of long section working between signal-boxes wherever traffic fluctuations allowed minor, intermediate signal-boxes to be switched out of use, although through trains could still operate in safety but without hindrance. Some reductions in rail services were initiated, particularly with Sunday services, but actual closures of lines or stations were kept to a minimum.

First to succumb to the rigours of the times was the Old Meldrum line, with its terminus right outside the town, and a circuitous route (compared with the road) to Inverurie and the main line; the branch lost its passenger service on 2 November 1931. A year later, on 31 October 1932, a similar fate overtook the unsuccessful branch to Boddam. Freight service continued on both these branches, and at Cruden Bay the tramway remained in use to carry coal and stores to the hotel and linen to and from the adjoining laundry. The hotel remained open to the public and to try to encourage custom, the LNER introduced for the summer season of 1933 express carriage road services between Ellon station and the hotel, in connection with certain of the Buchan line trains and between Aberdeen Joint Station and the hotel. From June 1934, however, a Rolls-Royce 7-seater motor car, owned by the LNER, provided a service each summer directly between the hotel and Aberdeen Joint Station, until September 1939.

The changes in ownership of road services did stimulate their development, often to the detriment of the railway serving a mainly rural area, in which short journeys predominated. Passenger traffic declined, particularly at small and inconveniently situated stations.

Moreover, certain bus routes which had been intended to feed the railway were extended, and became its active competitors for passenger revenue. Competition from road transport also seriously affected the goods traffic which was important to the railway; stones from the quarries around Aberdeen which were shipped out from the city's harbour; esparto grass and other raw materials for the Deeside and Donside paper mills, which passed inwards over the quays and, in the past, over the harbour rails. The movement of agricultural produce and supplies in country districts benefited from the convenience and mobility of motor vehicles and to secure a share of this trade the railway encouraged the larger traders to establish rail-head distribution depots at strategic stations around the North-East. In the reverse direction, however, the patterns of livestock transport changed; no longer did the farm-hands have to rise at 3 a.m. to gather cattle or sheep and drive them to the nearest station in time to load and dispatch them by train to market. Once the motor float became commonplace, direct transfer of animals from farm to market was the inevitable consequence, although longer journeys with livestock or with dead meat continued to involve rail. Even fish traffic, which had always been of major importance to the railway, now attracted road competitors. At Peterhead, the greater part of the extension from the goods station to the harbour had been closed by 1938 and the remainder of the line fell into disuse during World War II. The removal of the track was completed after the railways had been nationalised.

STAFF CHANGES

By the early 1930s, several links with the pre-Grouping period had been broken by changes among the directors and officers of the LNER. Alexander Duffus, the only director of the Great North to join the board of the new company, survived for little more than a year, and died in March 1924. The first of the officers to go were Simon Willox, the goods manager, who resigned at the end of April 1923, and James Parker, the engineer, who retired two years later. Both had remained in Aberdeen. From 1 May 1923 the officers of super-intendent of the line and of goods manager were combined under the charge of William Johnston, who became traffic superintendent, Northern Scottish Area, LNER based at Aberdeen. However, several of the former headquarters' departments were transferred soon there-after to Edinburgh, among them being the audit office and the general accounts office.

FREIGHT TRAINS

(59) *J36 no 65251 trundles a Deeside line freight through Cutler in the early 1960s. A dozen of this class were transferred to the Great North lines in BR days for freight work.*

(60) *LMS 2P 4-4-0 40622 shunting at Buckie in 1960. Nine of this class were used on the Great North, this example being transferred there in March 1948.*

DIESEL-HAULED FREIGHT

(61)   Barclay 204hp diesel mechanical loco D2420, shunting at Lethenty on the Oldmeldrum branch. Note the wagon turntable in the foreground, leading to the mills.

(62)   Fraserburgh in 1969, after the withdrawal of the passenger service. D6123 shunts the daily freight. This class, built by the North British Locomotive Company, were not a success despite being re-engined early in their lives.

DIESEL MULTIPLE UNITS

(63)   One of the Swindon-built 3 car cross-country sets at Dyce on an up train
        in 1968. The Buchan line platforms are to the right.

(64)   Cravens twin unit at Spey Bay on an up train in the mid 1960s. The loop
        here was taken out before the line closed in 1968.

GREAT NORTH REMAINS

(65)   Knockando station converted into a visitor centre for the adjacent Tamdhu distillery. The trackbed now forms part of the Speyside Way.

(66)   The Portsoy Harbour branch in 1988, converted into a footpath. This line ceased to be used about 1888.

George Davidson, the last general manager of the old company, died suddenly in summer of 1928; and Thomas Macintosh, the secretary, and William Johnston, the passenger superintendent, retired in 1932. Davidson had been successively solicitor for the LNER in Scotland and, in 1924, general manager of the North-Eastern Area, at York. Macintosh had been appointed rating agent for the new company in Scotland, with headquarters in Edinburgh; but Johnston had continued in post at Aberdeen. Shortly before he retired in September 1932, Johnston had completed fifty-two years of railway service. He was succeeded by J. G. Singer, who had been his chief assistant since the Grouping. Thomas Heywood, the last locomotive superintendent for the Great North, was appointed mechanical engineer and locomotive running superintendent, LNER (NSA), but was promoted in 1924 to district mechanical engineer at Gorton, where he remained for three years. In 1927 he returned to Scotland to take up the appointment of mechanical engineer for the LNER, based in Glasgow, a position which he held until he retired in 1942; the year after the death of his superior, Sir Nigel Gresley.

LOCOMOTIVE CHANGES

Even before Heywood returned from England, the LNER was faced with motive-power problems, not least on the lines of his old company. Of the hundred 4—4—0 tender engines which came to the LNER from the Great North, nineteen were between forty-five and fifty-seven years old and twenty-two others had seen at least thirty-five years' service. With four exceptions, the twenty-two tank engines also were far from new. The veterans began to pass to the scrap heap soon after the Grouping; twenty-seven in all during the period 1924 to 1928. Axle weight restrictions, associated with the ex-GNSR track and bridges, imposed limitations on the choice of replacements from the locomotive stock of other constituents of the LNER. To work long or heavy trains, the old company had resorted to double-heading with its general purpose 4—4—0 locomotives. However, the steady post-war rise in fuel and manpower costs rendered this an increasingly expensive solution. Moreover, the weight of trains was increasing, as modern corridor stock replaced older coaches, and larger wagons were used in place of the relatively low capacity vehicles used by the Great North.

In the spring of 1923, an ex-North British Railway 0—6—0 goods engine arrived on trial in the NSA and became the first six-coupled tender locomotive to work on regular service on the former GNSR system. The experiment was short-lived, as was another soon after, with a similar type of SSA engine. The problem of replacement power remained, but a partial solution was found in 1925 when five ex-NBR 4—4—0 tender engines (LNER Class D31) were transferred north following the arrival in the SSA of several locomotives of Great Northern Railway origin. Eight more D31s arrived in 1926 and a further four between 1927 and 1929. Later, an additional nine reached North-East Scotland during and after the war, although not all of those transferred necessarily remained in the north.

More far-reaching change was heralded in 1926, when a 4—6—0 tender engine, of a design by Samuel Holden for the former Great Eastern Railway, visited the NSA to participate in loading tests on bridges, particularly the one over the Spey at Craigellachie. This LNER Class B12 type from East Anglia offered the prospect of increased tractive effort in association with suitably low axle weight, and a short, rigid wheelbase for both the engine and the tender a combination likely to suit the sharp curves and light track bed on such lines as the Glen road between Keith and Elgin. Prospect it was to remain for another three years until new locomotives suited to the ex-GER lines could be delivered, and thus release some B12s to the NSA.

The first four 'Hikers', as the Aberdeen men were to come to call them, arrived at Kittybrewster shed in 1931, to be followed by one the next year and six in 1933. Another came north in 1937, while no fewer than eight were transferred during 1939. During and after the war, five more of the type were allocated to the Aberdeen District (as the former Great North had then become), although some of the engines in the overall group did return south, at different times. The majority of these fine machines remained in North-East Scotland to spend the rest of their working lives as the backbone of the area's motive power for nearly thirty years. Concurrently with their introduction to the NSA, a modern mechanical coaling plant was erected at Kittybrewster and brought into use in 1932. It stood as a landmark until the end of steam traction and the closure of the depot in 1961.

Tank engines presented less of a problem on the NSA lines than had tender ones, although in the mid '30s six former North Eastern Railway six-coupled locomotives of LNER Class J72 were transferred in to assist with yard shunting. A particular problem existed, however, with the unfenced St Combs light railway, where even the Great North's 4—4—0 tender engines had been prohibited from regular use. The line had been the preserve of cowcatcher-fitted ex-

GNSR 0—6—0 tank engines, but in 1926 and 1927 two small Drummond 4—4—0 tanks of NBR origin (LNER Class D51) were assigned to the service. Another two of the type went to Kitty-brewster in 1930 and 1932, but all four had been withdrawn by mid 1933. As had happened earlier in the Edinburgh area, the replace-ments for these diminutive tanks were obtained from the ranks of former GER 2—4—2 tank engines (LNER Class F4). Three of the latter came to the NSA in 1933; a fourth did not arrive until just after Nationalisation. Two of the group were fitted with push-pull opeat-ing gear in 1941, and in conjunction with an appropriate set of carri-ages, provided auto-train working of the light railway for some three years. One F4 was withdrawn in 1943 but the others survived at least eight years longer.

ROLLING STOCK CHANGES

With coaching stock, too, the LNER obtained from the Great North quite a mixture of vehicles. These ranged in age and structure from some fine, pre-war and post-war bogie coaches of modern design and equipment, to antiquated four-wheelers, long overdue for with-drawal. The latter did prove to have one useful contribution to make, however; two Firsts, four Thirds and one Third Brake, all over forty-five years old, were restored at Inverurie works along with locomotive 45A, to provide a genuine vintage train, in GNSR livery, which took part in the Railway Centenary parade between Stockton and Darlington in early July 1925. None of these exhibits survived thereafter for preservation.

The immediate problem after the Grouping was to find more up-to-date stock with which to replace as many as possible of the old four-wheelers, as soon as possible. In 1924–25 transfers of ex-NER carriages, fifteen six-wheelers and six bogie vehicles, afforded some relief. Further stock appeared from the south between 1926 and 1929, but from the Great Eastern section, which provided fifty six-wheeled coaches, mostly of Third Class compartment type, for introduction on the Aberdeen suburban services. Some seven years later, the North-Eastern Area again became a source for transferred coaches, when forty compartment vehicles of bogie type were re-allocated between 1936 and 1938. By that time, the first of the more modern, Gresley-designed, bow-ended bogie corridor stock had been placed in primary service on the former Great North, and the ex-NER coaches appeared more usually on secondary trains.

With wagons, the GNSR had had a preponderance of small capacity (mostly 8 tons) open box wagons in its fleet, with grease-type axleboxes and hand-brakes which bore on only one of the two pairs of wheels in the running-gear set. A group of some 200 wagons for fish traffic did have fittings which allowed running in passenger train formations, as did a number of express cattle trucks. These apart, the average ex-GNSR wagon was outmoded, and seldom ventured far outside its own lines, either before or after the Grouping. The LNER pursued a programme for scrapping NSA stock, from about 1924 to the mid '30s, by which time most of the elderly vehicles had been eliminated. Wagons from the other constituent companies, especially the NBR, served as replacements within an overall policy of retaining only those with capacity of 10 tons or more. During the '30s, containers became a popular means of conveyance for certain commodities, particularly furniture and meat; small, wooden containers were used in association with four-wheeled flat wagons, designed specially for such use. A development of this concept was the road-rail conveyance of milk in road-trailer tanks which traversed country districts to collect milk from farms but were transferred to rail flat-wagons for the trunk journey to a major dairy or creamery. Also introduced were vans for the carriage of fish from North-East ports to the principal markets in southern Scotland and in England. Just before Nationalisation, Aberdeen fish merchants started to use solid carbon dioxide as a coolant in the fish vans, to improve the quality of the fish during its delivery journey.

THROUGH WAR TO NATIONALISATION

From about 1933 onwards, hopes began to rise in Britain that the 'Depression' years were passing and that recovery of the country's economy would be achieved. Wage restrictions were relaxed gradually, business activity increased, and as a measure of the better times to be enjoyed, excursion traffic showed improved demand. In 1933 the first major, all-rail 'land cruise' in Britain departed from King's Cross, London, on the evening of Friday 16 June. A 15-coach train, conveying only sixty passengers, steamed north on a circular tour which reached Aberdeen and Royal Deeside, as its northern-most destinations, the West Highlands, the Borders and northern England. Named the *Northern Belle*, the train was a hotel on wheels, at a fare of £20 per person for the long weekend's varied programme. That year three of these very special excursions were operated and similar land cruises were offered each summer thereafter until war put an end to them after 1939.

Further evidence of rising public confidence encouraged the LNER to inaugurate a brief era of fast trains on the East Coast main line, in competition with the LMSR on the West Coast route; shades of the 'Railway Races' of some forty years earlier, although Edinburgh and Glasgow were now the focal destinations instead of Aberdeen. Nevertheless, improved timings over both companies' lines to and from the 'Granite City' were accompanied also by tightening of the principal schedules of the LNER (NSA). Much publicity was garnered from the revived rivalry, particularly between the LNER 'Coronation' train and the LMSR 'Coronation Scot', with interest in rail travel heightened, at least in the context of main-line expresses.

In the Aberdeen district, however, the suburban services had been worked at a loss for a considerable time, mostly as a result of continuing bus competition. In March 1936 a local bus strike afforded some temporary relief but on 5 April 1937 the end came; the withdrawal of both the Dyce and the Culter trains. Between Aberdeen and Dyce all the intermediate stations were closed, except for Kittybrewster and Bucksburn, while on the Deeside line only Cults remained open between Aberdeen and Culter. Many local people expressed regret at the demise of the 'subby' trains, but from the LNER standpoint there was a share to be had still from the profit the bus operations (which it had started) were earning!

In the sphere of goods transport, the railways remained aggrieved that road haulage charges had not been subjected to regulation after the 1933 Road and Rail Traffic Act took effect, whereas railway charges continued to be subject to control. In 1938, the 'Big Four' promoted a 'Square Deal Campaign' which was overtaken by events before it could have much real impact. In Europe, Germany once again was pursuing expansionist policies which threatened to induce full-scale and widespread hostilities. In September 1938 the Government appointed a Railway Executive Committee as its advisory body pending any actual start to a war involving Britain. Sir Ralph Wedgwood, LNER chief general manager, was made chairman and retained the post after he retired from the LNER in the following year. By the summer of 1939, war appeared imminent such that on 1 September the REC was authorised to change to become an executive organisation, on behalf of the Minister of Transport, to run the railways in the 'national interest'.

Rather hastily at first, train services were curtailed and schedules eased. By 2 October, however, proper 'Emergency Time Tables' were issued by the railways, and in the absence of attacks on Britain by the enemy, some easing of restrictions followed from 4 December onwards. As part of the efforts to harness the railway network to the needs of war, a Scottish Central Control was established in Edinburgh, with overall authority to determine the distribution and availability of locomotives, carriages and wagons on the LMSR and LNER lines in Scotland. Local versions of this Control were established progressively, with the Aberdeen district brought into the scheme by 1943.

Much as had happened during World War I, the railways had to shoulder the load which road transport and coastal shipping were obliged to relinquish. The consequent demands on motive power, men and rolling stock proved once again to be a heavy burden. Although distanced from many of the front-line problems, especially heavy bombing, the former Great North lines still played a part in the general war effort. Canadian forestry teams arrived on Deeside, Donside and Speyside to set up lumber camps and sawmills. Men and supplies came in by rail and the finished wood went out the same way. The Grampian highlands offered good training areas for troops and special trains for men and equipment met their transport needs. Airfields were established at several locations around the North-East coast, and again it was the railway which handled the movements of personnel and supplies.

The only wartime casualty among the lines north of Aberdeen was the tramway to the hotel at Cruden Bay, on which all traffic ceased in March 1941. The railway from Ellon to Boddam remained open for goods until shortly after the end of the war, but was closed completely on 7 November 1945, although much of the track was not lifted until early 1951. The Cruden Bay Hotel had been requisitioned for use as an army hospital on the outbreak of war, but had been handed back to the railway company by the autumn of 1945. The premises were then advertised for sale, but no definite offers were received. Eventually, it was decided that the heavy cost of maintaining the hotel was not justified, and in July 1947 it was sold to a demolition contractor. The work of clearing the site was not completed until 1952.

In Aberdeen, the Station Hotel was taken over by the Admiralty in July 1940, and used as an administrative centre until January 1946. It was reopened as an hotel in March 1950, after undergoing extensive modernisation. The Palace Hotel was not requisitioned but on 30 October 1941 was completely destroyed in a fire in which six chambermaids lost their lives. The ruins lay derelict until after the war had ended, but in September 1945 the Aberdeen Town Council approved plans for the rebuilding of the hotel. This work was never undertaken, and the site was sold eventually for a department store.

Recovery after the war had ended was slow, and was far from complete when the railways were nationalised on 1 January 1948. The railways in Scotland were separated from the English lines administratively, and were placed in the Scottish Region of the new British Railways. The route mileage of the region was rather more than 3,700, to which the surviving lines of the Great North contributed 318 miles formerly owned by the old company, and 3½ miles over which it had had running powers.

CHAPTER 15

British Railways and Retrenchment

THE FIRST YEARS

Nationalisation did not see great changes: instead there was some tinkering with the time-tables such as cutting out some stops and some trains, but the service continued much as before.

Attempts to restore pre-war through coach facilities in north-east Scotland after the railways were nationalised did not meet with lasting success. The service between Edinburgh and Elgin, which had run in summer only after 1931, was reinstated on a similar basis in 1949, but survived only until 1952. Even shorter was the life of a through coach for Elgin in the principal night train between London and Aberdeen, in place of the sleeping car of pre-war years. This coach, which ran throughout the year, and not in the summer only, was introduced in September 1957, and was withdrawn two years later.

On the other hand, a through coach on summer Saturdays between Glasgow (Buchanan Street) and Elgin, *via* the coast, lasted from 1949 to 1962. This service, which included a through coach between Glasgow and Keith Town, attached and detached at Cairnie Junction, recalled the all-the-year-round through working by the Great North and the Caledonian which had not survived World War I.

One of the most serious difficulties that beset the railways after the end of the second world war was a prolonged shortage of coal, and early in 1951 passenger services had to be reduced on many lines. In north-east Scotland, these economies resulted in an interval of more than six hours between the departure from Aberdeen of the trains for Elgin connecting with the principal night service from London and with the mid-morning train from Edinburgh. This gap, extending through the morning into the early afternoon, persisted until the summer of 1959, and another two years elapsed before the mid-morning service from Aberdeen to Elgin was again maintained throughout the year.

DIESEL REPLACES STEAM

By the time the services between Aberdeen and Elgin had been restored, diesel traction had almost completely replaced steam on the lines north of Aberdeen. An augmented service between Aberdeen and Ballater was provided from 21 April 1958 by a two-coach battery-electric railcar. The North of Scotland Hydro-Electric Board agreed to supply current at a reduced rate from charging equipment at the terminal stations. The changeover to diesel began with the Deeside steam services from the following 7 July. A further improvement on the line was the opening of a halt at Dee Street, Banchory in February 1961.

Steam trains on the Strathspey line were replaced by a diesel railbus in the autumn of 1958. To widen the scope of the services, certain journeys were extended from Boat of Garten to make connection with the main Highland line at Aviemore, and (by reversing at Craigellachie) to Elgin.

To enable the railbus to serve some of the rather isolated communities at whisky distilleries and farms in Speyside, halts were opened in the summer of 1959 at Imperial Cottages, and Gilbey's Cottages (between Carron and Knockando), at Dalvey Farm (between Advie and Cromdale), and at Ballifurth Farm (between Grantown and Nethy Bridge).

In June 1959, multiple-unit diesel trains took over all the passenger services between Aberdeen and Peterhead and Fraserburgh, and on the St Combs branch. Cross-country type diesel multiple units, with miniature buffets, were introduced in July 1960 for an accelerated service between Aberdeen and Inverness. West of Keith, these trains used the former Highland Railway route, and were allowed 2½ hours for the 108-mile journey, with four intermediate stops. In the summer of 1961, the service was increased from two to four in each direction.

The Great North contributed forty-four locomotives to British Railways, but withdrawal proceeded rapidly after nationalisation. All the same, it is clear that the surviving D40s were worked appreciably harder late in life than any other pre-grouping engines on the former LNER in Scotland. Newcomers to the area included North British 'Glen' class 4—4—0s, LMSR Midland-type 4—4—0s, LNER class 'B1' 4—6—0s, and British Railways 2—6—0s, and 2—6—4 tank engines. From 1959, diesel locomotives appeared in increasing numbers, and by the summer of 1961 steam traction had been almost superseded, except on the branch from Tillynaught to Banff. Timetable alterations during this change-over period included the closure on 7 March 1960 of the short loop from Grange to Grange North Junction.

The Manning Wardle tank engines continued to work on the Aberdeen harbour lines, and Nos. 68190 and 68192 (GNSR Nos. 43 and 30 respectively), which were withdrawn in April 1960, were the last two locomotives of the Great North to remain in service.

In 1958 there was a move towards using preserved locomotives for special trains. Apart from the Manning Wardle tank engines, the only locomotive of the old company then surviving was one of Heywood's 4—4—0s, No. 62277, *Gordon Highlander* (originally No. 49). The engine was restored at Inverurie Works and displayed at an open day in June 1958. Prior to its withdrawal that month it was used on shunting duties at the Works.

Although considerable care was bestowed on the restoration, the locomotive appeared in the green livery abandoned during the latter part of the first world war, which had never been used for engines built as late as 1920. However, it was considered that this anachronism was justified, because green, rather than black, was the colour most representative of Great North locomotives. After withdrawal, *Gordon Highlander* was replaced in store until its first excursion on 13 June 1959 from Glasgow to Dumfries. It hauled special trains for railway enthusiasts until 1965, when it was placed in the Glasgow Museum of Transport.

The continued increase in operating costs, and the decline in local traffic after the end of the second world war, resulted in the closure to passengers of the Alford branch on 2 January 1950, and of the Macduff branch on 1 October 1951. The northern end of the latter line, the 11¾ miles from Turriff to Macduff, was closed completely nearly ten years later, on 1 August 1961, and the track was dismantled soon afterwards. Several individual stations on other lines also became unprofitable and had to be closed, in some cases to all types of traffic. On the Deeside line, the ten miles from Ferryhill Junction, Aberdeen, to Park were reduced to single track in December 1951.

THE BEECHING REPORT

In March 1963 'The Reshaping of British Railways' (the so-called Beeching Report) was published, which proposed drastic action. The withdrawal of passenger services and closure of stations received most publicity, and other aspects of the report, such as improved

InterCity passenger services, block freight trains and the introduction of freightliner services tended to be overlooked.

On the former Great North, the plan was to close all the lines and stations except the main line between Aberdeen and Keith and the stations at Huntly and Keith Junction. There would be a limited service of trains between Aberdeen and Inverness: most of these closures were carried out in the following seven years. Thus the system was reduced to what it was in 1856, but without most of the intermediate stations and the Lossiemouth and Banchory lines.

The Transport Act of 1962 laid down the procedures for the closure of passenger stations and the withdrawal of passenger services. The Transport Users' Consultative Committee (TUCC) was required to hold an inquiry, whenever an objection to a proposed closure was lodged, during the appropriate time given in the legal notice. At these inquiries the committee considered possible hardships which might be caused. It was not allowed to discuss the financial aspects, and the savings which were claimed from the closures were thought by many to be questionable. The committee then reported to the Minister of Transport who could approve with or without conditions or, very rarely, refuse approval for the closure. On the Great North the only closures refused were Inverurie and Insch stations. The Minister's usual conditions which were often applied were that appropriate bus services had to be provided; these had to be licensed by the Traffic Commissioners, a separate procedure in which the TUCC and the Minister had no official part, although an appeal could be made to the Minister. In recent years there has been a drastic change in these services and very few still survive in the form originally envisaged.

The first passenger service to be withdrawn under Beeching was the Lossiemouth branch as from 6 April 1964, to be followed by the Banff branch on 6 July. In the following year the St Combs branch closed on 3 May and passenger services were withdrawn on the same day between Maud and Peterhead, followed by Dyce-Fraserburgh on 4 October. The Speyside service between Boat of Garten and Craigellachie was withdrawn two weeks later, there having been a delay in arranging substitute bus services. In 1966 the Deeside service, after much protestation and attempts to save it, ceased on 28 February. On the main line the Inverurie local service was withdrawn on 7 December 1964 with the closure of the stations at Pitmedden, Kinaldie and Kintore, although two trains continued to run daily between Aberdeen and Inverurie, mainly for the employees at the Locomotive Works.

During this period many of the smaller intermediate stations were unstaffed and the passengers bought their tickets on the train. Many sidings were also unstaffed and only full wagon loads were handled there.

There was a lull before the last passenger withdrawals—the main line services between Aberdeen and Elgin via the Coast and Craigellachie. On 6 May 1968 all services on these two lines were withdrawn except for a goods service between Keith and Rothes. In approving the closure the Minister of Transport included the condition 'to retain for the time being the formation of the lines'. However, latterly sections have been sold off or included in road improvement schemes.

In 1969 there was a passenger service between Aberdeen and Inverness of five trains in each direction usually worked by diesel multiple units, together with two trains between Aberdeen and Elgin and an early morning train to and from Inverurie; there was also an early morning train from Elgin to Inverness which gave a connection into the 08.20 from Inverness to Edinburgh. This train was the former 05.00 from Aberdeen, running as a parcels train between Aberdeen and Elgin. In 1971 the mid-afternoon Aberdeen to Elgin train was extended to Inverness and gave a later return at 19.40 from Inverness. The mid-morning train (09.43 hours from Aberdeen) continued to terminate at Elgin until 1978, when it was also extended to Inverness. This produced a service of seven trains each way between Aberdeen and Inverness on weekdays. Thus, despite the general retrenchment, patrons of the remaining Great North stations were offered a more frequent and faster service to Aberdeen and Inverness than ever before.

GOODS TRAFFIC

The changes in the goods traffic were not so obvious. The typical goods train calling at wayside stations picking up and setting down the odd wagon of timber, coal or general merchandise was no longer economic as British Railways sought to establish regular flows of traffic between a few points. Traffic was discontinued from all livestock depots except Kittybrewster at the end of 1963 and from Kittybrewster on 24 July 1967. To close a freight depot or public siding in Scotland required only a notice in *The Scotsman* on the first day of the month giving, at least, one month and one day's notice of the closure which could then take place.

The goods service on the St Combs branch was provided by mixed trains which were discontinued from 7 November 1960. Goods facilities at stations between Buckie and Elgin ceased by 1964 and services over the whole line, together with the Banff branch, ceased on 6 May 1968 with the passenger withdrawals. On 3 January 1966 the goods only services provided on the Oldmeldrum, Alford and Turriff branches were withdrawn, while later on 28 March Lossie-mouth was closed.

The Deeside line was closed west of Culter on 18 July 1966 and the Aberdeen-Culter section, retained to serve the paper mill, shut as from 2 January 1967, the last train being steam worked. The other goods closure of 1966 was the line to Parkmore and Glendullan on 7 November, the line on to Mortlach having closed on 23 March 1964. On 4 November 1968 the Speyside line between Boat and Garten and Aberlour was closed, although the signalboxes did not close until 16 December, to allow the men to work out their notice. The last train was a special excursion from Aberdeen on 2 November organised by the GNSR Association and on this day the goods depots at Craigellachie and the line on to Rothes also closed. Except for Strathisla near Keith and Ardmore at Kennethmont, no distilleries were then rail-connected to the former Great North. The milk traffic from the creamery siding near Bucksburn ceased on 26 January 1969.

One of the main customers on the Peterhead line was Crosse & Blackwell who received empty cans from Metal Box near Arbroath and sent them out, in wagon loads to various parts of Britain, filled with their products. It was an ideal traffic situation, but with the establishment of a freightliner depot at Aberdeen in November 1966, the products were taken in containers from Peterhead to Aberdeen by road. The empty cans were also moved on to road transport so that finally on 7 September 1970 the service between Maud and Peterhead ceased, the last train on 5 September again being a GNSR Association excursion; this left the freight trains to Fraserburgh.

Another major casualty during this period was the Locomotive Works at Inverurie which closed in 31 December 1969, having carried out locomotive and rolling stock repairs and scrapping to the end. The works site has been significantly redeveloped by private industry having provided facilities for a number of engineering and oil-related firms.

On 15 November 1971 Aberlour was closed to goods traffic and the section from there to Dufftown closed completely. By 1979 the system had stabilised as a main line of 53¼ miles with four stations and a goods siding at Kennethmont, with freight only branches from Keith to Dufftown and from Kittybrewster to Waterloo. In under ten years the system had shrunk from 303 miles serving 100 passenger and 87 goods stations; the railway was no longer part of the general community. Outside Aberdeen only just over 30,000 people stayed near a railway station compared with almost 98,000 in 1961.

TRACK AND SIGNALLING

The reorganisation of the service was paralleled by a rationalisation of track and signalling. Although there had been some other double track sections, the main line to Keith from Aberdeen formed the major part. Between 30 November 1969 and 13 December 1970 the line between Dyce and Keith was singled and operated with 'Tokenless Block' while Aberdeen–Dyce was singled and Track Circuit Block introduced on 20 June 1971. One section, Insch–Kennethmont, was left as double track to facilitate the crossing of trains. The only signalboxes left north of Aberdeen were Dyce, Inverurie, Insch, Kennethmont, Huntly and Keith. Except for the double section between Insch and Kennethmont the crossing loops controlled by the boxes allowed bi-directional working on each line. Apart from several 'distants' which have been converted to colour-light, the signals remain semaphore.

From 1965 the three main level crossings left on the line at Gartly, Oyne and Boat of Kintore were converted to automatic half barriers; the only conventional crossing left was at Insch station. It has since been converted to lifting barriers, operated by the signalbox. At Pitmedden, the road user raises the barriers using a pumping action with a lever at the side, when the miniature traffic lights show 'green' to the road; the user also has to restore the barriers across the road.

Rationalisation during this period also affected Aberdeen station. The bay platforms (10—13) at the north end of the station were taken out of use, along with the adjoining sidings. The four through platform tracks (6—9) were reduced to three with platform 7 becoming a siding; the remaining tracks merged into a single track at the north signalbox which, despite the reduction in facilities survived. 'Directional lever' signalling was instituted with Dyce, while a ground frame was installed at Kittybrewster to control access to the remaining sidings there and the Waterloo branch.

With the service reductions, Kittybrewster motive power depot also closed on 14 August 1967, the remaining locomotives being withdrawn or transferred. The original main line diesel locomotives allocated to the Great North section (the series built by the North

British Locomotive Company in Glasgow numbered D6138—D6157) were by this time in course of withdrawal after a very short life. They were replaced on the remaining duties by locomotives which worked in from elsewhere in the system, but principally class 24 and class 26 Sulzer engined machines based in Inverness. The Cravens built twin railcar sets were transferred elsewhere and the remaining pre-nationalisation passenger rolling stock was also displaced as a result of the Beeching closures.

CHAPTER 16

North Sea Oil and the Future

OIL TO THE RESCUE

1964 saw the first licences being issued for exploratory drilling for oil and gas in the North Sea. Gas was brought ashore in eastern England in 1965. In 1973 the oil-producing countries of the Middle East raised the price of oil considerably, and this gave additional impetus to exploration in the North Sea. The first oil brought ashore in Scotland was in 1975, at Cruden Bay. Aberdeen was to become known as the 'Oil Capital of Europe' with far reaching changes in the community.

The question of re-opening the line to Peterhead, also an important oil centre, was raised. It was eventually decided that the oil should be transported to Grangemouth by pipeline. Pipes were coated with concrete at Invergordon and then conveyed to Maud and Inverurie by special 'Company Trains'. Oxygen was handled at Maud, while Waterloo yard became mainly a private siding for British Steel.

Oil had other consequences; homes and offices were required and the drilling rigs needed services. British Rail took on extra staff for the first time in many years, but also lost employees to the oil related industries. Passenger and parcels traffic increased, mainly to the south of Aberdeen but also on the former Great North, and overcrowding became more common. The parcels delivery and collection service was discontinued from 1 June 1981, but the Red Star station-to-station service became very popular, with all the stations on the line except Dyce providing the service. In May 1983 Night Star, a guaranteed service with collection and/or delivery was instituted. The line also saw 'Company Trains' for grain to Dufftown and Burghead, and whisky traffic from Keith. Until 1987 a Freightliner service was provided south of Aberdeen with a mini service from Elgin where the Customs & Excise had an office for dealing with the whisky traffic. A trial Freightliner service ran from September 1983 to March 1984 between Aberdeen and Thurso using specially adapted air-braked freightliner wagons in the passenger trains which were then still vacuum braked. This was a modern form of mixed train, unusual also in that it was dual braked. All freight trains in the Great North area have been composed of fully fitted vehicles since 27 July 1981.

On 5 April 1978 a High Speed Diesel Train ran from Aberdeen to Inverness in a flag-showing exercise of what was to come between Aberdeen and London. Later there was an HST 125 service on Sundays on the line for a few years—an early morning Inverness to Kings Cross *via* Aberdeen train. These trains were to bring Aberdeen nearer the other business centres of Britain in journey time.

At Aberdeen the station offices were altered and a Travel Centre, incorporating the booking and the enquiry offices, was opened on 10 September 1978 to cater for over a million passengers each year, with the official opening on the following 5 October. Also incorporated in the building was the Great North of Scotland Railway War Memorial which had been displayed originally in the former company headquarters at 80 Guild Street, Aberdeen. This was made of oak with the names inscribed in gilt; in the Travel Centre it could be seen by the public and still be preserved. When there was a further extension of the Travel Centre in 1985, the Memorial moved again, but still within the Travel Centre and its preserving atmosphere.

From 1970 to 1985 the revenue at Aberdeen increased more than tenfold and a further reorganisation of the station and track layout was carried out during the early 1980s. A new signalling centre was built south of the station and bi-directional working introduced from the south to give greater flexibility of operation. Platforms 6 and 7 provided through lines to the north, and platforms 8 and 9 became a single headshunt for the Clayhills carriage sidings. The North box closed along with all the boxes as far as Craiginches South. The interior of the station was smartened up with white floor tiling, brighter lighting, an electronic information indicator, a newsagent's shop and new offices for the area manager. As the open station system introduced on 2 November 1982 was working well, the ticket barriers were removed while television-type monitors were provided to relay information to each platform, the Travel Centre and to the taxi stands. The station has become a showpiece in contrast to the dingy scene of earlier British Railways years. The Travellers Fare buffet was extended and modernised in 1988.

CHARTER TRAINS

The 1970s saw the return of charter trains for the general public, recalling the popularity of the Speyside excursions started by the GNSR. 1970 was the centenary of the opening of the line from Dingwall to Strome Ferry, and the enthusiast GNSR Association chose Kyle of Lochalsh as a destination, because it could not be reached in a day by scheduled train. The charter was so successful that it was repeated many times during the ensuing five years by a number of organisations, which included the local newspaper and railway societies south of the Border. Other destinations were also reached but none achieved the popularity of Kyle. The introduction of railcards made the charters less attractive and led to a decline in the numbers run. Instead a new type of charter became popular; twice a week each summer since 1984, Grampian Railtours have run the *Northern Belle* from Aberdeen to Dufftown, providing a package inclusive of meals and a visit to a distillery at Dufftown. There is also the *Royal Scotsman* which started in the summer of 1985 as an up-market venture with passengers staying on the train for three or six days while touring many parts of Scotland, including the former Great North line, in historic rolling stock elegantly refurbished. British Rail's InterCity charter unit operates long weekend excursions from London to the northern Highlands which include a trip on the Dufftown branch.

With the reduction in the number of signalboxes, the change to automatic half barriers at level crossings and the open station concept, it has been possible to provide a service economically on Sundays; the only previous Sunday service in British Railways' days was a brief service on the Deeside line, plus summer excursions and charters.

In the 1980s various factors, such as increasing population and greater road congestion, have encouraged a climate of opinion that the railway should not only be maintained, but also improved further to enable it to play a greater part in the transport scene than it has in recent decades. While no closed ex GNSR lines have been seriously considered for reinstatement, the reopening of certain closed passenger stations has been discussed and one, Dyce, was reopened on 17 September 1984 with support and financial assistance from Grampian Regional Council, the local district authority, and also, as it adjoins the airport, the British Airports Authority! It has proved successful. In fact ScotRail (as British Rail now markets itself in Scotland) has publicly stated that Dyce is top of the list of ten stations opened in Scotland for passenger journeys in its first year of operation. The traffic initially was almost three times what had been estimated. All trains call and additionally three services have been extended there from the south. The journey time between Dyce and Aberdeen is nine minutes, much less than the time normally taken to the city centre by road, especially at peak periods.

Other stations on line have been improved. In particular, reconstruction of the station at Keith was completed in 1988 and the new facilities officially opened on 19 August. The terminal bay platforms, which dated from 1856, had been disused for many years while the accommodation for both staff and customers was outdated. Only the canopy of the surviving through platform, linking the former GNSR and Highland territories, and the track side weather screen associated with it, have been retained. All other buildings were demolished and an entirely new structure provided. The space released in the angle between the present main line and the Dufftown line has been used to make an enlarged car park, Grampian Regional Council contributing towards the costs.

SERVICE IMPROVEMENTS

Improvements to the Aberdeen–Inverness service continue to be made. The total journey time including all stops was cut by ten minutes to 2 hours 20 minutes from 16 May 1983. Two minutes were added when the stop at Dyce was instituted, but further reductions have taken place since and more are planned. From May 1984 a new train was introduced between Aberdeen and Penzance which was started at Elgin, having run there empty, to provide a connection with the early morning Aberdeen–London train. From May 1985, a train was run from Inverness at 05.02 to provide the connection and the Penzance train reverted to starting from Aberdeen. This addition brought the service up to eight trains each way daily, plus two short workings to and from Huntly and one to and from Inverurie. The Sunday service has grown to five trains each way daily.

The quality of the rolling stock is being progressively improved. The Swindon-built cross country diesel multiple units which had arrived in November 1959 and had worked the line since 1960, were withdrawn from 10 March 1980 and transferred elsewhere; they were replaced by sets of Mark 1 compartment coaches which, in turn, were later replaced by sets of mainly Mark 2 open saloon coaches. First class facilities ceased just prior to the withdrawal of the multiple units. A mobile trolley service provides the catering on most trains. Locomotive power changed from Class 27s to Class 47s which, in normal circumstances, were well able to maintain the schedules. Occasionally a Class 37 did duty on passenger service. The next change was the introduction in 1989 of class 156 Super Sprinter diesel multiple units. These brought about further reductions in the journey time with more promised, together with increases in frequency. The level of passenger patronage is well maintained, being over a million passenger journeys each year, and is believed to amply justify this investment. There is also the possibility of further upgrading to Class 158 Express units when they become available.

When the line between Aberdeen and Keith was largely singled in 1969 and 1970, tokenless block signalling was introduced and there was no need to use the Manson tablet exchange apparatus. This had been installed in the cross-country diesel multiple units for use on the line west of Keith; in this unique system the apparatus was placed in the guard's van and bell codes operated between the guard and the driver to assure the driver that the train had the correct token. The line to Keith is also the last in Scotland with overhead telegraph wires slung from poles.

Signalling remains basically as it was when the line was singled but its life expectancy must now be limited. Radio Electronic Tokenless Block was considered but this could not handle the necessary level of service and train speed. Other possibilities, making use of modern electronics, are being investigated. Improvements are also being made to the track alignment at selected locations to raise the line speeds.

Inevitably, in recent years the freight traffic has undergone changes. The line to Dufftown had little freight after 1982 and was closed in 1985 except for charter traffic. The freight service on the Fraserburgh line ran for the last time on 5 October 1979 although the solum was retained initially by Grampian Regional Council in the hope of sufficient oil traffic to justify its reopening. However, several bridges have been removed and the embankments cut back. There has been a notable decline in the number of company bulk grain trains, but grain remains an important long-distance traffic for the railway. There are flows in each direction from time to time—grain from the south and malt from the north for export—which are usually conveyed in large bogie vehicles. Other long-distance incoming traffic, conveyed by Speedlink service, includes coal (now concentrated at the former Deeside yard in Aberdeen and at Keith), calcium carbonate and china clay (for the paper mills), fertiliser, oil products and rock-salt for roads. Outgoing loads include seed potatoes, whisky, paper and an important new traffic in felled timber, destined for points in Wales and the western side of England. Yards on the Great North which remain open are Inverurie, Port Elphinstone (for the paper mills), Huntly, Keith and Elgin. Waterloo is also nominally open as a private siding but sees little use. British Fuels, who used Kittybewster, moved to the former Deeside yard at Guild Street, Aberdeen, and Kittybrewster was closed. Freight trains are normally worked by classes 37 and 47.

GREAT NORTH REMAINS

It seems fitting, finally, to mention some of the disused Great North buildings and other features which have been preserved. In 1978 the original viaduct over the River Deveron at Rothiemay, disused since 1898, was demolished. This apparently skew viaduct was in fact five arches slightly staggered side by side. The viaducts on the Coast line at Spey Bay and Cullen survive, the latter having been saved from demolition following a planning enquiry, the former being used as a footpath.

Many stations have been demolished but at least two survive in preserved form; Aberlour is now a refreshment centre with an historic photographic display, and Knockando is a visitors' centre for the nearby Tamdhu Distillery. The latter station contains several railway relics, although most of them relate to the Highland Railway. Another, the 1884 Portsoy station, has been renovated without much exterior structural alteration for use as a Scout and Guide Hall. The original train shed there, which was under threat of demolition for many years, has been incorporated into an advance factory complex. At Alford the original station, which was not typical of the Great North style, was demolished and a replacement inspired by Aviemore was built by the local Regional Council to house the railway relics of the Grampian Transport Museum, which is also located at Alford. At Elgin the former Great North station and associated buildings are listed Grade B and are expected to see use as a business centre. At Boat of Garten, a Highland Railway station, the Strathspey Railway Company operates the preserved line to Aviemore and maintains a Great North presence in its museum.

On Deeside, Ballater station building is now owned by Kincardine & Deeside District Council and is well utilised. The former Royal waiting room is used as Council offices, the station restaurant is still used as such, and a shop and storage accommodation are also provided. The refurbished Albert Hall, across the road, houses the local tourist information centre and a display of Great North material which emphasises the connection with royalty. Aboyne station has been converted to shop units by the Regional Council, and many other buildings survive throughout the area as workshops, offices and houses.

Of the Great North hotels, only the Station Hotel in Aberdeen survives but was sold by British Rail in February 1983 along with the former Head Office building of the GNSR at 80 Guild Street; the former GNSR boardroom and office suite in the old Head Office are still much as they were at the Grouping.

Some of the former trackbeds have been converted to footpaths and bridle paths. The Deeside Walkway extends from near Ferryhill Junction in Aberdeen to Culter and from Cambus O'May to Ballater, while the Speyside Way has been conceived on a greater scale, extending from Nethy Bridge to Spey Bay and using forest tracks north of Craigellachie. Unfortunately, the section south of Ballindalloch may never be opened because it seems the GNSR did not obtain the title for the land. Another walkway is planned from Dyce to Ellon on the former Buchan railway.

The one surviving GNSR locomotive, No 49 *Gordon Highlander*, is preserved in the Glasgow Transport Museum while the former Royal coach saloon No. 1, is preserved by the Scottish Railway Preservation Society at Bo'ness along with an open wagon. The Strathspey Railway have two 6-wheeled coaches under restoration. Some restoration work has been undertaken on the remains of the bodies of the Cruden Bay trams. The former coach bodies which were a characteristic sight on the farms for many miles around Inverurie, in use often as hen hutches, are seen less often, but a few survive.

With the interest and enthusiasm to be found today, the heritage and mystique of the Great North past is preserved for present and future generations. After the retrenchment of the Beeching years and a period of relative stability in the '70s, the last few years have seen a noticeable revival affecting the remaining part of the Great North. The main line, with more through trains than ever, plays an important link in the modern ScotRail. Yesterday the Railway played a great part in the community; in time to come it will continue to do so but in a different way.

1 : AUTHORISATION AND OPENING DATES FOR RAIL AND ROAD MOTOR SERVICES

Line	Authorised	Opened to Public Traffic
Kittybrewster to Huntly	26 Jun 1846	12 Sep 1854 (g)
		20 Sep 1854 (p)
Elgin to Lossiemouth	16 Jul 1846	11 Aug 1852
Aberdeen (Ferryhill Jct) to Banchory	28 May 1852	8 Sep 1853
Kittybrewster to Aberdeen (Waterloo)	24 Jul 1854	24 Sep 1855 (g)
		1 Apr 1856 (p)
Huntly to Keith	25 May 1855	11 Oct 1856
Inverurie to Old Meldrum	15 Jun 1855	1 Jul 1856
Inveramsay to Turriff	15 Jun 1855	5 Sep 1857
Kintore to Alford	23 Jun 1856	21 Mar 1859
Orton to Rothes	14 Jul 1856	23 Aug 1858
Rothes to Dandaleith	14 Jul 1856	24 Dec 1858
Grange to Banff	27 Jul 1857	30 Jul 1859
Tillynaught to Portsoy (a)	27 Jul 1857	30 Jul 1859
Banchory to Aboyne	27 Jul 1857	2 Dec 1859
Turriff to Banff & Macduff (b)	27 Jul 1857	4 Jun 1860
Dyce to Mintlaw	23 Jul 1858	18 Jul 1861
Mintlaw to Peterhead	23 Jul 1858	3 Jul 1862
Peterhead Harbour Branch	23 Jul 1858	9 Aug 1865
Keith to Dufftown	25 May 1860	19 Feb 1862 (g)
		21 Feb 1862 (p)
Elgin to Rothes	3 Jul 1860	30 Dec 1861 (g)
		1 Jan 1862 (p)
Dufftown to Nethybridge	17 May 1861	1 Jul 1863
Dandaleith to Craigellachie	17 May 1861	1 Jul 1863
Maud to Fraserburgh	21 Jul 1863	24 Apr 1865
Kittybrewster to Aberdeen (Joint)	23 Jun 1864	4 Nov 1867
Nethybridge to Boat of Garten	5 Jul 1865	1 Aug 1866
Aboyne to Ballater	5 Jul 1865	17 Oct 1866
Banff & Macduff (b) to Macduff	30 Jul 1866	1 Jul 1872
Portsoy to Tochieneal	12 Jul 1882	1 Apr 1884
Elgin to Garmouth	12 Jul 1882	12 Aug 1884
Tochieneal to Garmouth	12 Jul 1882	5 Apr 1886 (g)
		1 May 1886 (p)
Grange South Jct to North Jct	19 Jul 1887(c)	5 Apr 1886 (g)
		1 May 1886 (p)
Ellon to Boddam	24 Aug 1893	2 Aug 1897
Fraserburgh to St Combs	8 Sep 1899	1 Jul 1903

(a) Original terminus for Portsoy, closed to passengers 1 April 1884
(b) Original terminus, closed 1 July 1872
(c) Act was to authorise line already built without powers
(g) Opened for goods traffic
(p) Opened for passenger traffic

Road Motor Routes (d)   Opened to public
                                                         traffic (e)

Ballater (Station) to Braemar (Fife Arms Hotel)   2 May 1904 (f,h)
Udny (Station) to Methlick   15 Nov 1904
Huntly (Square and Station) to Aberchirder   1 May 1905
Culter (Station) to Echt and Midmar   1 Jun 1905
Alford (Station) to Strathdon (Bellabeg)   1 May 1906
Aberdeen (Schoolhill Station) to Skene and Cluny   1 Sep 1906
Aberdeen (Schoolhill Station) to Echt and Midmar   1 Nov 1906
Aberdeen (Schoolhill Station) to Newburgh   1 Apr 1907
Strathdon (Bellabeg) to Cockbridge (Allargue Hotel)   1 Jul 1907 (i)
Ballater to Dinnet and Strathdon   1 Jul 1907 (i,j)
Ballindalloch (Station) to Tomintoul   1 Jul 1907 (i,j)
                                                         1 Jul 1910 (k)
Fraserburgh to Rosehearty and New Aberdour   18 Nov 1912
Aberchirder to Turriff (Station)   31 May 1921

Cluny to Millbank   1 Jun 1925 (l)
Aberdeen (Schoolhill) to Inverurie   1 Oct 1927
Aberchirder to Banff, via Alvah   1 Jun 1928 (l)
Aberchirder to Banff, via Cornhill   1 Apr 1929 (l)
Aberdeen (Schoolhill) to Alford (and Strathdon)   8 Apr 1929 (l,m)
Inverurie to Chapel of Garioch   15 May 1929 (n)
Elgin to Fochabers, Portgordon, Buckie, Cullen,
        Portsoy, Banff and Macduff   17 Jun 1929 (o)
Ballater to Aberdeen   1 Jul 1929 (p)

(d)   The GNSR road motor routes and services were originally operated
without specific powers. The Great North of Scotland Railway Order,
1906, granted the necessary Parliamentary authority.
        The LNER inherited such powers in respect of its Northern Scottish
Area and obtained more general powers under the London and North Eastern
Railway (Road Transport) Act, 1928.
(e)   Public traffic refers to omnibus services for passengers (and
parcels), including availability for intermediate traffic. After 1906,
the GNSR was empowered to enter into agreements with the Postmaster-
General for the conveyance of mails. See also note (f).
(f)   From 1 November 1908, a specially designated 'Mail' road motor
service was introduced involving the use of an adapted omnibus.
(h)   Between 7 December 1912 and 1 May 1913, exclusive, the operation of
the service reverted to a horse-drawn conveyance during road repairs.
(i)   A seasonal service, usually July to September but with some
additional services during June and the early part of October.
(j)   Charabanc service as part of the inclusive rail/motor tours and not
available for intermediate traffic. The service between Ballindalloch
and Tomintoul may have been provided privately during 1907-1909.
(k)   Omnibus service, as described under note (e)
(l)   Extension of existing service.
(m)   Also operated in the summer only from Strathdon to Cockbridge.
(n)   Extension of an existing service consequent on the takeover by the
LNER of J S Mitchell of Inverurie, whose services were integrated into
LNER operations.
(o)   Including local services between Portgordon and Cullen.
(p)   Including local services between Aberdeen and Culter.

2 : DOUBLING AND SINGLING OF LINES

	Doubled	Singled
Aberdeen to Kittybrewster	4 Nov 1867	20 Jun 1971
Kittybrewster to Dyce	before 31 Jul 1861	20 Jun 1971
Dyce to Kintore	1 Jun 1880	30 Nov 1969
Kintore to Inverurie	1 May 1882	30 Nov 1969
Inverurie to Inveramsay	1 May 1882	7 Dec 1969
Inveramsay to Insch	27 Oct 1888	7 Dec 1969
Insch to Kennethmont	1 Aug 1896(a)	---
Kennethmont to Gartly	20 Sep 1896	6 Dec 1970
Gartly to Huntly	30 Nov 1896	6 Dec 1970
Huntly to Avochie	19 Jan 1898	13 Dec 1970
Avochie to Rothiemay	30 Apr 1900	13 Dec 1970
Rothiemay to Keith	17 Jan 1898	13 Dec 1970
Grange South to North Jct	17 Jan 1898	(b)
Buckie to Portessie	1 May 1886	(b)
Ferryhill Jct to Cults	14 Jun 1884	2 Dec 1951
Cults to Murtle	13 Jul 1892	2 Dec 1951
Murtle to Culter	24 Sep 1892	2 Dec 1951
Culter to Park	28 Aug 1899	2 Dec 1951
Parkhill to Elrick	31 May 1920	23 Aug 1925 (c)

(a) Used as double track for goods trains from 6 Jul 1896.
(b) Double at closure.
(c) This section was in use as double track during busy periods only.

3 : CLOSURES

Line	Passengers	Completely
Main Line		
Rothes to Elgin	6 May 1968	6 May 1968
Craigellachie to Rothes	6 May 1968	4 Nov 1968
Dufftown to Craigellachie	6 May 1968	15 Nov 1971
Keith Jct to Dufftown	6 May 1968	1 Oct 1985 (a)
Coast Line		
Grange to Grange North Jct	7 Mar 1960	7 Mar 1960
Cairnie Jct to Elgin via Tillynaught	6 May 1968	6 May 1968
Alford Branch		
Paradise Siding to Alford	2 Jan 1950	3 Jan 1966
Kintore to Paradise Siding	2 Jan 1950	7 Nov 1966
Banff Branch		
Tillynaught to Banff	6 Jul 1964	6 May 1968
Peterhead Branch		
Maud Jct to Peterhead	3 May 1965	7 Sep 1970
Peterhead to Peterhead Harbour	-	late 1930s
Buchan Section		
Dyce to Fraserburgh	4 Oct 1965	8 Oct 1979
Cruden Section		
Ellon to Boddam	31 Oct 1932	7 Nov 1945
Deeside Section		
Culter to Ballater	28 Feb 1966	18 Jul 1966
Ferryhill Jct to Culter	28 Feb 1966	2 Jan 1967

```
Lossiemouth Branch
    Lossie Jct to Lossiemouth          6 Apr 1964      28 Mar 1966
Macduff Branch
    Turriff to Macduff                 1 Oct 1951       1 Aug 1961
    Inveramsay to Turriff              1 Oct 1951       3 Jan 1966
Oldmeldrum Branch
    Inverurie to Oldmeldrum            2 Nov 1931       3 Jan 1966
Rothes to Orton
    Orton to Sourden                   1 Aug 1866       1 Aug 1866
    Sourdén to Rothes                  1 Aug 1866          c 1880
St Combs branch
    Fraserburgh to St Combs            3 May 1965       3 May 1965
Speyside Section
    Aberlour to Boat of Garten        18 Oct 1965       4 Nov 1968
    Craigellachie to Aberlour         18 Oct 1965      15 Nov 1971
```

(a)   Subsequently retained for charter passenger traffic.

Road Motor Routes	Closed (b)
Culter (Station) to Echt and Midmar	31 Oct 1906
Udny (Station) to Methlick	31 Dec 1906
Aberchirder to Turriff	29 Oct 1921
Aberdeen (Schoolhill) to Echt and Midmar	28 Feb 1922
Aberdeen (Schoolhill) to Newburgh	28 Feb 1922
Ballater (Station) to Dinnet and Strathdon	30 Sep 1925 (c)
Ballindalloch (Station) to Tomintoul	30 Sep 1925 (c)
Aberdeen (Schoolhill) to Dunecht (Skene) and Cluny	31 Dec 1925 (d)
Fraserburgh to Rosehearty and New Aberdour	10 Jul 1927
Strathdon (Bellabeg) to Cockbridge	4 Oct 1929
Elgin to Fochabers, Portgordon, Buckie, Cullen, Portsoy, Banff and Macduff	15 Feb 1930 (e)
Aberdeen to Alford and Strathdon (Bellabeg)	30 Jun 1930 (f)
Aberdeen to Inverurie and Chapel of Garioch	30 Jun 1930 (f)
Aberdeen to Culter, Banchory, Aboyne, Ballater, and Braemar	30 Jun 1930 (f)
Huntly to Aberchirder and Banff via Alvah or Cornhill	30 Jun 1930 (f)

(b)   Date given is last day of public service by railway company's road motor
(c)   Seasonal service in summer only - service not resumed in 1926
(d)   Cluny to Millbank section ceased operation during Autumn 1925
(e)   Route and services transferred to Scottish General (Northern) Omnibus Co. Ltd. of Elgin, part of the Scottish Motor Traction (SMT) group of companies.
(f)   Routes and services transferred to W. Alexander & Sons Ltd of Falkirk, part of the SMT group of companies.

The LNER obtained general powers under the London and North Eastern Railway (Road Transport) Act, 1928 to operate road motor services and to purchase shares in other companies operating road motor services. Agreement was reached on 15 August 1929 for the reconstructed Scottish Motor Traction Co Ltd, with the LNER taking a share in the company and transfering to one of its subsidiaries all the routes which it operated. The transfer took effect in 1930, on the dates shown above.

4 : ROUTE INFORMATION

This appendix lists all passenger and goods stations by line, with any additional signal boxes. Some of the stations dealt only with goods (G) or passengers (P). Those still open are shown in capital letters. Stations opened by the LNER are suffixed with (+) and by BR with (*).

The suffixes 'Halt' and 'Platform' have generally been omitted from the above list since their use was inconsistent and they were often not applied throughout the life of the station.

Main Line

ABERDEEN (JOINT)	0
Schoolhill (P)	0 3/8
Hutcheon Street (P)	0 7/8
Kittybrewster	1 3/8
Don Street (P)	2 1/4
Woodside	2 5/8
Persley (P)	3 1/4
Bucksburn	4 1/8
Bankhead (P)	4 5/8
Stoneywood (P)	5 1/8
DYCE (2nd location)	6 1/4
Dyce (1st location)	6 1/2
Pitmedden (P)	8 1/4
Kinaldie	10 1/2
Kintore	13 1/4
Port Elphinstone (G)	15 1/2
Inverurie (1st loc)	16
INVERURIE (2nd loc)	16 3/4
Inveramsay	20 1/2
Pitcaple	21 1/4
Oyne	24 1/2
Buchanstone	25 3/4
INSCH	27 1/2
Wardhouse (P)	31
Kennethmont	32 3/4
Gartly	35 3/4
HUNTLY	40 3/4
Rothiemay	45 1/4
Cairnie Jct (P)	48 1/4
Grange	48 3/4
KEITH JUNCTION	53 1/4
Keith Town (P)	54
Strathisla Mills (G)	54 1/4
Auchindachy	56 3/4
Towiemore (+)	58 1/4
Drummuir	59 1/2
Parkmore Siding (G)	63 1/2
Dufftown	64
Craigellachie	68
Dandaleith	68 3/4
Rothes	71
Birchfield (P)	74
Coleburn (G)	75 1/2
Longmorn	77 3/4
Elgin	80 3/4

Waterloo Branch

Kittybrewster	0
Waterloo	2

Buchan Section

Dyce	0
Parkhill	1 1/4
Elrick S.B.	3 3/4
Newmachar	5 1/4
Udny	8 1/4
Logierieve	10
Esslemont	11 1/2
Ellon	13 1/4
Arnage	16 3/4
Auchnagatt	20 3/4
Maud Jct	25
Brucklay	26 3/4
Strichen	30 3/4
Mormond	33 1/4
Lonmay	35 3/4
Rathen	38 1/4
Philorth	39 1/2
Fraserburgh	41

Cruden Section

Ellon	0
Auchmacoy	3 1/2
Pitlurg	5 1/2
Hatton	8 1/4
Cruden Bay	10 1/4
Bullers O'Buchan (P)	12
Longhaven	13 1/2
Boddam	15 1/2

Peterhead Branch

Maud Jct	0
Mintlaw	4
Longside	7 1/4
Newseat (P)	9 1/2
Inverugie	11
Peterhead	13
Peterhead Harbour (G)	14

St Combs Light Railway

Fraserburgh	0
Kirkton Bridge (P)	1
Philorth Bridge (P)	2 1/4
Cairnbulg	3 5/8
St Combs	5 1/8

Alford Branch

Kintore	0
Paradise Sdn (Private)	3 3/4
Kemnay	4 1/2
Monymusk	7 1/2
Tillyfourie	10 3/4
Whitehouse	13
Alford	16

Oldmeldrum Branch

Inverurie	0
Lethenty	2 1/4
Fingask (P)	3 1/2
Oldmeldrum	5 1/4

Macduff Branch

Inveramsay	0
Wartle	3 3/4
Rothienorman	7 1/2
Fyvie	10 3/4
Auchterless	14
Turriff	18
Plaidy	22 1/2
King Edward	24 3/4
Banff Bridge (P)	29 1/2
Macduff	29 3/4

Grange Curve

Grange	0
Grange North Jct SB	0 3/4

Mortlach Siding

Parkmore (G)	0
Glendullan (G)	0 1/2
Mortlach (G)	1

Rothes to Orton

Rothes	0
Sourden	1 1/4
Orton (H.R. station)	3 1/4

Coast Line

Cairnie Jct (P)	0
Grange North Jct SB	0 1/2
Millegan	1 1/4
Knock	3 1/4
Glenbarry	4 1/2
Cornhill	7 3/4
Tillynaught Jct	10
Portsoy	12 3/4
Glassaugh	14 3/4
Tochieneal	17
Cullen	18 1/4
Portknockie	20 1/4
Findochty	21 1/2
Portessie	23
Buckie	24 1/4
Buckpool	25 1/4
Port Gordon	26 3/4
Spey Bay	29
Garmouth	30 1/4
Urquhart	33 1/2
Calcots	36
Lossie Jct SB	38
Elgin	39

Banff Branch

Tillynaught Jct	0
Ordens (P)	1 1/4
Ladysbridge	3 1/2
Bridgefoot (P)	4 3/4
Golf Club House (P)	5 1/4
Banff	6

Speyside Section

Craigellachie	0
Aberlour	2 1/4
Dailuaine Halt (P)(+)	4 3/4
Carron	5 1/2
Imperial Cottages (P)(*)	6
Knockando House (P)	6 3/4
Gilbey's Cottages (P)(*)	7 3/4
Knockando	8
Blacksboat	10 1/4
Ballindalloch	12
Advie (1st location)	c14 3/4
Advie (2nd location)	15 1/4
Dalvey	c17 1/2
Dalvey Farm Halt (P)(*)	17 3/4
Cromdale	21
Grantown-on-Spey	24
Ballifurth Farm (P)(*)	26 1/2
Nethybridge	28 1/2
Broomhill Jct (site of)	c30 1/4
Boat of Garten (HR sta)	33 1/4

Lossiemouth Branch		Murtle	5 3/8

Lossiemouth Branch

		Murtle	5 3/8
		Milltimber	6 1/4
Lossie Jct SB	0	Culter	7 3/8
Linksfield	0 1/2	Drum	9 3/4
Greens of Drainie (P)	2 1/2	Park	10 3/4
Lossiemouth	4 1/2	Mills of Drum (P)	13
		Crathes	14 1/4
Deeside Section		Banchory	16 3/4
		Dee Street (P) (*)	17 1/2
ABERDEEN (JOINT)	0	Glassel	21 3/8
Ferryhill Jct S.B.	0 5/8	Torphins	23 3/4
Holburn Street (P)	1 3/8	Lumphanan	26 7/8
Ruthrieston (P)	1 3/4	Dess	29 1/2
Pitfodels (P)	3	Aboyne	32 1/4
Cults	3 5/8	Dinnet	36 3/4
West Cults (P)	4 1/8	Cambus O'May	39 3/8
Bieldside (P)	4 3/4	Ballater	43 1/4
(continued in next column)			

5 : OFFICERS

Great North of Scotland Railway

Chairmen		Passenger Superintendants	
1846-1849	Thomas Blaikie	1854-1865	William Walker
1849-1867	Sir James Elphinstone	1865-1867	Samuel Bates
1867-1872	John Duncan	1867-1880	Forbes Morrison
1872-1879	William Leslie	1880-1900	Alexander Reid
1879-1904	William Ferguson	1900-1918	William Deuchar
1904-1919	Sir David Stewart	1918-1922	William Johnston
1919-1922	Andrew Bain		
Feb-Dec 1922	Andrew Duffus	Goods Managers	

Secretaries		1854-1878	William Walker
		1878-1910	Alexander Ross
1846-1851	William Leslie	1910-1922	Simox Willox
1851-1868	Robert Milne		
1868-1880	William B Ferguson	Engineers	
1880-1906	William Moffat		
1906-1922	Thomas Macintosh	1846-1851	William Cubitt
		1851-1856	Benjamin Hall Blyth
General Managers		1856-1867	Alexander Gibb
		1867-1868	Alexander Fraser
1856-1880	Robert Milne	1868-1906	Patrick Barnett
1880-1906	William Moffat	1906-1922	James Parker
1906-1922	George Davidson		

Locomotive Superintendants

1853-1855	Daniel Kinnear Clark	1890-1894	James Johnson
1855-1857	James Ruthven	1894-1914	William Pickersgill
1857-1883	William Cowan	1914-1922	Thomas Heywood
1883-1890	James Manson		

Alford Valley Railway

Worked by GNSR, and merged with it as from 1 Aug 1866. From 1856-1866, Chairman was Sir James Elphinstone, Secretary Robert Milne and Engineer Alexander Gibb.

Aberdeen & Turriff Railway

Worked by GNSR, and merged with it as from 1 Aug 1866. From 1855-1866, Chairman was Sir James Elphinstone, Secretary Robert Milne and Engineer Alexander Gibb.

Banff, Macduff & Turriff Extension Railway

Worked by GNSR, and merged with it as from 1 Aug 1866. Chairman was Sir James Elphinstone from 1857-1859 and William Tayler 1859-1866. From 1857-1866 Secretary was Robert Milne and Engineer Alexander Gibb.

Formartine & Buchan Railway

Worked by GNSR, and merged with it as from 1 Aug 1866. From 1858-1866, Chairman was Sir James Elphinstone, Secretary Robert Milne and Engineer Alexander Gibb.

Inverury & Oldmeldrum Junction Railway

Worked by GNSR, and merged with it as from 1 Aug 1866. From 1855-1866, Chairman was Beauchamp Urquhart, Secretary James Chalmers and Engineer John Willet.

Keith & Dufftown Railway

Worked by GNSR, and merged with it as from 1 Aug 1866. Chairman was John Grant 1857-1859 and James Findlater 1859-1866. Secretary was John Allan 1859-1861 and Robert Milne 1861-1866. Engineer was Alexander Gibb 1857-1861.

Strathspey Railway

Worked by GNSR, and merged with it as from 1 Aug 1866. From 1861-1866, Chairman was Sir James Elphinstone, Secretary Robert Milne and Engineer Alexander Gibb.

Banffshire Railway

Worked by GNSR from 1863, and merged with it as from 12 Aug 1867. From 1857-1867 Chairman was Hon. Thomas Bruce and Secretary John Forbes. General Manager in 1859 was Joseph Grierson and 1859-1867 George Morison. He was designated general superintendant after GNSR took over working of line in 1863. Engineer 1858-1863 was William Keir and Locomotive Superintendant 1859-1863 John Jeffrey.

Deeside Railway

Leased by GNSR in 1866, and merged with it as from 1 Aug 1875.

Chairmen		Engineers	
1846-1849	Thomas Blaiklie	1846-1849	William Cubitt
1849-1875	John Duncan	1849-1864	John Willet
1875-1876	.Patrick Davidson	1864-1866	William B Ferguson

Secretaries		Locomotive Superintendants	
1846-1849	William Leslie	1853-1864	John Willet
1849-1876	William B Ferguson	1864-1866	William B Ferguson

General Manager

1849-1866   William B Ferguson

Aboyne & Braemar Railway

Worked by GNSR, and merged with it as from 31 Jan 1876. From 1865-1876 Chairman was James Farquharson and Secretary William B Ferguson.

Morayshire Railway

Worked by GNSR from 1863, and merged with it from 1 Oct 1880.

Chairmen		Engineers	
1846-1851	Alexander Forteith	1846-1853	James Samuel
1851-1855	David Manson	1853-1857	Joseph Taylor
1855-1872	James Grant	1857-1858	Robert Blackwood
1872-1881	Alexander Urquhart	1858-1863	William Mills

Secretaries		Locomotive Superintendants	
1846-1855	James Grant	1851-1853	Joseph Samuel
1855-1857	Charles Cranstoun	1853-1857	Joseph Taylor
1857-1859	William Topp	1857-1858	Robert Blackwood
1859-1861	William Mills	1858-1863	George Golightly
1861-1881	Alexander Watt (a)		

General Managers			
1855-1857	Charles Cranstoun	1859-1861	William Mills
1857-1859	James Jenkins	1861-1881	Alexander Watt (a)

Note : (a) Relinquished general managership when GNSR took over working of line in 1863 but continued as secretary.

Aberdeen to Elgin

Date	Total trains	Via Craigellachie No.	Best	Worst	Via Coast No.	Best	Worst	Via Mulben No.	Best	Worst
Jun 1863	3 Dn							3	3h 53m	4h 00m
	3 Up							3	3h 50m	3h 54m
Mar 1891	7 Dn	3	2h 43m	3h 40m	5	2h 40m	5h 00m	5	2h 32m	3h 20m
	7 Up	6	2h 49m	3h 50m	5	2h 40m	4h 20m	5	2h.35m	4h.10m
Jun 1914	7 Dn	4	2h 24m	3h 10m	3	2h 22m	3h 30m	4	2h 34m	3h 36m
	6 Up	4	2h 28m	3h 11m	6	2h 28m	4h 05m	5	2h 10m	2h 42m
Jul 1938	7 Dn	6	2h 10m	3h 55m	6	2h 38m	4h 11m	3	2h 14m	2h 56m
	7 Up	5	2h 30m	3h 03m	5	2h 35m	3h 35m	3	2h 05m	2h 45m
Sep 1964	10 Dn	4	2h 33m	2h 48m	5	2h 37m	3h 21m	5	1h 31m	2h 12m
	9 Up	5	2h 22m	2h 54m	4	2h 39m	3h 04m	4	1h 37m	1h 38m
May 1989	10 Dn							10	1h 24m	1h 42m
	10 Up							10	1h 26m	1h 42m

		Aberdeen to Fraserburgh No.	Best	Worst	Aberdeen to Peterhead No.	Best	Worst
Jun 1863	Down	1	4h 10m (a)		3	2h 30m	2h 40m
	Up	1	4h 10m (a)		3	2h 30m	2h 40m
Mar 1891	Down	5	1h 45m	2h 25m	5	1h 40m	2h 15m
	Up	5	1h 45m	2h 30m	5	1h 40m	2h 20m
Jun 1914	Down	6	1h 40m	2h 10m	6	1h 34m	2h 00m
	Up	6	1h 46m	2h 15m	6	1h 37m	2h 05m
Jul 1938	Down	5	1h 45m	2h 00m	5	1h 36m	1h 51m
	Up	5	1h 38m	2h 07m	5	1h 30m	1h 54m
Sep 1964	Down	5	1h 32m	1h 35m	3	1h 30m	1h 35m
	Up	5	1h 29m	1h 36m	4	1h 24m	1h 31m

Note : (a) By coach to and from Mintlaw.

		Aberdeen to Ballater No.	Best	Worst	Craigellachie to Boat of Garten No.	Best	Worst	Inveramsay to Macduff No.	Best	Worst
Jun 1863	Dn	4	1h 50m	2h 50m	3	1h 45m	2h 00m	4	1h 32m	1h 50m
	Up	4	2h 00m	2h 30m	3	1h 30m	1h 50m	4	1h 37m	1h 45m
Mar 1891	Dn	4	1h 40m	2h 00m	3	1h 20m	1h 55m	4	1h 15m	1h 45m
	Up	4	1h 47m	2h 00m	3	1h 30m	2h 00m	5	1h 19m	1h 50m
Jun 1914	Dn	7	1h 05m	1h 40m	3	1h 05m	1h 45m	5	1h 05m	1h 15m
	Up	7	1h 06m	1h 40m	3	1h 10m	1h 50m	5	1h 03m	1h 06m
Jul 1938	Dn	6	1h 12m	1h 36m	3	1h 07m	1h 17m	4	1h 02m	1h 04m
	Up	6	1h 09m	1h 29m	3	1h 12m	1h 15m	5	1h 02m	1h 14m
Sep 1964	Dn	5	1h 19m	1h 28m	3	1h 10m	1h 12m	-		
	Up	5	1h 16m	1h 25m	3	1h 08m	1h 09m	-		

Subbies : June 1914 - To Culter, 8 stops, first down train arrived Culter at 5.51am and last 11.16pm. First up train left 6.08am and last 11.23pm. There were 21 down and 22 up trains, plus 7 Deeside trains to and from Culter only. To Dyce, 9 stops, first down train arrived Dyce at 5.49am and last 11.10pm. First up train left at 5.25am and last at 11.15pm. There were 18 down and 20 up trains plus 12 down and 11 up trains with some intermediate stops to Dyce.

Summary of selected Official Returns made of Coaching and Goods Stock

Period	Route Mileage	1st	3rd	Com	P.O	Lug Tr. Bke	3rd Lug Bke	Hse Box	Fish Tr.	Total Coach Stock	Open Box	Cov Gds Tr	Cat Tr	Shp Van	Meat Van	Low Van Side +	Tim Side	Bal-last Rail	Brake Ord	Brake Spl	Total Goods Stock
Contracted for — Jul 1854		10	30	-	-	4	2	2	-	48	250	30	60	4	-	-	-	-	4	-	348
Delivered by — Sep 1854	39 1/4	7	17	-	-	4	2	2	-	32	149	-	1	4	-	-	-	-	-	-	154
Official returns at 31 Jan 1864																					
GNSR	195 1/2	28	72	4	-	13	2	5	-	124	535	180	90	4	-	100	-	-	16	3	928
BR (BPSR)	19	-	4	3	-	3	-	-	-	10	30	-	6	-	-	6	-	-	-	-	42
MR	11 1/4	-	2	5	-	-	-	-	-	7	42	1	3	-	-	20	-	-	1	-	67
Total	225 3/4	28	78	12	-	16	2	5	-	141	607	181	99	4	-	126	-	-	17	3	1037
31 Jul 1867																					
GNSR	243 3/4	31	86	14	-	15	2	5	-	153	822	176	99	4	-	133	-	-	20	3	1257
DR	43 1/4	12	27	1	-	1	1	-	-	42	104	19	12	-	-	60	-	-	5	-	200
Total	287	43	113	15	-	16	3	5	-	195	926	195	111	4	-	193	-	-	25	3	1457
31 Jan 1875	289 1/4	43	113	15	-	19	3	5	50	248	1265	192	111	4	-	157	-	-	28	5	1762
31 Jan 1887	315	55	141	31	2	45	9	8	100	391	1651	200	140	-	-	150	12	32	38	8	2231
31 Jan 1895	315	63	260	33	2	52	13	14	200	637	2033	200	250	-	50	150	12	56	44	8	2803
31 Jan 1915	330 1/2	43	363	69	2	75	16	20	200	788	3023	372	265	-	*	*	34	*	68	4	3767
31 Jan 1922	334 1/2	38	346	69	2	75	17	23	196	766	2625	565	262	-	*	*	79	*	67	4	3603
Ex-GNSR stock in LNER ownership passed to BR on 31 Dec 1947	319	-	22	21	-	21	-	2	6	72	178	239	3	-	-	-	2	8	57	-	494

* Vehicles listed as covered goods, open box or service stock respectively.

The categories changed over the years. The following categories were introduced in the years shown - composite coaches 1856, fish trucks 1874, Post Office vans 1874, lowside wagons and special brake vans 1855, ballast wagons 1878, timber wagons 1885 and meat vans 1891. Sheep vans dispensed with in 1875. An additional category - Vitriol tanks - was introduced in 1902 and is shown as one each in 1915, 1922 and 1947.

In the 1947 returns, Ballast were of GNS type but built at Inverurie in 1924. Open Box includes GNS type wagons built by LNER at Inverurie 1923-4. There were also 143 Open Box in service stock as Loco Coal.

During the years between the opening of the line in 1854 and the complete closure of the last locomotive depot, Kittybrewster, in August 1967, some 250 non-GNSR locomotives as well as about 30 rail-car units were based on the system. The list below details most of them. For brevity, those that appeared essentially for trials are ommitted. Not all members of the various classes were present for the entire period shown. Engines moved in by the LNER are identified by their 1924 numbers, except class B1. Those that remained after nationalisation have their 1946 numbers in brackets.

Before 1923

An L & Y engine arrived Aug and left Nov 1855.
The Glenlossie Distillery Aveling-Porter 3766/98 for some time, possibly in 1915.
Great Central nos 425B, 428B, 429B, 442B and 444B between June 1920 and January 1921.

1923-1947

Class	Period	Numbers
B1	1946-53	1064/67, 1132-34/46-48, 1242
B12	1933-54	8500-5/7/8/11/13/21/24/26/28/29/31/32/36/39/43/48/51/52 8560/62/63. These became 15XX. 8531 withdrawn 1947.
D31	1925-49	9037, 9211/12/15/16, 9404(2062), 9575, 9634/42, 9729/30 9731-33(2064-66), 9734-40/65/67-70
D51	1926-33	10456/58/61/62
F4	1933-51	7176, 7222(7164), 7236(7151)
G5	1940-55	1889(7287), 1914(7292), 2098(7327)
J36	1923-25 and 1946-47	9711/23/26/86
J72	1932-61	542(8749), 566(8750), 2183(8700), 2303(8710), 2310(8717) 2312(8719)
N14	1927-50	9863(9125)
Sentinel Railcar	1929-30	33

1948-61 : Ex LNER Locomotives

Class	Period	Numbers
B1	1948-61	61277/94, 61307/8/23/24/33/43/45-53, 61400-4
C15	1952-56	67455/78
C16	1956-57	67496, 67501
D34	1953-61	62469/79/80/82/89/93/97/98
F4	1948-56	67157
J35	1952-59	64482/83
J36	1948-61	65213/21/27/42/47/51/67/77/97, 65303-5/10/38
J69	1951-52	65825/52/68
K2	1952-60	61734/41/55/79/82/83/90/92/93
N15	1957-61	69180, 69201/24
V4	1954-55	61700/1

1948-61 : Ex-LMS Locomotives

Class		Period	Numbers
2P	2-6-2T	1958-59	40011
2P	4-4-0	1948-61	40600/3/4/17/18/22/48/50/63
Cl.5	4-6-0	1960-61	45167, 45469
Cl.2	2-6-0	1952-61	46460/1/4

```
CR      0-4-4T    1952-61    55185, 55221
CR      0-6-0T    1958-60    56348
CR      0-6-0     1954-61    57591, 57634/61
```

1952-61 : BR Steam Locomotives

```
Cl.4    2-6-0     1957-61    76104-8
Cl.2    2-6-0     1955-61    78045/53/54
Cl.4    2-6-4T    1952-61    80004/5/20/21/28/29, 80106-15/21/22
```

1958-67 : BR Diesel Locomotives

```
204hp   d/m       1958-67    D2414-24
225hp   d/h       1962-64    D2723/49/50
350hp   d/e       1961-67    D3546-53, D3930-36
1000hp  d/e       1960-67    D6138-57
1000hp  d/e       1960-66    D8028-31/34
```

1958-67 : BR Railcars

```
Derby Lightweight (Battery)   1958-62    Sc79998 (MBS), Sc79999(DTC)
Craven Twins                  1959-67    Sc51473-93(MBS), Sc56462-82(DTC)
Swindon 3-car Cross Country   1959-67    Sc51781-87(MBC), Sc59679-85(TBS)
                                         Sc51788-94(MS)
```

Railbuses - Examples of Bristol, Park Royal and Wickham units worked in the area, mainly on Speyside 1958-65, and were based at Aviemore.

Other units were drafted in temporarily from time to time for operational purposes.

9 : SELECTED ALTITUDES

Altitudes are shown in feet above sea level.

Aberdeen Joint	17	Kintore	164
Kittybrewster	100	(11 1/8 miles)	618
(32 1/8 miles)	590	Alford	460
Keith	357		
(62 1/8 miles)	590	Aberdeen Joint	17
Craigellachie	270	(26 1/4 miles)	604
Birchfield	450	Aboyne	390
Elgin	36	Ballater	660
Grange North Jct	308	Inveramsay	237
Glenbarry	476	(7 7/8 miles)	397
Tillynaught	180	Turriff	125
Portessie	88	(27 miles)	257
Spey Bay	18	Macduff	66
Dyce	174	Craigellachie	270
(12 1/4 miles)	430	(28 3/4 miles)	690
Ellon	65	Broomhill Jct	660
Maud	230	Boat of Garten	712
Peterhead	35		
Fraserburgh	16		

These appendices give only some of the information which has
been published by the Great North of Scotland Railway
Association. Separate publications are available covering such
subjects as details of all the lines, showing station locations
and opening and closing dates, bus routes, signal boxes and
single line working, the construction and history of selected
locomotive classes, and gradients profiles.

Details of the Association and its publications are given
occasionally in the Railway Press. The main Scottish Libraries
also receive the Associations quarterly journal, the Great North
Review, which shows the current office holders.

Index

Illustrations are indicated by heavy type

Aberdeen, Banff & Elgin Railway, 14
Aberdeenshire Canal 16–17, 22
Aberdeen harbour lines, 28, 129, 154, 163
Aberdeen–Inverness traffic, disputes over, 104–115
Aberdeen Junction Railway, 70
Aberdeen, Peterhead & Fraserburgh Railway, 62
Aberdeen Railway, 13, 19
Aboyne & Braemar Railway, 78–79
Accidents,
  Buckpool (1887), 95
  Inverythan (1882), 92
  Kittybrewster (1854), 25
  Knock (1896), 101, 149
  Lossiemouth (1854), 151
  Nethy Bridge (1878), 89
  Wartle (1885), 95
Alford Valley Railway,
  Authorised, 61
  Financial difficulties, 61
  Fusion with GNSR, 65
  Opened, 61
  Original scheme, 60
  Rival lines, 60
  Train services, 61

Bain, Andrew, 141
Balmoral Castle, 75, 82
Banffshire Railway,
  BPSR authorised, 49
  Dividends, 50
  Fares on, 51
  Fusion with GNSR, 52
  No second class on, 51
  Opened, 50
  Original scheme, 48
  Portgordon extension, 51
  Portsoy harbour incline, 49, 52
  Title changed, 50

Train services, 51–52
Worked by GNSR, 50
Banff, Macduff & Turriff Extension Railway,
  Authorised, 58
  Financial difficulties, 59
  Fusion with GNSR, 65
  Macduff extension, 59
  Opened, 58
  Train services, 58
Banff, Macduff & Turriff Junction Railway,
  Authorised, 57
  Financial difficulties, 58
  Fusion with GNSR, 65
  Opened, 58
  Train services, 58
Banff, Portsoy & Strathisla Railway, 49
Barnett, Patrick, 73, 136
Bates, Samuel, 73
Beeching Report, 186
Blackwood, Robert, 151
Blaikie, Thomas, 13, 74
Blyth, Benjamin Hall, 22, 30
Brakes, automatic, 166
Bridges,
  Allt Arder (Knockando), 56
  Cullen viaducts, 93, 95, **plate 2**
  Deveron (Rothiemay), 30, 97
  Don (Inverurie), 23, **plate 1**
  Don (Parkhill), 63
  Fiddich (Dufftown), 54
  South Ugie Water (Longside), 63
  Spey (Ballindalloch), 56, **plates 5, 8**
  Spey (Carron), 56, **plate 4**
  Spey (Craigellachie), **plate 7**
  Spey (Garmouth), 93, **plates 3, 9**
  Spey (Nethy Bridge), 56
  Spey (Orton), 30, 31
  Ythan (Ellon), 63, **plate 6**
Bruce, Hon Thomas, 49

Caledonian Railway, 13, 72, 73, 130
Charter Trains, 194
Clark, Daniel Kinnear, 144–145
Closures,
    Aberdeen to Elgin, 188
    Aberdeen suburban services, 181
    Alford, 186, 189
    Banff, 187
    Beeching Report, 186
    Cruden Railway, 175, 182
    Deeside, 187, 189
    Dyce to Fraserburgh, 187, 196
    Freight, 188, 189, 196
    Lossiemouth, 187
    Macduff, 186, 189
    Maud to Peterhead, 187, 189
    Old Meldrum, 175, 189
    St Combs, 187, 188
    Speyside, 187, 189
Cowan, William, 147–150
Cruden Bay Hotel tramway, 96, 175,
    182
Cruden Railway,
    Authorised, 96
    Extension to Peterhead, 169
    Opened, 96
    Train services, 96, 169
Cubitt, William, 13, 22, 74

Davidson, George, 136, 168
Deeside Railway,
    Aboyne, extension to, 77
    Authorised, 78
    Ballater, extension to, 78
    Company works own line, 76
    Construction begun, 75
    Dividends, 81
    Fusion with GNSR, 81
    Lease to GNSR, 80–81
    Limpet Mill–Kintore scheme, 68, 79
    'Messenger Trains', 83–86
    No second class on, 76
    Opened, 75
    Original proposals, 74–75
    Re-authorised, 75
    Reduction to single track, 186
    Royal Trains on, 82–83
    Train services, 76, 82, 97, 132, 138,
        141, 142
Deeside Walkway, 198
Denburn Valley line, 70–71

Deuchar, William, 135, 140
Diesel traction, 185, 191, 195, 196,
    plates 45, 46, 61–64
Doubling of track
    Buchan Section, 139
    Craigellachie line, proposed, 97
    Cults to Park, 97
    Dyce to Insch, 90
    Elgin to Lossie Junction, proposed,
        97
    Ferryhill Junction to Cults, 92
    Insch to Keith, 97
    Kittybrewster to Dyce, 64
Dougall, Andrew, 113
Duffus, Alexander, 141, 143, 176
Duncan, John, 75, 77, 80, 82, 88, 89

Electric Battery Railcar, plate 45
Elgin to Edinburgh through coach,
    138, 143, 184
Elgin to Glasgow through coach, 107,
    143, 184
Elphinstone, Sir James, 17, 88

Ferguson, William (chairman), 90,
    135
Ferguson, William B. (secretary), 30,
    75, 76, 82, 90, 155
Forbes, John, 49
Formartine & Buchan Railway,
    Authorised, 62
    Financial difficulties, 64
    Fusion with GNSR, 65
    Line amended, 63, 64
    Opened, 63, 64
    Peterhead, Harbour branch, 63,
        187, 189
    Schemes for, 62
    Train services, 64
Fraser, Alexander, 73

Gibb, Alexander, 13, 30, 73
Glasgow & North Western Railway,
    103
Golightly, George, 151
Grampian Transport Museum, 197
Grange, Loop at, 94
Grant, James, 37, 39, 46
Great North of Scotland Railway,
    Aberdeen suburban trains, 99, 100,
        169, 170, 181

Amalgamation with Caledonian
  Railway proposed, 73
Amalgamation with HR proposed,
  133
Authorised, 15
Company's crest, **18**
Consolidation of system (1866), 65–
  66
Construction begun, 21–23
Dividends, 34, 36, 89, 92, 133, 143
Excursions, long-distance, 134, 170,
  194
Fares on, 16, 24, 25, 32, 35, 92
Financial difficulties, 19–21, 87–89
Formation of company, 13
Fusion with Aberdeen company,
  17, 20
GCR locomotives on, 143
GNSR (Eastern Extension), 61
GNSR (Western Extension), 57
Grouped into LNER, 141, 143
Highest summit on, 56
'Messenger Trains', 83–86
No second class on, 25
Offices moved to Guild Street, 101
Offices moved to Waterloo, 28
Opened to Aberdeen (Waterloo),
  28
Royal Trains, 82–83
Running powers, Elgin to Forres,
  93, 95
Slip coach service, 138
Staff receptions (1898), 102
Tickets, **91, 132**
Timetables, **106,** 137
Grierson, James, 49

Heywood, Thomas, 163–165, 177
Highland Railway,
  Carr Bridge line to Inverness, 104
  Formation of, 35
  Portessie branch, 93
  Running powers on Moray Firth
    Coast line, 93, 103
  Through loco working, 134
Hotels,
  Cruden Bay, 96, 182
  Palace, Aberdeen, 101, 182
  Station, Aberdeen, 133, 182, 198
Huntly, opening to, 23–24

Inverness & Aberdeen Junction
  Railway, 30, 31
Inverness & Elgin Junction Railway,
  14
Inverness & Nairn Railway, 29
Inverness & Perth Junction Railway,
  35
Inverurie, locomotive works, 129,
  189
Inverury & Old Meldrum Junction
  Railway,
  Authorised, 60
  Fusion with GNSR, 66
  Leased by GNSR, 60
  Opened, 60
  Train services, 60

Johnson, James, 159–160
Johnson, William, 177

Keir, William, 49
Keith & Dufftown Railway,
  Authorised, 53
  Financial difficulties, 54
  Fusion with GNSR, 65
  Line amended, 54
  Opened, 54
  Train services, 54
Keith, opening to, 30
Kittbrewster locomotive works, 129,
  144, 156, 161

Lenabo Airship base, 139
Leslie, William (chairman), 89, 90
Leslie, William (secretary), 13, 74
Level crossings, 190
Light railways,
  Aberdeen to Newburgh, 118
  Aberdeen to Skene and Echt, 117,
    118
  Alford to Bellabeg, 120, 127
  Ballater to Braemar, 120, 127
  Dufftown to Tomintoul, 118
  Fraserburgh to Rosehearty and New
    Aberdour, 119, 127
  Fraserburgh to St Combs, 118–119
  West Buchan line, 120, 127
Lineside mail apparatus, 99
Locomotives,
  Banffshire Railway, 152–153
  British Railways, 185, 186

Deeside Railway, 153–155
Designed by Clark, 144–145, **plate 47**
Designed by Cowan, 147–150, **plates 48, 49, 53**
Designed by Heywood, 163–165, **plates 57, 58**
Designed by Johnson, 159–160, **plates 51, 54**
Designed by Manson, 155, 159, **plate 50**
Designed by Pickersgill, 160, 163, **plates 55, 56, colour plate 2**
Designed by Ruthven, 145, 146, **plate 32**
EX-GER, **plate 40**
GNSR withdrawn, 177, 178, 185, 186
Liveries, 145, 150, 152, 153, 155, 158, 164
LNER, 177–179
Manning Wardle, **plate 52**
Morayshire Railway, 150–152
Preserved, 186, 198
London to Elgin through coaches (1869), 72
London to Elgin through coach (1957), 184
London to Lossiemouth through sleeping car (1923), 168, 169

Macintosh, Thomas, 136, 177
Manson, James, 153–156
Milne, Robert, 30, 90
Mitchell, Joseph, 15
Moffatt, William, 90, 135, 136
Montrose & Bervie Railway, 69–70
Moray Firth Coast Line,
  Authorised, 93
  Buckie to Portessie, double track, 94
  Opened, 93
  Projected, 92
  Train services, 95, **110**
Morayshire Railway,
  Agreement with GNSR, 42
  Authorised, 37
  Construction begun, 38
  Craigellachie line opened, 40
  Dispute with IAJR, 41
  Dividends, 39
  Elgin to Lossiemouth opened, 38

Fares, 39, 40
Fusion with GNSR, 47
Glen of Rothes line, 42–43
Junction with Strathspey Railway, 45
Orton to Rothes line closed, 45–46
Part abandoned, 37
Second class on, 39
Train services, 38, 44, 45
Morison, George, 49, 51
Morrison, Forbes, 73, 90
Motor bus services,
  Aberchirder to Turriff, 127
  Aberdeen to Cluny, 124, 171
  Aberdeen to Echt and Midmar, 124
  Aberdeen to Inverurie, 172
  Aberdeen to Newburgh, 124
  Alford to Bellabeg, 124
  Ballater to Bellabeg, 125, 171
  Ballater to Braemar, 121, 122
  Ballindalloch to Tomintoul, 125, 171
  Bellabeg to Corgaff, 123
  Culter to Midmar, 123
  Disposal of by LNER, 173
  Elgin to Macduff, 172, 173
  Fares on, 121, 124
  Fraserburgh to Rosehearty and New Aberdour, 125, 171
  Huntly to Aberchirder, 123, 172
  Huntly to Banff, 172
  Parliamentary authorisation, 124
  'Three Rivers Tours', 125
  Transfer of operation, 173
  Udny to Methlick, 123
Motor lorry services, 125
Motor vehicles, 121, 124, 126, 127, 171, **plates 34, 35**

North British Railway, 69, 72, 107, 138
Northern Belle, 180, 194, **colour plate 4**
North Sea Oil, 192

Parker, James, 136, 176
Perth & Inverness Railway, 14, 15
Pickersgill, William, 160–163

Railways Act (1921), 141, 143
Railway Mania, 19

Railways (Road Transport) Acts, 172
Reid, Alexander, 90, 135
Restaurant cars, **142**, 143, 168
Road Traffic Act, 173
Rolling stock, 165–167, **plates 32, 42–44**
  Liveries, 166, 167
  LNER changes, 179
  P.O. Sorting, 98, 99
  Preserved, 198
  Slip coach, 138
Ross, Alexander, 90, 136
Ruthven, John Folds, 145–146

Samuel, James, 41, 150, 151
Scottish Midland Junction Railway, 14
Scottish North Eastern Railway, 20, 72
Scottish Northern Junction Railway, 68–69
Sentinel Cammell railcar, 170
Singling of track, 186, 190
Signalling, 190, 196, **plates 36–38**
Smith of Echt, carrier, 124
Speyside Walk, 198
Stations,
  Aberdeen (Guild Street), 26, 27, 28
  Aberdeen Joint, 26, 67–71, 130, 136–138, **plates 10–12**
  Aberdeen (Waterloo), 26, 27, 33
  Aberlour, 196
  Abernethy (Nethy Bridge), 55
  Advie, 56
  Alford, 61, 197
  Ballater, **plate 27**
  Banchory, **colour plate 1**
  Banff, **plate 21**
  Banff Bridge, 59, **plate 29**
  Banff & Macduff, 58
  Barry (Glenbarry), 50
  Botriphnie (Auchindachy), 54
  Bridgefoot, 50
  Buchanstone, 25
  Buckie, **plate 60**
  Cairnie Junction, **plate 41**
  Cambus o'May, **plate 26**
  Carron, **plate 30**
  Craigellachie, **plate 18, 31**
  Cullen, **plate 19**
  Crathes Castle (private), 76
  Culter, **plate 59**
  Dailuaine, 169
  Dalbeallie (Knockando), 57
  Dalvey, 56
  Dandaleith, 56
  Dee Street, 185
  Dufftown, **plate 17**
  Dyce, 63, **plate 63**
  Earlsmill (Keith Town), 54
  Elgin, 40, 43, 44, 127, **plate 39**
  Fochabers (Spey Bay), 94
  Fraserburgh, **plate 24, 62**
  Golf Club House, 50
  Huntly, **plate 14**
  Inverurie, 126, **plate 13, colour plate 3**
  Keith Junction, 30, 31, 195, **plate 15**
  Keith Town, **plate 16**
  Kittybrewster, 28, 71
  Knockando, 197, **plate 65**
  Knockando House Halt, 57, 169
  Maud, 63, **plate 22**
  Millegan, 50
  Mills of Drum, 76
  Nether Buckie (Buckpool), 94
  Newburgh Road (Logierieve), 63
  Old Deer (Mintlaw), 63
  Ordens, 50
  Park, **plate 25**
  Philorth, 64, **plate 23**
  Portsoy, **plate 66**
  Rothienorman, **plate 28**
  St Combs, **plate 40**
  Spey Bay, **plates 20, 64**
  Strathspey Junction (Craigellachie), 56
  Towiemore, 169
Steel, Charles, 113
Stewart, Sir David, 135, 141
Strathspey Railway,
  Authorised, 54
  Extension to Boat of Garten, 55
  Fusion with GNSR, 65
  Opened, 55
  Train services, 57
Strathspey, Strathdon & Deeside Junction Railway, 104
Sunday trains, 24, 36, 84, 169–70

Tablet exchange apparatus, 94, 158–159, 196

Taylor, Joseph, 151
Train services (GNSR), 24, 31, 36, 71–
    72, **85,** 88, 98–100, 105–113, 115–116,
    131–132, 138, 140, 142, 168–169, 184,
    188, 195
Transport Committee, 1918, 127
Travelling Post Office, 98
Tunnels,
    Aberdeen, 71
    Aboyne, 78
    Craigellachie, 56

Urquhart, Alexander, 46

Walker, William, 73, 90
Watt, Alexander, 47
Willet, John, 76, 155
Willox, Simon, 136, 176
World war,
    First, 139–142
    Second, 180–182